The Origins of Fear

The Origins of Behavior

Michael Lewis and
Leonard A. Rosenblum, Editors

Volume 1
The Effect of the Infant on Its Caregiver

Michael Lewis and
Leonard A. Rosenblum, Editors

Volume 2
The Origins of Fear

Michael Lewis and
Leonard A. Rosenblum, Editors

The Origins of Fear

Edited by

Michael Lewis
 Educational Testing Service

and

Leonard A. Rosenblum
 State University of New York
 Downstate Medical Center

A Wiley-Interscience Publication

JOHN WILEY & SONS
New York • London • Sydney • Toronto

Copyright © 1974 John Wiley & Sons Inc.

All rights reserved. Published simultaneously in Canada.

No part of this book may be reproduced by any means, nor transmitted, nor translated into a machine language without the written permission of the publisher.

Library of Congress Cataloging in Publication Data:

Lewis, Michael, Jan. 10, 1937-
  The origins of fear.

  (The Origins of behavior, v. 2)
  "A Wiley-Interscience publication."
  Derived from papers presented and discussed at a conference sponsored by Educational Testing Service, Princeton, N.J.
    1. Fear—Congresses.   2. Child study—Congresses.
I.   Rosenblum, Leonard A., joint author.   II. Educational Testing Service.   III. Title.   IV. Series.

[DNLM: 1. Fear—Congresses. W10R687 v. 2 / WM178 069 1974]
BF723.F4L48   1974   155.4'18   74-9565
ISBN 0-471-53338-6

Printed in the United States of America

10 9 8 7 6 5 4 3 2 1

Contributors

Mary D. Salter Ainsworth
Department of Psychology
Johns Hopkins University
Baltimore, Maryland 21218

Stephanie Alpert
Primate Behavior Laboratory
Downstate Medical Center
450 Clarkson Avenue
Brooklyn, New York 11203

Inge Bretherton
Department of Psychology
Johns Hopkins University
Baltimore, Maryland 21218

Gordon W. Bronson
Department of Psychology
Mills College
Oakland, California 94613

Jeanne Brooks
Infant Laboratory
Educational Testing Service
Princeton, New Jersey 08540

William R. Charlesworth
Institute of Child Development
University of Minnesota
Minneapolis, Minnesota 55455

Howard S. Hoffman
Department of Psychology
Bryn Mawr College
Bryn Mawr, Pennsylvania 19010

Jerome Kagan
Department of Social Relations
William James Hall
Harvard University
Cambridge, Massachusetts 02138

Michael Lewis
Infant Laboratory
Educational Testing Service
Princeton, New Jersey 08540

Leah Matas
Institute of Child Development
University of Minnesota
Minneapolis, Minnesota 55455

Harriet L. Rheingold
Department of Psychology
University of North Carolina
Chapel Hill, North Carolina 27515

Henry N. Ricciuti
Department of Child Development
Cornell University
Ithaca, New York 14850

Leonard A. Rosenblum
Primate Behavior Laboratory
Downstate Medical Center
450 Clarkson Avenue
Brooklyn, New York 11203

H. Rudolph Schaffer
Department of Psychology
Turnbull Building
University of Strathclyde
Glasgow, C. 1, Scotland

Peter K. Smith
Department of Psychology
University of Sheffield
Sheffield S10 2TN, England

L. Alan Sroufe
Institute of Child Development
University of Minnesota
Minneapolis, Minnesota 55455

Daniel N. Stern
Department of Developmental
Physiology
New York State Psychiatric Institute
722 W. 168th Street
New York, New York 10032

Everett Waters
Institute of Child Development
University of Minnesota
Minneapolis, Minnesota 55455

Series Preface

*"The childhood shows the man,
as morning shows the day."*

Milton, Paradise Regained

None can doubt that the study of man begins in the study of childhood. Few would contend that the newborn lacks the challenge of his evolutionary heritage. This series addresses itself to the task of bringing together, on a continuing basis, that confluence of theory and data on ontogeny and phylogeny which will serve to illustrate *The Origins of Behavior*.

Whether our social, human, and professional concerns lie in the psychological disorders of childhood or adulthood or merely in the presumptively normal range of expression in development in different cultures, varied environments, or diverse family constellations, we can never hope to discern order and regularity from the mass of uncertain observation and groundless speculation if we fail to nurture the scientific study of development. Fortunately, the last two decades have seen an enormous burgeoning of effort toward this end, both at the human and nonhuman level. However, despite this growth of effort and interest, no single means of pooling our growing knowledge on development in children and animals and communicating that fusion of material to the broad scientific community now exists. This series seeks to fill the gap. It is our intention to have each volume deal with a specific theme that is either of social or of theoretical relevance to developmental issues. In keeping with the integrated perspective that we consider to be vital, and to provide a meaningful context within which these issues may be considered, each volume in the series will contain a broad range of material and will seek to encompass theoretical and sound empirical studies of the behavior of human infants as well as pertinent aspects of animal behavior with a particular emphasis on the primates. It is our view, furthermore, that not only is it necessary to focus our interest on both human infants and animals, but that the levels of analysis which will explicate the processes of development that are our concern must ultimately involve the study of behavior at all levels of discourse. Thus studies of developmental significance may be found in genetic, physiological, morphological, dyadic, and societal levels and an increased interdigitation of these separate disciplines is among the major goals of this series.

In light of the diversity of topics to be considered, the breadth of material to be covered, and the variety of orientations that will be included in these discourses on the origins of human behavior, we expect this series to serve the needs of the broad social science community, not merely of those interested in behavioral development alone. Just as the series itself will draw upon the knowledge and research of psychologists, ethologists, sociologists, psychiatrists, pediatricians, obstetricians, and devoted scientists and clinicians in a number of related disciplines, it is our hope that the material in this series will provide both stimulation and guidance to all among us who are concerned with man, his past, his present, and his future.

Michael Lewis
Leonard A. Rosenblum
Editors

June 1973

Preface

The present work represents the second in the series The Origins of Behavior. We have selected the topic of fear because it represents the conflux between the infant's emerging cognitive and affective systems. As an underlying principle of this series we have chosen to provide both the ontogenetic as well as the phylogenetic perspective. The chapters in this volume derive from papers presented and discussed at a conference on Fear held under the auspices and support of Educational Testing Service, Princeton, New Jersey. The chapters reflect the integration of the original papers and the critical comments and thematic discussions of the conference participants. In addition, the four conference discussants have supplied written comments on the theme. These, together with the introductory chapter, provide an overview and assessment of the most salient research issues and conceptualizations.

The participants in the conference were Dr. Mary D. Salter Ainsworth, Ms. Stephanie Alpert, Dr. Norbert Bischof, Dr. Gordon W. Bronson, Ms. Jeanne Brooks, Dr. William R. Charlesworth, Dr. Howard S. Hoffman, Dr. Jerome Kagan, Dr. Michael Lewis, Dr. Harriet L. Rheingold, Dr. Henry N. Ricciuti, Dr. Leonard A. Rosenblum, Dr. H. Rudolph Schaffer, Dr. Peter K. Smith, Dr. L. Alan Sroufe, and Dr. Daniel Stern.

Michael Lewis
Leonard A. Rosenblum

Princeton, New Jersey

Brooklyn, New York

April 1974

CONTENTS

Introduction

MICHAEL LEWIS
Educational Testing Service
LEONARD A. ROSENBLUM
Downstate Medical Center

To understand the problems set forth in this volume it is necessary for us to present several examples of the phenomena we wish to discuss.

Example 1. A 10-month-old infant and its mother sit in their pediatrician's office. It is their turn to see the doctor. As they enter the room, the child stares at the doctor and his white coat, screams, turns away from the doctor, and clutches its mother.

Example 2. A 4-month-old infant is lying in its crib looking at the mobile above it. Suddenly a loud bang sounds behind the crib. The infant startles, throwing out its limbs, and starts to cry.

Example 3. An 8-month-old infant is being walked in the park with its mother. A stranger walks over to the infant, bends over the stroller and says "What a pretty baby." The mother smiles. The infant freezes and stops playing with its rattle; then the infant turns toward its mother, back to the stranger, and starts to whimper.

Example 4. A 7-month-old infant is sitting in its mother's bedroom. In the bathroom its mother is dressing for the evening and puts on her new long-haired wig. As she steps into the bedroom, the infant stares at her and suddenly begins to cry.

Example 5. A year-old infant is playing in a sand box in the park. Its mother is standing close by. As he glances up from the sand he sees her walking away. He begins to call "Mommy, mommy" and starts moving toward her.

We might be willing to say that the infant in each of these examples is fearful. However, we quickly recognize that there are large and important differences among the five situations.

1

The first example appears to be a case of learned fear. The infant more than once has experienced some unpleasant action, the agent of which was the doctor. On the last visit, 2 months earlier, for example, the infant may have received an injection and by its behavior may have indicated that it was hurt. Now (2 months later) we see that in some sense the child remembers or at least associates the previous noxious event with the current situation. Its reaction to the present situation is affected by the past event; thus we might consider Example 1 to be a case of conditioned or learned fear. Moreover, we might imagine that such fear could generalize to other situations—that is, whenever the infant is taken to an office where there are men in white coats, it becomes fearful. (Many infant researchers soon learn to remove laboratory jackets for this reason.) Learned fear and its generalization must surely account for a portion of the child's fearful behavior.

In the second example the infant experiences an *intense, sudden* and *unexpected* change in the level of energy reaching its sensory systems. Without question, stimulus events having these three elements seem to be capable of eliciting behaviors commonly considered fearful. It should not be surprising that the nervous system of the young (or of any age for that matter) is designed to respond to such stimuli as noxious. Thus it would be reasonable to consider a class of events that produces unlearned, fearful behavior. We suggest that such events probably account for a relatively small percentage of fearful responses; moreover, since events become more associated with other events with increasing age, we would find clear examples of this phenomenon only in the very young.

The third example has most commonly been called stranger fear or anxiety. In this situation the child becomes frightened of new people and shows positive behavior toward its caregivers. The development of this pattern of behavior usually occurs after an initial period in which the infant exhibits positive behavior toward all social experiences. Thus at an earlier age this stranger must have evoked a smile and coo. This phenomenon has been likened to imprinting and as such has been considered to be a biologically derived response. Alternatively it has been considered to be a manifestation of the child's cognitive ability in comparing the various social events (people) to an internal representation of its caregivers. Most researchers have thought of it as an index of the infant's attachment toward its primary caregivers, since it represents a discriminably *different* response toward various adults in its world. Why these discriminably different actions to various adults should take the form of a fearful response is not easily explained. It is tempting to postulate some conditioned fear response. For example, the appearance of a stranger—say, the arrival of a baby sitter—may be associated with the loss of the mother. Alternatively, although less plausible, is the possibility that the infant has a schema of its familiar caregivers only, and violation of that schema by the appearance of a stranger elicits fear. One might anticipate the stranger producing interest (or arousal), but why they cause fearful behavior is not yet clear.

In the fourth example we see a clear case of the violation of expectancy. The child has formed a schema of its mother. This includes a complex integration of the stimulus properties of this person. The sudden and unexpected change in this schema results in interest or arousal. The resulting affective response can occur from the infant's inability to assimilate and accommodate its schema to this new event. Alternatively, one might argue that the infant, failing to perceive in this "new" mother its "old" mother, thereby is confronted with the loss of its "old" mother. This loss itself, whether through conditioning or innate mechanisms, is fear inducing. As in the previous example, we see the effect of novelty as an elicitor of interest, the specific affect being determined by some alternative process or cognition.

The final example involves the child's fear of the loss of its mother. It is clear that in primates the loss of the primary caregiver increases the probability of death. Thus it is extremely important for the infant to help regulate the physical distance between itself and its mother. This regulation, which is performed by both members of the dyad, consists of a wide variety of behaviors. Initially, due to the infant's helplessness, the mother is the most active regulator. However, she is by no means the only one. Through crying, eye contact, and smiling the infant also helps regulate this distance. As the infant matures and is able to both leave and follow, it becomes increasingly capable of assuming a major role in the regulation. Thus we see attempts at both movement toward the mother and signaling for her return as she leaves. For the species as a whole, we can justify calling these behaviors fearful because it is biologically useful; but unless we wish to postulate some innate releasing mechanism, we must again rely on cognitions having to do with past experience.

These examples are quite different, but they can be characterized by an affective response in the infant which most of us would readily label "fear." Even though we might have little trouble with the label of fear, it becomes evident that the boundaries of what we mean by "fearful" are not at all clear. This is rather surprising because it is a widely used term, thought to convey a plethora of meanings. The issue, however, is not simple. Fear, like all affective responses, is not itself available for study. Since it is an experience of an individual, it cannot be experienced by another. Nor for that matter, since infants are nonverbal organisms, is it available through the verbal report of the subject.

What do we mean when we say that the infant is fearful? We mean that there exists a set of behaviors in a particular context that we use to infer that the infant feels fearful. Clearly we cannot state that the infant is fearful, since we can never know this. All one can claim is that "If I did this [set of behaviors] when this occurred [context including stimulus] I would feel fearful." Since it is epistemologically impossible to know whether the infant is fearful, we must be willing to settle for the statement "acting as if he is fearful." Notice that we have signified that *both* a set of behaviors and a particular context are necessary for the statement, "I think the infant is fearful." This requirement is particularly important because neither the behaviors independent of the context nor the context independent of the behaviors will help us define the infant's feeling. Crying at a funeral or crying at the unexpected appearance of a loved one cannot lead us to assume the same internal state, although in both cases crying behavior occurs. Likewise, in considering reunion with the mother, the same context does not always suggest happiness, since one infant may be happy whereas another becomes angry at the mother's reappearance.

Our brief discussion indicates that the meaning of fear must give way to a taxonomy of context and of behavior, merged in a matrix of interaction. In the following sections we approach each aspect separately to highlight some specific issues, either to be raised as problems for future research or as topics that are dealt with in this volume.

ORGANISMIC VARIABLES

The specific examples discussed previously suggest an ordered set of general issues and problems on whose clarification our ultimate understanding of the dynamics of fearful behaviors depends. We must consider first the characteristics of the organism in which the behavior is being evaluated. Given highly divergent genetic structures and experiential backgrounds, as well as their interaction, it is not surprising that individuals nominally classified together should differ markedly in their responses to a particular, complex stimulus situation. Nonetheless, certain overtly identifiable features that distinguish taxonomic classes of individuals (e.g., species, age, and sex) have some predictive capacity in determining the likely pattern of response to a given stimulus event. Different members of the primate order, for example, respond quite differently to stimuli even in the first weeks of life, conspecifics being responded to more positively than alien species. Similarly, studies carried out under a variety of conditions indicate that at most ages, male and female infants may respond fearfully to different stimuli, and such stimuli may evoke dissimilar patterned arrays of behaviors. Perhaps the most frequently identified independent variable influencing fearful behavior is the infant's chronological or developmental age. Studies using diverse groups of infants have attempted to determine the ages of onset, course of development, and often the terminal points of fearful behaviors. Here, a major theoretical and methodological dilemma must be confronted. How shall we judge the presence or absence of fear at various ages, knowing that the capacities that are critical to the expression of our criterion behaviors themselves may vary with age. Can withdrawal serve as a measurement of fear in a child too young to locomote easily? Does eye aversion index fear in the prelocomotive child, but merely distraction or disinterest in the toddler? In short, does a given behavior maintain a unitary relation to the fear concept, or shall we accept a more fluid complex of behaviors as our index?

PROBLEMS OF BEHAVIOR MEANING

Thus our understanding of the organismic variables affecting the expression of fearful behavior inevitably involves a careful scrutiny of the behavioral measurements themselves. The chapters that follow indicate clearly that no single behavior may act as a necessary and sufficient referent for fear. As suggested earlier, even crying—perhaps the most likely candidate for such a position—fails to meet our requirements in this regard. A given stimulus may initially evoke smiles and laughter, yet on repeated presentations evoke the cry. Indeed, nominally identical stimuli may at different moments be maximally suitable for producing either pattern in a given infant. Similarly, neither approaching nor withdrawing, looking toward or looking away, reaching for or holding back, among many other possibilities, offers the investigator the simple, operationally defined distinctions he seeks. It would appear at this point that the pattern of interdigitated response elements, not the individual elements themselves, shows systematic changes in response to a given stimulus configuration. These coherent patterns may differ between classes of individuals, between members of a class, and even within the same individual at different times. Genetic factors, cognitive and motor capacities, prior life experiences, as well as immediately antecedent events, all serve to alter the structure of these response configurations in a given individual.

The viewpoint featuring a pattern of response elements has led to the postulation of a fear system in the infant; that is a uniquely organized set of responses integrated within the central nervous system and functionally independent of other such systems in terms of the stimuli that elicit it and the neural structures that subsume it. This system approach, however, has its own pitfalls. We are too often led to assume that if a particular central system has been activated, other, presumably opposite structures have been either unaroused or actively inhibited. Regardless of the nature of the pattern of fearful behavior, as the work described in this volume attests, the entire array of behaviors usually identified as reflecting positive, affiliative (cf. attachment) responses to a stimulus may be evidenced simultaneously with or in intimate temporal proximity to, the fear system. This fact—that a stranger, for example, may evoke both smiling and prolonged gaze interspersed with aversion and lip quivering or even crying—must have an impact on our measurement techniques. Clearly, global, unitary rating scales that serve to grade the infant's response along a single continuum belie this multidimensional response array.

In an effort to delineate degrees of fearfulness, the term "wariness" has come into use. This is an attempt to recognize that although we talk of fear in early childhood, relatively few infants in relatively few situations show behavioral patterns we would choose to call fearful. The problem of the measurement of wariness is a good example of the kinds of difficulty that befall the investigator. It has been widely recognized that the appearance and approach of the new, or the loss of the familiar, results in an inhibition of ongoing activity, attentive behavior (eye gaze, heart rate changes, etc.) often referred to as a general state of alerting or arousal. If one calls that set of behaviors "wariness," one has already biased the response as a negative affective behavior. One could consider this set of behaviors as a general arousal state preparatory to any number of responses, some of which might be positive or negative in affective tone. Clearly these two alternatives have different theoretical and practical implications. In labeling the set of behaviors, care must be taken not to prejudge the nature of the response.

The types of behavior we choose to observe represent another measurement concern. For the most part we have been discussing the overt manifestations of behavior; however, several studies have employed techniques to obtain physiological data. The history of the use of physiological data in the study of affect is long and involved. To summarize such a literature is difficult, however there appears to be no simple or exact relationship between the overt manifestation of a behavior, the reported occurrence of an affective response, and the physiological process being monitored. Thus it is not possible to infer from the physiology the nature of either the overt behavioral manifestations or the reported affective responses. We do not yet know whether improved measurement procedures will alter these findings, but we must not assume that the act of measuring an internal response brings us any closer to those internally perceived affective responses having some relationship to overt behavior. Such a belief not only belies the historical evidence, it is somewhat naïve. We are no closer to understanding the phenomenon of fear when we measure heart rate changes than we are when we look at overt behavior. For example, heart rate acceleration may be a function of general arousal, specific fear, or the problem-solving activity of the infant. Thus the introduction of these physiological measures at this time offers us little immediate hope of solving our specific problems.

A final measurement issue deals with a measurement–context interaction and as such will lead to a context discussion. The question of a "natural" versus an "experimental" situation continues to be an important one. The primary issue is whether meaningful data can be generated in a nonnatural situation. Of course the definition of "natural" is significant here, and it becomes apparent that no situation in which observation is made can be natural. Observation by definition distorts. Thus we turn to degrees of naturalness, itself a rather misleading topic. The issue is the generation of meaningful data, and by "meaningful" we imply (1) that the data are reliable—can be repeatedly observed in the same or like situations, and (2) that the situation bears on events that occur with some frequency in the infant's life. Thus the question is not whether the situation is natural but whether it can be generalized to other events in the infant's life. Only observation across a number of different situations can determine this. Thus the research strategy should be tuned to repeated observation over a variety of situations rather than the observation of behavior in a single natural or laboratory situation. This point needs to be emphasized, since many researchers feel the laboratory situation does not generate characteristic behavior, which, they believe, can be collected only in the natural situation of the home or the field. Of actual importance, however, is the generalizability of the behaviors, not the place of observation.

PROBLEMS IN STIMULUS MEANING

Regardless of the measurements employed or the labels applied, our systematic understanding of the nature of fear responses and their antecedents depends on our ability to specify the stimulus conditions within which our assessments are made. Although for discussion purposes it is feasible to consider two dimensions of the stimulus configuration with which the infant is confronted (i.e., the physical properties of the focal stimulus and the contextual cues provided by prior events and current conditions), it must be remembered that both dimensions coalesce in forming the stimulus array to which responses occur.

In terms of the physical characteristics of specific stimuli, particularly social stimuli, the studies described herein indicate that assessments of infant response must at the very least take into account and control for *(a)* the distance at which the stimulus is first perceived and how close it ultimately comes, *(b)* the relative speed with which the approach is made, *(c)* whether the social stimulus makes eye contact with, speaks to, and/or touches the infant, and *(d)* the size, age, and sex of the stimulus event. Thus it is now clear that an infant may show marked disturbance and fear when a stranger appears suddenly nearby and/or rapidly approaches and touches it, but show prolonged gaze and reaching toward one who approaches slowly from a distance. It is unclear in human infants whether young and adult conspecifics, of each sex, produce different responses as a result of some innately differentiated response, as has been indicated in nonhuman primates, or primarily as a result of prior experience with such stimulus figures, or their interaction. However, it is clear that different classes of stimulus may produce markedly different patterns of response.

Prior experience itself must be considered in a number of ways, and none has yet been adequately studied. For the specific stimulus event, it must be known whether the stimulus is a stranger, a familiar, or an attachment figure, bearing in mind the obvious potential gradations of experience that may occur along such an ordinal continuum. Furthermore, one must remember that the infant's experience with the class to which the individual belongs (e.g., a man in a white jacket) may have an important impact on the infant's response to an individual, even on first exposure to that specific person. More generally, on repeated exposure, through processes ranging from simple stimulus habituation to more complex assimilations, the infant shows changing response to the same,

originally novel stimulus whether animate or inanimate, even when such repetitions are temporally quite distinct. A consideration of this temporal sequencing
of stimuli, in terms of both immediately and more remotely antecedent events,
invokes some hypothesized memory capacity, which allows the infant to recognize previously experienced figures, either positive or negative in character, and
to alter its response configuration accordingly. Thus the effects of particular
types of prior experience may be expected to change as the infant's memory
apparatus matures. Even on a most limited time scale (i.e., within the time
frame of a given testing condition), the temporal and ordinal sequencing of
stimulus events must be carefully controlled for to prevent confounding of the
response to a given stimulus event (e.g., with such apparently benign but in
fact significant factors as the total time the infant is in the test situation when
the stranger appears and the place of the stimulus within a fixed sequence of
stimulus events). Despite the practical difficulties that might be involved in
more balanced test orders, it now seems reasonable to assume that the response
to a stranger is not the same at the beginning of even a 15-minute test as it
is at the end, nor is it the same when the entrance of the stranger precedes and
when it follows the departure of the mother or her return.

This brings us to our final concern regarding the contextual circumstances
that form a part of the stimulus conditions for assessment of fear in infants.
As discussed earlier, whether observations take place in the home or the laboratory or the field, we must concentrate on the determination and specification
of the most salient features of the test situation in terms of elements that may
readily be generalized beyond the initial test environment. Thus we must be
prepared to consider in some detail (a) the size and complexity of the test environment, (b) its actual familiarity to the infant (e.g., merely being in a room
in the home does not ensure total familiarity in the young infant), (c) the presence or absence of the mother at each test point and her juxtaposition to the
infant when present (e.g., on her lap, seated nearby, within the sight of the infant or not, (d) the mother's means of departure and reentry if such events are
instituted as part of the testing (e.g., exiting through a previously observed pas-
sageway through which the mother has previously left or returned).

In all these considerations of stimulus factors, both the more specific as well
as the contextual ones, it is necessary to bear in mind that the infant's perception and cognitive integration of these factors should provide the perspective for
viewing and controlling them. The maturational capacity of the infant's sensorimotor apparatus as well as his prior experiences will determine what he "sees"
and what he fails to detect. At later ages his anticipation of events and behaviors he has learned to expect, as well as his recognition of events reproduced
in whole or in part from his past, act as part of the codeterminants of his perception of and reaction to a given stimulus event. Finally, his developed range
of responses, as well as the degree to which the situation allows free expression

of such responses, may also influence the way in which a stimulus is perceived and the way in which it is reacted to. An infant, already able to locomote freely but restrained for testing in a Baby Tenda, may be unable to modulate through locomotion the stimulation derived from an approaching stranger in a way to which it has become accustomed; thus it may show more marked fearfulness than it would if free to regulate its exposure to the stimulus.

GENERAL THEORETICAL CONSIDERATIONS

We have been dealing with some of the important specific issues in the study of fear. Let us reconsider our original examples, attempting to summarize some of the general theoretical systems proposed for the eliciting of fear. It should be noted that these may have a more general use in describing other affective responses or systems.

At least in infancy it is reasonable to discuss the possibility that there exists a series of events having the innate biological capacity to elicit fearful behaviors. We need to consider events having intensive, sudden, and unexpected qualities (a loud sound) as well as more complex stimulus arrangements such as the departure of a familiar object (mother). The underlying mechanism may be related to some *innate releasing mechanism* built into the organism and designed for survival value. Thus there may exist predetermined response systems associated with specific events.

A large proportion of fear-producing events are learned. The conditioned fear paradigm in which a conditioned stimulus is paired with an unconditioned one to produce a conditioned response is highly likely. Ontogenetically this may develop from the organism's innate unconditioned responses. The bite of the dog and its pain associated with the configuration of the dog itself results in the conditioned response of fear to the sight of the dog. Fearful reactions to the doctor and the painful examination or injection are well-known, documented examples of this phenomenon. Furthermore, it is possible to include the mother's departure in this example, since the departure may have been associated with the mother's absence, itself a painful experience. Finally, the animal literature is replete with demonstrations of conditioned fear. In some sense it is the familiarity of the event that causes the fearful response, that is, the presence of the learned fearful event in the organism's schema. Thus although insufficient attention has been given to the formation of such fears during normal development in most infants, it is clear that learning accounts for a significant amount of fear-producing events.

Discrepancy, incongruity, and violation of expectancy are all similar constructs and are treated as similar in order to offer a third explanation. When an event is perceived as discrepant, it results in a state of arousal for the organism. This state can be characterized by inhibition of activity, including motor activity, attentive behavior, and specific physiological responses. This arousal precedes the specific affective response. The specific affective response is determined by the specific consequences of this arousal. In one theoretical scheme, it is related to the degree to which the infant can assimilate the arousing event. In another scheme, it is related to the specific cognition, needs, and plans the organism has at the time of the arousing event. In either scheme, however, the function of discrepancy is to arouse the organism; and arousal, though insufficient in itself, may lead to the specific affect.

It is interesting to note that both the presence of the schema, in the case of learned fear, and its absence, in the case of incongruity, have been hypothesized as affect producing. This should signify to us that the specific affective response is the result of a complex and poorly understood process involving the organism's status and its cognitions, plans, and strategies, as well as the stimulus properties and the contextual elements.

CHAPTER 1

Cognitive Components of the Infant's Response to Strangeness

H. RUDOLPH SCHAFFER

University of Strathclyde

In the growing literature on the infant's behavior toward strangeness, there is considerable agreement on a number of points. Since discussion so often tends to center on disagreements, it may be useful to begin by listing the issues on which empirical findings from a number of diverse studies indicate similar conclusions:

1. In the early months of life there is a fearless period, during which no avoidance responses are shown to any object (social or inanimate) on the basis of its unfamiliarity alone.

2. During the later stages of the fearless period, differential behavior toward unfamiliar individuals can be found, but it takes the form of diminished responsiveness and less enthusiastic proximity seeking rather than proximity avoidance and emotional upset.

3. The first onset of fear generally occurs in the third quarter of the first year. Although Spitz's (1950) term "8-months-anxiety" has been criticized for giving too precise an age of onset and not making sufficient allowance for individual differences, 8 months has in fact been found by most investigators (with the notable exception of Bronson, 1972) to represent the mode for the age of first appearance of fear responses.

4. Individual differences exist not only in the age of onset of fear but also in its intensity. It is likely that both genetic and experiential factors play a part in this respect, but their precise nature remains uncertain.

5. Both short-term and long-term stability of fearfulness is poor. Fluctuations occur according to many state and situational variables.

6. Fear is more easily induced by strange people than by strange objects.

7. Fear of strangers is not merely the opposite side of the coin to attachment behavior: there are differences both in age at onset and in the intensity of the two behavior systems. Nevertheless, the joint importance of these two developments lies in the indication that the infant is now truly capable of selective social behavior; that is, he can direct his proximity-seeking responses to certain

11

specific, familiar individuals while greeting all others with caution or outright avoidance.

There are, admittedly, disagreements in the literature, with particular reference to the incidence of fear, the age of peak intensity, and the conditions required to elicit the syndrome. To a large extent these are a function of methodological considerations, which have been reviewed elsewhere (Schaffer, 1971a). We have, however, established a descriptive account of the early developmental course of this syndrome that indicates clearly the progression from indiscriminate to increasingly selective behavior, reaching its culmination generally in the third quarter of the first year. It is of no small significance that a similar progression has also been outlined for a number of other species.

When we turn from descriptive to explanatory accounts, we are on much less firm ground. What are the factors responsible for the emergence of fear of strangers? Why, in particular, does it generally make its first appearance around the age of 8 months? To these questions we still have no firm answers. We may, however, be taken at least some of the way toward understanding if we pay attention to the specifically cognitive components of fear and examine the operations that the infant must perform in order to show awareness of strangeness. By reviewing the development of these operations, we find that a considerable amount of cognitive restructuring goes on in the third quarter of the first year, with particular reference to three kinds of fundamental change that can be detected in the infant's behavior at that time. These changes are, I want to suggest, implicated in the onset of fear of strangeness; thus they require examination here.

FROM IMPULSIVENESS TO WARINESS

Let us first note that fear-related behavior refers not to a unitary pattern of responses that invariably occur in conjunction with one another, but rather to a syndrome of diverse reactions, only some of which will enter into any one act that we call fearful. Even in infancy, the diversity is considerable, including such responses as staring, frowning, freezing, head turning, trembling, hand withdrawal, trunk twisting, crawling, running, and a fairly extensive range of vocalizations. "Fear" is thus an umbrella term for a variety of behavior patterns, linked, however, by their common function—namely, proximity avoidance.

To discuss fear as a unitary phenomenon, without due reference to its specific behavioral manifestation, may thus be misleading—particularly when we describe its developmental course. As Sluckin (1972) has pointed out, if distress calls are taken as an indication of fear, then fear in domestic chicks might be said to be in evidence from hatching onward. If, however, flight is taken as the criterion, fear responses do not become pronounced until about 24 hours of age. It seems, therefore, that the different components of the syndrome may appear as predictable reactions to strange stimuli at different ages rather than all together. This has obvious implications for apparently discrepant findings in studies using different indices.

What applies to chicks applies also to human infants. It appears that some behavior systems are sensitive to the effects of strangeness earlier than others, with particular reference to a developmental discrepancy between receptive and expressive functions. This conclusion has emerged from a series of studies in which we experimentally familiarized infants of various age groups within the second half-year on initially strange objects (see Figure 1) and in which we obtained measures of both visual and manipulative behavior (Schaffer, 1971b; Schaffer, Greenwood, & Parry, 1972; Schaffer & Parry, 1969, 1970, 1972). In all these experiments an age-by-response division occurred, the age break being located somewhere around 8 months. Before this age infants were already well capable of visual sensitivity to variations along the familiarity–unfamiliarity continuum: on its first appearance the strange object was greeted with prolonged staring (as indexed by both the length of the first visual fixation and the total amount of fixation during the trial), whereas on subsequent trials, with growing familiarity and increasing ability to assimilate the stimulus, visual attention gradually habituated and became progressively briefer. On the introduction of a second, incongruous object, attention once more revived, only to return to its

FIGURE 1.   "Wariness": 9-month-old infant confronted by unfamiliar object.

former level when the previous object was brought back again on the next trial. Thus infants at the beginning of the second half-year were as competent in responding differentially to the strange object by visual means as older infants. Manipulative measures, on the other hand, provide a different picture. Among infants older than about 8 months, latency to contact at the beginning of each trial was also found to be differentially influenced by variations in familiarity: when first confronted by the unfamiliar object, there was relatively prolonged hesitation to approach the stimulus (sometimes accompanied by avoidance responses and crying), and when contact was finally made, the first touch was mostly brief and cautious. With further familiarization, however, there was an increasingly greater readiness to reach for the object on its first appearance at the beginning of trials and to handle it with confidence. In younger infants, on the other hand, no such variation occurred in the manipulative measure, for from the very first trial on they approached the object impulsively and immediately—despite their ability perceptually to categorize the stimulus in terms of its degree of familiarity.

These data make it apparent that at the earlier age strangeness is responded to by one behavioral system but not yet by another—hence the disjunctive effect, which means that the ability to register information in terms of a familiarity–unfamiliarity dimension is not yet accompanied by selective approach–avoidance behavior as expressed by the infant's manipulative responses. It is as though action remains shielded from the effects of visual memory, and it is not until 8 months or so that the latter begins to exert control over the former and the two systems become truly coordinated. The differential sensitivity of different behavior systems to the effects of strangeness throws an interesting light on the information-processing operations of the young infant, in that it suggests the existence of modality-specific memories at this age; it also counsels caution in the choice of response indices, for one's knowledge of the effects of experimental familiarization may well depend (especially at this early age period) on the particular index chosen (Schaffer, 1973).

Clearly the third quarter of the first year witnesses a marked change in the infant's response to strangeness. But in what way does this change manifest itself? The usual answer to this question refers to the onset of avoidance responses. Whereas previously all stimuli, familiar or strange, were responded to positively, now the individual sometimes reacts with negative responses—that is, with fear and withdrawal. Our studies, however, suggest a somewhat different interpretation.

The change in manipulative behavior found to occur around the age of 8 months did not refer primarily to the beginnings of avoidance, but rather to the onset of the ability to check impulsive approach responses. Instead of indiscriminately making immediate reaching movements toward the strange object (as they had done previously), the infants showed a period of hesitation during which they generally subjected the stimulus to intense and uninterrupted visual inspection—as though appraising it before selecting a response deemed suitable in terms of the individual's past experience of that stimulus. Impulsiveness thus gave way to wariness, and the response that emerged after the period of immobility could take the form of approach *or* avoidance (i.e., cautious exploration or a fear reaction). Our first concern should therefore be with the development of the capacity for "not-approach"—that is, the ability to withhold the response—not with the onset of fear as such. Wariness is the primary problem; the direction ensuing behavior takes, whether toward or away from the stimulus, represents another, separate problem.

The developmental literature is full of studies showing how children learn to make responses, but very little has been said about the capacity *not* to respond. A number of animal studies, however, have addressed themselves to this problem. Vince (1961), for instance, compared young with adult birds in a problem-solving situation and found the juveniles to be superior at learning tasks requiring approach responses but inferior at tasks requiring avoidance: the ability of the young, that is, to inhibit responses that were not rewarded was found to be impaired. Working with rats, Riccio, Rohrbaugh, and Hodges (1968) found young animals to be inferior to adults in passive avoidance tasks involving the withholding of a response; yet no age differences were observed in other simple conditioning tasks, including active avoidance learning. To remain in one location and *not* to make a response was thus more difficult for the younger animals, yet they were just as capable as mature rats in learning to escape. A simi-lar conclusion emerges from a study by Brunner (1969), who also noted that younger rats in a passive avoidance situation appeared to be deficient in inhibiting an established response. There are thus some indications that the capacity for response inhibition is initially weak in the course of development.

Unfortunately the applicability of this proposition to human development has not been subjected to systematic inquiry. Other than the above-mentioned studies on manipulative wariness, relevant data on infants come from only one study by Siqueland (quoted by Lipsitt, 1970), in which 4-month-old infants were required to withhold sucking to obtain visual feedback. A slight decrease in the amount of sucking was found as a result of the contingency experience, but this appears to be no different from the decrease in rate shown by a baseline control group. A third group, on the other hand, who were reinforced for active sucking, produced rapid and marked response acquisition. Although no age comparisons were included in this study, we do have a hint that the capacity for response inhibition may be deficient in early human development, too.

It is, of course, possible that inhibitory capacity emerges at different times in different response systems and that some of the "older" systems show the effect earlier than the "younger." Indeed, according to Luria (1961) the inhibitory effect of speech on motor behavior does not occur until the fourth year or so: up to this age speech has only an impelling function, in that verbal commands cannot inhibit ongoing activity and tend to intensify it. Although the situation is psychologically very different from that concerned with the onset of wariness, the developmental sequence is the same: a period of impulsive and indiscriminate responding takes place first, and the capacity for inhibition manifests itself only subsequently. To respond is clearly easier than not to respond, and though the capacity for the latter may first manifest itself at various ages depending on particular conditions, it does seem that a major transition point in the development of this capacity is to be found in the third quarter of the first year.

FROM SEQUENTIAL TO SIMULTANEOUS CONSIDERATION

It is useful, as we turn to our second developmental theme, to make a distinction between two aspects of the fully developed (i.e., post-8-months) response to strangeness. This response is based in the first place on a *failure to recognize*—that is, an awareness that the stimulus does not match existing representations established as a result of previous experience and that it cannot therefore be readily assimilated. This is a relatively simple cognitive process: to see a stranger as unfamiliar (or, for that matter, mother as familiar) involves merely a match–mismatch judgment; that is, the infant searches for the counterpart of that particular stimulus and concludes that he either has or has not previously experienced it. His attentional behavior will then vary accordingly, visual fixation responses being particularly sensitive in this respect. It is this process that underlies the various indications of perceptual differentiation between familiar and unfamiliar people that appear as early as the third month.

The second aspect is a cognitively more sophisticated accomplishment, for it requires the stimulus to be seen as *different* in relation to another stimulus. It is based, in other words, on an active process of comparison, as a result of which the individual may conclude that the stimulus is like yet not the same as some standard. Thus instead of treating the stimulus in its own right isolated from other events, it requires that two different stimuli be related to one another. The stranger is not merely strange, he is different from mother; he is not seen only as initially unassimilable but is responded to as one element that may be related to other elements within a wider context. The first aspect refers to the question, Have I or have I not seen this stimulus before?; the second involves asking, How does this stimulus compare with my other experiences? Not surprisingly, the ability to deal with the latter appears developmentally well after the former, and again there are indications that the third quarter of the first year contains a major transition point in this respect.

Let me illustrate, although the data available to plot this development are still scarce. In a longitudinal study (Schaffer, Greenwood, & Parry, 1972) in which a group of infants was seen at 4-weekly intervals between 6 and 12 months, an initially unfamiliar object was exposed for seven 30-second trials. It was, replaced by another object (differing in color but of the same size and shape) on the eighth trial, whereas on the ninth trial the original object was brought back again. As Figure 2 indicates, measures of the length of the first visual fixation show an interesting change across age in the relative amounts for trials 1 and 8. At the youngest age level the unfamiliar stimulus encountered on the first trial elicited a great deal of attention—rather more than was shown to the incongruous stimulus subsequently exposed on trial 8. With increasing age, however, and particularly after 8 months, the relative attention paid to the novel

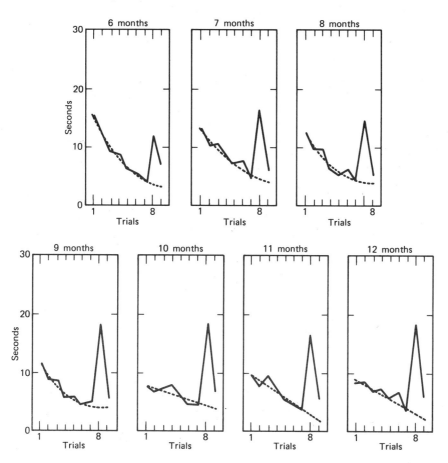

FIGURE 2.   Length of first visual fixation per trial obtained at monthly intervals from a group of 20 infants (broken lines represent regression curves based on the observed data obtained on the first seven trials).

and to the incongruous stimuli changed, in that the latter elicited far more prolonged fixations than the former. It is tempting to speculate that, with increasing
age, deviations from an established norm become more attention-worthy than
unfamiliarity *per se*. The interest of the stimulus thus derives not merely from
its absolute but also from its relative novelty—relative, that is, to other stimuli
to which it may be related and with which it may be compared and contrasted.
The infant, it seems, can now hold in mind more than one stimulus: it can consider several at the same time and has thus progressed from sequential to simultaneous consideration of different experiences.

The evidence is, of course, only indirect; nevertheless, these data hint that a
change occurs later in the first year in the infant's ability to connect different
stimuli with one another. Behavior in the early months of life has frequently
been characterized as "stimulus-bound," denoting a tendency to be absorbed in
one particular feature of the environment without regard to any other feature.
This gives early behavior its rather rigid character, for the young infant lives
in the here-and-now without concern for any event separated in time and space
from that which happens to preoccupy him at the moment. We may here recall
Piaget's (1950) description of sensorimotor intelligence as "a slow motion film,
in which all the pictures are seen in succession but without fusion, and so without the continuous vision necessary for understanding the whole." The ability
to connect various events is thus as yet absent. It is only later that the infant
can break out of these confines and begin to consider different events simultaneously and jointly instead of sequentially and separately, thereby bringing
about a marked increase in the temporal integration of his behavior.

In the response to strangeness, the younger infant also shows stimulus-bound
behavior. The stranger elicits a marked orienting response, he is stared at and
closely examined, yet without apparent reference to the mother. Even when the
mother is present as a possible standard of comparison, infants in the first half-
year do not use her as a source of reference by the to-and-fro looking behavior
that has been observed to occur subsequently and to precede the manifestation
of fear (Schaffer, 1971b). An observation by Morgan and Ricciuti (1969) may
be interpreted in the same light. These authors found that before the age of 8
months there was no difference in the form or intensity of the response to a
stranger, whether the child was sitting on his mother's lap or some feet away
from her, whereas thereafter proximity to the mother became increasingly important. A similar observation has been reported by Bronson (1972): he too
noted that the mother's presence initially did not affect the response to a stranger, whereas subsequently tactual contact with her (and still later also visual contact) did make a difference. Again the distinction arises between the stranger
as merely an unfamiliar stimulus on the one hand and, on the other hand, as
an individual whose appearance and location are related to those of other people
such as, in particular, the mother. As long as the infant's attention is com-

pletely preempted by the one ongoing event—namely, the stranger—the infant is unlikely to be affected by any other consideration, such as the whereabouts of the mother. Once he becomes capable of relating several stimuli to one another, however, he will not only be able to see the stranger as *different* but will also have reached the stage of being able to organize his behavior such that he not merely flees *from* the stranger but also *to* the mother.

The capacity for relating different stimuli to one another is thus an essential precondition for the more mature form of the stranger reaction. Under most circumstances, however, the comparison involves a centrally stored rather than a perceptually available standard—the sensory experience of the stranger, that is, is compared with a representation of the mother that is retrieved from memory. It thus becomes necessary to give some attention to the way in which changes in memory functioning are implicated in the onset of fear of strangeness.

FROM RECOGNITION TO RECALL

Although our knowledge of the role of memory in infancy is still scant, it is apparent that the infant's changing responsiveness to strangeness is in some way based on changes in memory functioning. This point has been generally accepted ever since Hebb (1946) placed the onus for the development of fear squarely on the part played by past experience. Fear accordingly requires the previous encoding of a familiar standard, which is established through repeated encounters with the relevant stimulus. Subsequent exposures to stimuli sufficiently like the familiar standard to arouse incompatible processes will produce disruption and emotional upheaval, which the individual will then attempt to reduce by means of avoidant behavior. As subsequently expressed by Hunt (1963), it is the perception of incongruity brought about by the unfamiliar stimulus that causes fear.

Although a number of writers (e.g., Moltz, 1963; Salzen, 1962; Scott, 1962) seem to regard the ability to differentiate between the familiar and the unfamiliar as the only condition necessary to produce fear or wariness, it has become apparent that such ability is not a sufficient condition. Both observational and experimental studies (cf. Schaffer, 1971a) have shown that differential behavior toward familiar and unfamiliar people can be found as early as the third month, yet fear of strangers does not set in until several months later. Similarly our studies, referred to previously, on wariness of strange objects indicate the disjunctive effect between visual differentiation and motor approach–avoidance responses. The role of memory in the production of fear is clearly more complex than the mere appreciation of lack of familiarity.

If, however, fear of strangers generally involves access to a centrally stored. rather than a peripherally available standard, the capacity to retrieve such a standard even in the physical absence of the corresponding stimulus is essential, and there are now a number of lines of evidence to indicate that such a capacity is absent in the first half-year or so. The infant, that is, can recognize but cannot as yet recall; he behaves differentially to the mother but in her absence shows no orientation toward her (such as separation upset), and similarly he cannot use her as a means of comparison when confronted by a stranger.

It is here that we learn why a number of writers (Décarie, 1972; Scarr & Salapatek, 1970; Schaffer, 1966) have suggested a link between the fear-of-strangers syndrome and the object concept. In the conventional test for the latter, the child is asked to retrieve a hidden object. To succeed, he must be able to remain oriented to the perceptually absent stimulus and continue this orientation despite his necessary preoccupation with the cover. If he cannot synthesize these two stimuli and is instead immediately distracted by the cover, he will not show the required searching behavior; if he can recall the object, however, and is not dependent on continuing sensory stimulation, he is deemed to have achieved conservation of the object. Both this test and the fear-of-strangers phenomenon are thus dependent on the capacity for spontaneous retrieval of stored information, and it is therefore unlikely that their occurrence at about the same age level is coincidental.

It is interesting that other studies also point to the third quarter of the first year as the time when memory functioning undergoes this fundamental change. In an operant conditioning study, Millar and Schaffer (1972) tested infants aged 6, 9, and 12 months under three conditions of spatial displacement of feedback source and manipulandum. In one condition (the 0° condition), feedback emanated from the manipulandum itself; in the second condition feedback was provided by a spatially separate source displaced 5° to the subject's midline; in the third condition the feedback source was displaced 60° to the side, so that it was no longer visually directly accessible when fixating the manipulandum. Feedback took the form of a brief flash of light accompanied by a bleep and was obtained by discrete touches of the manipulandum. Results indicate that all three age groups learned under the 0 and 5° conditions, but under the 60° condition the 6-month-old group failed to acquire the contingency. It appeared that the behavior of these younger infants became disrupted when the displacement was such that manipulandum and feedback source were no longer both directly within the same visual field. A memory factor is thus implicated, in that a successful solution demanded that infants bear in mind a stimulus that was no longer perceptually accessible.

This interpretation was investigated in a second experiment (Millar & Schaffer, 1973) by obtaining visual as well as manipulative measures from 6- and 9-month-old infants confronted by the 60° task. The data not only confirm the previously obtained age difference but also throw light on its cause. The older infants, it appears, were able to solve the task by visually fixating the feedback source while at the same time repeatedly touching the manipulandum. The younger infants, on the other hand, were not able to adopt such a "simultaniz-ing strategy"; these infants, it was observed, could not maintain tactual contact with the manipulandum without at the same time visually fixating it. To them, out of sight was out of mind, and the response strategy adopted by the older group was thus cognitively beyond them. Although capable of all the individual components (touching the manipulandum, fixating the feedback source), the younger infants treated them as separate categories of events which they were unable to integrate into a unitary whole.

We have here an illustration of the theme mentioned previously (the development from sequential to simultaneous processing) and the present theme (the ability spontaneously to retrieve central representations). Initially, it seems, each event experienced by the infant is so preemptive of attention that it cannot be related to any other event, particularly when such other event is not directly perceptually experienced. Only after the age of about 8 months are there indications that infants become able spontaneously to retrieve information and to relate it to concurrent activity. To act in the absence of the corresponding object seems to be a task beyond the cognitive capabilities of the younger infant. Thus Gratch (1972) has shown that 6-month-old infants will remove a transparent cloth from their hand after grasping a toy but will not remove an opaque one: in the absence of continuing visual input the appropriate motor response is not made, for at this age visual perception is required to guide action, visual memory being insufficient. A similar conclusion arises from a study by Millar (unpublished): in an operant conditioning situation, infants' manipulative responses were reinforced by a brief flash of light coming from behind a translucent panel in front of the subject. In one condition the precise feedback locus remained marked throughout the procedure by a ring, thus enabling the infant to remain oriented to this location during interresponse intervals; in the other condition such a cue was not available. Operant acquisition was found under both conditions in 9-month-old infants; 6-month-old infants, however, could learn only under the cue-assisted condition. In the absence of a visual prop these younger infants were unable to remain oriented to the source of task-relevant information: memory, once again, was found not to act as a guide under such circumstances.

Recall, it may be asserted, is a phenomenon that occurs developmentally later than recognition. As the various experimental situations described indicate, it does not appear until the age of about 8 months; thus from then on the role of past experience becomes far more important. Any explanation of fear of strangeness based on a comparison of the unfamiliar with the previously experienced familiar must take cognizance of the child's ability to recall. It is suggested that the same age of onset for the two phenomena is more than coincidental.

CONCLUSIONS

We have been concerned with three developmental themes that may be detected in early behavior, referring to these as the transitions from impulsiveness to wariness, from sequential to simultaneous consideration, and from recognition to recall. Each theme refers to a widening of the infant's capacity to handle his experience, and there are indications in each case that a significant transition point is reached in the third quarter of the first year. Together they thus indicate that this age range constitutes a period of major cognitive restructuring, with implications, it has been suggested, for the onset of the fear-of-strangeness syndrome.

We have so far treated the three themes in isolation, but it seems likely that the onset of fear is the result of the three forces operating jointly. To substantiate this point, let us return to Luria's account of the influence of speech on motor behavior. Initially, according to Luria, speech has only a releasing function—the command "Don't press" immediately results in pressing responses to the bulb held by the child. To withhold the response is not yet possible for the younger child: he behaves impulsively and indiscriminately to all verbal stimuli. The capacity for inhibition appears later, and one of the conditions for inhibition is the ability to take into consideration two different events (e.g., "When you see the red light, don't press the bulb"). Instead of responding to each event separately and sequentially (by orienting and pressing), the child is now able to consider both instructions simultaneously and jointly—even when the command was given previously and must therefore be retrieved. The conflict of intention thus induced by the two simultaneous excitations, Luria believes, gives rise to a state of inhibition, which takes the place of the previous impulsive behavior triggered by each separate event.

A similar process may be hypothesized as underlying the onset of fear of strangeness. Initially each stimulus is treated in isolation; and although the memory store may be checked for representations of that same stimulus, it is not compared with different stimuli or their representations. In time, however, the infant becomes capable of relating stimuli to one another—Piaget's slow-motion film is speeded up and the infant is made aware of the connections between the various images. As a result, the strange stimulus can be considered simultaneously with the familiar standard, even though the latter is centrally stored and must therefore be retrieved. The ensuing conflict (which, following Hebb, we may ascribe to perceived incongruity) leads to the inhibition of the primary approach response and results in the wariness phenomenon which, we have suggested, underlies and precedes any manifestation of fear. Wariness therefore occurs when the infant becomes able to consider two different elements simultaneously, even though one is centrally rather than peripherally available.

References

Bronson, G. W. Infants' reactions to unfamiliar persons and novel objects. *Monographs of the Society for Research in Child Development*, 1972, **37** (3, Serial No. 148).

Brunner, R. L. Age differences in one-trial passive avoidance learning. *Psychonomic Science*, 1969, **14,** 134–136.

Décarie, T. G. *La réaction du jeune enfant à la personne étrangère*. Montreal: University of Montreal Press, 1972.

Gratch, G. A study of the relative dominance of vision and touch in six-month-old infants. *Child Development*, 1972, **43,** 615–624.

Hebb, D. O. On the nature of fear. *Psychological Review*, 1946, **53,** 250–275.

Hunt, J. McV. Piaget's observations as a source of hypotheses concerning motivation. *Merrill-Palmer Quarterly*, 1963, **9,** 263–275.

Lipsitt, L. P. Developmental psychology. In A. Gilgen (Ed.), *Contemporary scientific psychology*. New York: Academic Press, 1970.

Luria, A. R. *The role of speech in the regulation of normal and abnormal behaviour*. Oxford: Pergamon Press, 1961.

Millar, W. S. The role of visual-holding cues in infant operant learning. Unpublished.

Millar, W. S., & Schaffer, H. R. The influence of spatially displaced feedback on infant operant conditioning. *Journal of Experimental Child Psychology*, 1972, **14,** 442–453.

Millar, W. S., & Schaffer, H.R. Visual-manipulative response strategies in infant operant conditioning with spatially displaced feedback. *British Journal of Psychology*, 1973, **64,** 545-552.

Moltz, H. Imprinting: An epigenetic approach. *Psychological Review*, 1963, **70,** 123–138.

Morgan, G. A., & Ricciuti, H. N. Infants' responses to strangers during the first year. In B. M. Foss (Ed.), *Determinants of infant behaviour*. Vol. 4. London: Methuen; New York: Wiley, 1969.

Piaget, J. *The psychology of intelligence*. London: Routledge & Kegan Paul, 1950.

Riccio, D. C., Rohrbaugh, M., & Hodges, L. A. Developmental aspects of passive and active avoidance learning in rats. *Developmental Psychobiology*, 1968, **1,** 108–111.

Salzen, E. A. Imprinting and fear. *Symposia of the Zoological Society of London*, 1962, **8,** 197–217.

Scarr, S., & Salapatek, P. Patterns of fear development during infancy. *Merrill-Palmer Quarterly*, 1970, **16,** 53–90.

Schaffer, H. R. The onset of fear of strangers and the incongruity hypothesis. *Journal of Child Psychology and Psychiatry*, 1966, **7,** 95–106.

Schaffer, H. R. *The growth of sociability*. Baltimore: Penguin, 1971a.

Schaffer, H. R. Cognitive structure and early social behaviour. In H. R. Schaffer (Ed.), *The origins of human social relations*. London: Academic Press, 1971b.

Schaffer, H. R. The multivariate approach to early learning. In R. A. Hinde & J. S. Hinde (Eds.), *Constraints on learning: Limitations and predispositions*. London: Academic Press, 1973.

Schaffer, H. R., Greenwood, A., & Parry, M. H. The onset of wariness. *Child Development*, 1972, **43**, 165–175.

Schaffer, H. R., & Parry, M. H. Perceptual-motor behaviour in infancy as a function of age and stimulus familiarity. *British Journal of Psychology*, 1969, **60**, 1–9.

Schaffer, H. R., & Parry, M. H. The effects of short-term familiarization on infants' perceptual-motor coordination in a simultaneous discrimination situation. *British Journal of Psychology*, 1970, **61**, 559–569.

Schaffer, H. R., & Parry, M. H. Effects of stimulus movement on infants' wariness of unfamiliar objects. *Developmental Psychology*, 1972, **7**, 87.

Scott, J. P. Critical periods in behavioral development. *Science*, 1962, **138**, 949–958.

Sluckin, W. *Imprinting and early learning*. (2nd ed.), London: Methuen, 1972.

Spitz, R. A. Anxiety in infancy: A study of its manifestations in the first year of life. *International Journal of Psychoanalysis*, 1950, **31**, 138–143.

Vince, M. A. Developmental changes in learning capacity. In W. H. Thorpe & O. L. Zangwill (Eds.), *Current problems in animal behaviour*. Cambridge, England: Cambridge University Press, 1961.

CHAPTER 2

Fear-Mediated Processes in the Context of Imprinting[1]

HOWARD S. HOFFMAN
Bryn Mawr College

The concept of fear is basic to the analysis of imprinting. Indeed, there is hardly an aspect of this phenomenon in which fear, in one form or another, fails to play a role. My purpose here is to analyze that role by examining the several kinds of fear-mediated processes that are known to occur in the imprinting situation. Before attempting to do so, however, it is necessary to define the term "imprinting" as clearly as possible, for despite its widespread usage, there is little agreement about exactly what imprinting entails.

WHAT IS IMPRINTING?

As commonly conceived, imprinting represents an essentially irreversible process in which a young developing organism establishes an enduring social bond with the first appropriate stimulus that it encounters. Because the word "imprinting" connotes stamping in, the process is often thought to occur more or less instantaneously, and, like the placing of a seal, to leave an indelible impression. Based on such conceptions, Moore and Shiek (1971) have suggested that infantile autism may represent imprinting in the womb. Presumably this can occur when the infant is so precocious that the critical period for imprinting occurs prior to birth. As a result, the neonate becomes imprinted on the stimulation provided by its own body and so is precluded from forming subsequent social attachments. As is discussed here, such suggestions bear little relation to the conceptions of imprinting that have emerged from recent investigations. Based on studies in my own and other laboratories, for example, it is clear that imprinting is neither instantaneous nor irreversible. Moreover, it does not represent the kind of exclusive fixation process implied by Moore and Shiek in their attempt to explain autism.

[1]Preparation of this manuscript, as well as much of the research on which it is based, was supported by NIMH Grant no. 19715. I wish to thank Katharine J. Boskoff, Leonard A. Eiserer, and Alan M. Ratner, who participated in many phases of the research and made substantial contributions to the concepts elucidated here.

The view of imprinting to be developed here has been elaborated fully else-where (Hoffman & Ratner, 1973). Basically it is quite simple. It asserts that certain aspects of imprinting stimuli are primary reinforcers that innately elicit filial behavior. In doing so, these aspects serve as unconditioned stimuli, ena-bling the development of familiarity with the other characteristics of a given im-printing stimulus through classical conditioning. Familiarity serves to prevent novelty-induced fear reactions that would otherwise compete with the filial re-sponse at later stages of ontogenetic development.

When viewed in this way, imprinting is less a means of establishing and fixating a filial reaction on a given stimulus than a means of preventing future competing reactions that would interfere with an innate tendency to react filial-ly. Interestingly, each of the behavioral processes contributing to this phenom-enon is quite well known. For example, to suggest that an imprinting stimulus innately elicits filial behavior is merely to identify that stimulus as an uncondi-tioned stimulus (US). There is scarcely a behavioral scientist who has not em-ployed the notion of an unconditioned stimulus at one time or another. Similar-ly, every behavioral scientist is familiar with the idea that pairing a US with a neutral stimulus under appropriate circumstances can lead to the establishment of a conditioned response. To suggest that imprinting entails a form of classical conditioning is merely to identify the various elements of the imprinting situ-ation with the appropriate elements of the classical conditioning paradigm. Sur-prisingly, however, this task has been rather difficult. The problem has been succinctly described by Rajecki (1973). In examining the role of classical condi-tioning in imprinting, Rajecki asks:

"Is it then a classical conditioning paradigm? An unconditioned response is indeed present, approach and following, and this can become the conditioned response. An unconditioned stimulus is also present, the conspicuous stimulus, for this stimulus can automatically elicit the response on first presentation and hence reinforce the conditioned response to the conditioned stimulus. But if the unconditioned stimulus is the conspicuous stimulus, what is the conditioned stimulus?"

Fortunately, the resolution to this paradoxical question is now at hand. It stems from the finding that the nervous systems of many organisms include highly refined detector mechanisms that are responsive to specific forms of stim-ulation only. Thus in the cat, as well as a number of other organisms such as the pigeon, the rabbit, and the frog, it has been possible to isolate detectors that respond only when the subject is exposed to stimulation provided by the motion of an object across the visual field. Since these detectors are silent when the same object is stationary, they have been identified as "motion detectors" (McIlwain, 1972). Their relevance to imprinting becomes apparent when one considers the finding (Hoffman, Eiserer, & Singer, 1972) that while an appropriate imprinting stimulus (e.g., a moving object) immediately elicits a filial reaction in newly hatched precocial birds, the same object presented stationary fails to do so until the subject has been exposed to it in motion. In short, the static features of an imprinting object (e.g., its size, shape, and color) may not innately elicit filial reactions, but they can acquire the capacity to do so and in this sense can function as conditioned stimuli if they are paired with the stimulation provided by the object in motion.

In an apparatus used to investigate this process (Figure 1), a moving white foam rubber object serves as an imprinting stimulus for a newly hatched duckling; since it is located behind a controllable one-way-vision screen, its presence or absence can be readily manipulated by the experimenter. Unlike most imprinting arrangements, in which interest focuses only on the ducklings' tendency to follow the imprinting stimulus, this apparatus is especially designed also to permit assessment of the ducklings' distress calls. Because these calls are quite intense and have a limited frequency range (3000–4000 Hz), they can be unambiguously detected by employing a voice-activated relay that incorporates an appropriate filtering circuit.

The use of distress calling as a quantitative index of the ducklings' filial reactions to the imprinting stimulus has several advantages over the assessment of its tendency to follow that stimulus (the more usual index of a duckling's filial reaction). First, although a duckling's locomotor abilities are not completely developed when it hatches, its capacity to emit distress calls is evident even before it is free of its shell. Second, whereas assessment of following behavior focuses mostly on the reactions that occur in the presence of the imprinting stimulus, assessment of distress calling focuses on the *changes* in behavior that occur when the imprinting stimulus is presented and then withdrawn. This strategy is

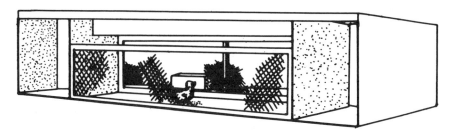

FIGURE 1.   Apparatus used to study imprinting. The imprinting stimulus (visible behind the rear screen) consists of a block of foam rubber mounted over the cab of a model train engine. With this apparatus, stimulus presentation is produced by illuminating the stimulus compartment and initiating back-and-forth movement of the engine. When its compartment is darkened, the stimulus is not visible. The vertical pole in the center of the screen can be used as a manipulandum. Under an appropriate arrangement, pecks at the pole will initiate stimulus presentation.

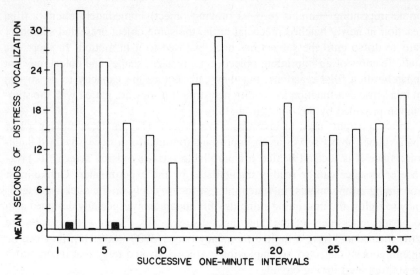

FIGURE 2.   Mean number of seconds of distress vocalization during alternating periods of stimulus presentation and withdrawal. Ducklings were placed in individual housing units when they were first free of their shell. They remained there undisturbed until testing began (17 hours later). Stimulus presentation occurred during even-numbered minutes. (From Hoffman, Eiserer, Ratner, & Pickering, 1974.)

particularly useful when one is interested in the subjects' earliest reactions, because it provides unambiguous behavioral measurements before, during, and after the imprinting stimulus is first presented. Obviously, if one assessed following behavior only, the measurement interval would be limited to the period when the imprinting stimulus was present.

Figure 2 shows the average number of seconds of distress calling prior to, during, and following each of a sequence of 1-minute presentations of a moving imprinting stimulus to a number of newly hatched ducklings. These birds had been individually hatched in an incubator, and then they were transferred to individual housing units. When a given duckling was 17 hours old, it was placed alone in the imprinting apparatus for the first time. As Figure 2 indicates, distress calling occurred at a high rate until the imprinting stimulus was first presented. Although the ducklings had not previously seen either the imprinting stimulus or any other moving object, ongoing distress calls were almost completely suppressed during the initial stimulus presentation, and their subsequent occurrence was largely limited to periods when the stimulus was withdrawn.

This finding, together with those of several other experimenters (Hoffman, Stratton, Newby, & Barrett, 1970; Bateson & Reese, 1968), implies that ducklings are predisposed to react positively to the special class of visual stimula-

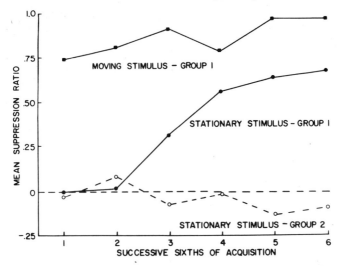

FIGURE 3. Acquisition of control over distress vocalization by a stationary stimulus. Ducklings in group 1 were exposed to trials in which the stimulus was stationary, interspersed among trials in which the stimulus moved. Ducklings in group 2 were never exposed to the stimulus in motion. (From Hoffman, Eiserer, & Singer, 1972.)

tion provided by moving objects. For this reason, it gives a clear indication that the filial reaction to visual motion is innately determined.

It was noted earlier that although the initial presentation of a moving stimulus completely suppresses a newly hatched duckling's distress calls, presentations of the same stimulus stationary do not, and they only gradually acquire the ability to do so if the subject is also exposed to the stimulus in motion.

Figure 3 illustrates the acquisition of control over distress vocalization by the static features of a stationary imprinting stimulus. One group of previously isolated 17-hour-old ducklings was repeatedly exposed to the same imprinting stimulus in an arrangement where trials in which the stimulus was moving were alternated with trials in which the stimulus was stationary. A second group of ducklings was also repeatedly exposed to the same imprinting stimulus, but the stimulus was stationary on all trials. With the response index used here, a suppression ratio of 1.0 indicates that ongoing distress vocalization was completely suppressed during stimulus presentation, whereas a ratio of zero indicates that ongoing distress vocalization persisted, undiminished, throughout stimulus presentation. As revealed by the flat function for the subjects that never saw the stimulus move, mere exposure to the static features of the imprinting stimulus failed to endow those features with the capacity to control distress calls. When, however, presentations of the moving stimulus were interspersed among presentations of the stationary stimulus, its features gradually acquired the capacity to suppress distress calls. These findings provide a direct and unambiguous illustration of the role of classical conditioning in imprinting. They indicate that the stimulation arising from visual movement innately suppresses distress calling, and that by virtue of their association with this reinforcing stimulation, the other, initially neutral, features of the stimulus gradually acquire the capacity to themselves function in this fashion. Of course, this is not to suggest that visual movement is the only innately reinforcing stimulation in the imprinting situation. Several species of precocial birds have been found to display an immediate filial response to flickering lights (James, 1959, 1960) and to appropriate, often species-specific forms of acoustic stimulation (Gottlieb, 1965; Gottlieb & Simner, 1969). Indeed, in a natural setting certain forms of stimulation may be even more effective than visual movement in eliciting and controlling the filial response. There is, however, no reason to suspect that these forms of stimulation function in a manner basically different from the one revealed here for visual movement.

It is of interest that Mason, Hill, and Thompson (1971) have performed an experiment with infant monkeys that is strikingly similar in procedure and results to the one we conducted. The work of Harlow and his associates had made it clear that for infant monkeys the tactile stimulation that arises from a claspable mother surrogate was sufficient to innately elicit a filial response. In accord with this proposition, Mason *et al.* found that infant monkeys emitted few distress calls in the presence of the surrogate when contact with it was permitted; this control was evident during the first test session and each subsequent one. However, the ability of the surrogate to control distress calling when encased in plastic (i.e., unavailable for contact) became apparent only after the subject had been raised with the claspable surrogate for several weeks. This finding suggests that the specific visual characteristics of a surrogate mother become familiar to an infant monkey and acquire the ability to elicit filial behavior through a classical conditioning process that closely resembles the one that we are postulating for imprinting. At this point, the only major differences appear to be that the conditioning process requires more time with the slower maturing primate than it does with a newly hatched precocial bird and that the reinforcing stimulation that subserves the conditioning process for primates is contact rather than movement.

Among the most salient characteristics of imprinting is that once a bird has been imprinted to a given stimulus, its filial behavior tends to be restricted to that stimulus, or at least the class of stimuli that include it. The development of this stimulus specificity was recently examined in my laboratory. In that study (Hoffman, Ratner, & Eiserer, 1972) previously isolated 17-hour-old ducklings were individually afforded a series of five brief (30-second) exposures to the moving foam rubber object illustrated in Figure 1. In the same session they also received a series of five brief exposures to an amber rotating lamp

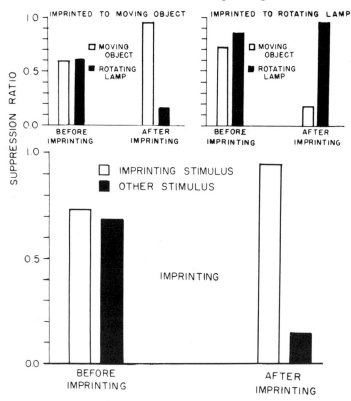

FIGURE 4.   The suppression of distress vocalization during initial (preimprinting) and final (postimprinting) tests. In the interval between tests, a given duckling received a sequence of extended imprinting exposures to either the moving object (Figure 1) or a rotating lamp. The upper graphs plot the data from subjects imprinted to either the moving object or the rotating lamp. The larger graph combines these data. With the index of suppression used here, a ratio of 1 indicates that ongoing distress calls were completely suppressed during stimulus presentation, whereas a ratio of zero indicates that distress calling continued unabated. (From Hoffman, Ratner, & Eiserer, 1972.)

(like those seen on the top of many police vehicles). Next, a given duckling received extended imprinting exposure (six 20-minute sessions) to one or the other object. When the birds were 5 days old, they were again tested by presenting one and then the other stimulus in a sequence of brief exposures. As revealed in Figure 4, prior to extended imprinting exposure, both objects exhibited a strong tendency to suppress ongoing distress vocalization. After imprinting, the control exhibited by the imprinting stimulus increased slightly, and the control exerted by the nonimprinted stimulus declined. This finding is clearly representative of the stimulus specificity that characterizes imprinting. Before

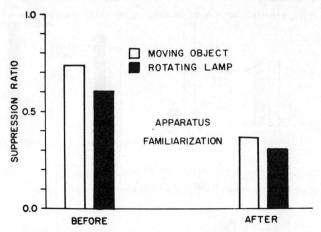

FIGURE 5.   The suppression of distress vocalization during initial (preimprinting) and final (postimprinting) tests. In the interval between tests the ducklings
received extended exposure to the imprinting apparatus, but neither imprinting
stimulus was presented. With the index of suppression used here, a ratio of
1 indicates that ongoing distress calls were completely suppressed during stimulus presentation, whereas a ratio of zero indicates that distress calling continued
unabated. (From Hoffman, Ratner, & Eiserer, 1972.)

lengthy imprinting exposure, each of two quite different stimuli could control
the ducklings' distress calls. After imprinting, however, the control was largely
limited to the stimulus that had been employed in the lengthy imprinting exposure.

Figure 5 shows the performance of a second group of ducklings that received
identical brief test exposures to the moving object and the rotating lamp, but
these subjects were denied exposure to either stimulus in the 4-day interval between the two tests. As revealed in Figure 5, both stimuli strongly suppressed
distress calls during the initial test (when the ducklings were 17 hours old).
When, however, the ducklings were again tested with the same stimuli on day
5, both stimuli exhibited a decline in their capacity to suppress distress calling.[2]
This finding provides evidence that the loss in control by a nonimprinted
stimulus is not merely a product of imprinting to some other stimulus. Apparently the factors responsible for this loss can be found in a process that would
be expected to increase as a duckling grows older, regardless of whether it was

[2] The finding that some suppression of distress calling occurred on day 5 is deceptive because
observation of the ducklings revealed that rather than representing a low, but positive, filial reaction, it reflected a strong initial tendency to either freeze or flee when the stimulus was presented.
That distress calling is sometimes suppressed in strong fear has been recently documented by Montevecchi, Gallup, and Dunlap (1973). Their findings, in conjunction with those revealed here, indicate that the distress call has more than one determinant, and they highlight the need to take account
of the total behavioral milieu in assessing the significance of a given behavioral index such as distress calls. This issue is discussed more fully in Hoffman and Solomon (1974).

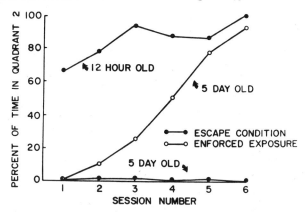

FIGURE 6. The percentage of time that previously isolated 12-hour-old and 5-day-old ducklings spent in close proximity to a moving imprinting stimulus. For ducklings in the control condition, the imprinting stimulus was presented throughout each session regardless of where the duckling was situated. For subjects in the escape condition, the stimulus was withdrawn whenever the duckling left the region of the experimental space immediately adjacent to the stimulus (quadrant 2). (Adapted from Ratner & Hoffman, in press.)

imprinted to a given stimulus. One such process is novelty-induced fear.

The results of a number of investigations have indicated that in precocial birds, the tendency to react fearfully increases gradually as ontogenetic development proceeds (Hess, 1959, 1972; Hess & Schaefer, 1959). In ducklings, for example, such fear reactions are quite weak during the first few hours posthatch, but by the time a duckling is 5 days old, they are likely to be extremely strong. A recent experiment (Ratner & Hoffman, in press) provides a good example of the way in which novelty-induced fear functions in the context of imprinting. In that experiment we arranged that several groups of ducklings received their initial exposure to an imprinting stimulus under conditions in which the stimulus was withdrawn whenever the duckling attempted to retreat from it. Figure 6 shows the percentage of time, in each of the six daily sessions, that the ducklings in each group spent near the stimulus. Subjects in one group were first exposed to the stimulus at 12 hours posthatch. Subjects in the second group were maintained in isolation until day 5 posthatch, whereupon they were individually exposed to the stimulus. Figure 6 also shows the percentage of time that a third group of previously isolated 5-day-old ducklings spent near the stimulus. However, the attempts of these subjects to escape did not lead to stimulus withdrawal. As revealed in Figure 6, even though escape was possible, the 12-hour-old ducklings spent most of their time in the immediate vicinity of the stimulus. Five-day-old ducklings, on the other hand, given the opportunity to escape, did so, and this behavior persisted throughout the six sessions of testing. When, however, 5-day-old ducklings were exposed to the condition in which retreat did not lead to stimulus withdrawal, their attempts to escape gradually ceased, and they spent increasing amounts of time in the immediate vicinity of the stimulus. These findings verify the assertion that in newly hatched (12-hour-old) duck-lings, novelty-induced fear is too weak to interfere appreciably with the in-nately elicited filial reaction, whereas in older (5-day-old) ducklings, the tendency to react fearfully is overwhelmingly strong. They also point to the conclusion that despite its strong tendency to evoke fear in an older duckling, an appro-priate imprinting stimulus maintains its potentiality to elicit a filial reaction. This follows because when complete escape is precluded, rather than merely stopping its efforts at escape, an older duckling begins to actively ap-proach and stay nearby the stimulus. Clearly these findings, considered in their entirety, provide strong support for the conclusion that imprinting serves to pro-tect an innate tendency to respond filially against future interference by a com-peting fear reaction.

THE DEVELOPMENT OF NOVELTY–INDUCED FEAR

As suggested by the terms used to describe it, novelty-induced fear cannot occur unless the subject recognizes that a given stimulus is unfamiliar. This implies the need for a history of experience with what comes to be familiar stimulation against which the new stimulus can be contrasted. Several investigators (Salzen, 1970; Bateson, 1971; Dimond, 1970) have suggested that this is the only condi-tion required for the emergence of novelty-induced fear. According to this posi-tion, once a newly hatched duckling has formed a conceptual (neuronal) model of the conspicuous stimuli in its environment (i.e., is familiar with them), stim-uli that are discriminably different would fail to match the neuronal model, and this would automatically generate aversive reactions.

A recent experiment in my laboratory, however, asked whether this is a suffi-cient condition for the occurrence of novelty-induced fear, or whether certain other factors must also be considered. Hints that this might be the case were provided by the data presented in Figure 5: when 5-day-old ducklings were con-fronted with two different imprinting stimuli that had been seen for a brief (25-minute) period earlier, but not subsequently, they responded fearfully rather than filially. This suggests that a factor other than extensive exposure to a given imprinting stimulus may also be important in the emergence of novelty-induced fear.

One way to examine this possibility is to ask whether newly hatched duck-lings that respond filially rather than fearfully to each of two different sequen-tially presented imprinting stimuli are able to recognize that the stimuli are dif-ferent. That is, one may ask whether a newly hatched duckling's lack of an appreciable fear reaction when confronted with various imprinting stimuli is pred-icated on its lack of a conceptual model against which a given imprinting stimulus can be contrasted. If it could be shown that very young ducklings can differentiate between two imprinting stimuli, both of which elicit filial reactions, it would imply that the recognition of novelty might be a necessary but not a *sufficient* condition for the occurrence of novelty-induced fear.

To examine this issue, we used an experimental procedure in which young (10- to 14-hour-old) ducklings were exposed to a counterbalanced sequence of presentations of moving and stationary stimuli. The rationale for this procedure was derived from the finding illustrated in Figure 3, which indicates that although the presentation of a moving stimulus immediately suppresses distress calls, stationary presentations of the same stimulus fail to do so until the duckling has been given adequate exposure to that stimulus in motion. We capitalized on that finding by employing a design in which newly hatched ducklings were sequentially exposed to two different stationary stimuli after they had received lengthy exposure to one of them in motion. Under such circumstances, only the static features of the now-stationary but previously moving stimulus would be expected to suppress distress calls. The other stationary stimulus, never having been seen in motion, would not be expected to function in this way. To the extent that such a differentiation was evident, it would suggest the existence of a conceptual model of the familiar stimulus against which the static features of the novel stimulus was contrasted. In addition, by subsequently presenting the novel stimulus in motion, it would be possible to replicate the earlier findings of nondifferentiated emission of filial reactions to *moving* stimuli by subjects of this age.

In this experiment, half the subjects were initially exposed to the foam rubber object seen in Figure 1 and subsequently exposed to the lamp stimulus, described earlier. The other subjects were initially exposed to the lamp stimulus and subsequently exposed to the foam rubber object. For expository purposes, the stimulus used first (either the lamp or the foam rubber object) is identified as S_1 and the other stimulus is identified as S_2. For both groups of ducklings, initial exposure to the S_1 occurred after a 60-second adaptation period in the apparatus. It consisted of five 20-second periods in which the stimulus was presented stationary. The birds were then given five 20-second periods in which the same stimulus was presented in motion. Each stationary presentation and each moving presentation was preceded by a 20-second baseline period in which the stimulus was withdrawn.

Immediately following the completion of these tests, the ducklings were given continuous 20-minute exposure to the S_1 in motion. Half these subjects were then again exposed to the S_1 stationary for five 20-second periods (each preceded by a 20-second stimulus-absent period). The remaning ducklings were exposed to the stationary S_2 in an identical fashion. Then the birds that had been tested with the stationary S_1 were tested with the stationary S_2, and vice versa. Following this, each subject was given five 20-second presentations and withdrawals of the S_2 in motion and then a continuous 20-minute exposure to the S_2 in motion. Finally the ducklings were again tested by repeatedly presenting and withdrawing the stationary S_2. With this experimental design, both stimulus and order effects were completely counterbalanced.

The study revealed that the ducklings immediately began distress calling when they were introduced to the novel test apparatus, and except during presentation of one or the other stimulus, they continued to emit distress calls throughout the test session. Figure 7 illustrates the mean suppression of the ongoing distress calling that each stimulus afforded. As can be seen in this figure, both the S_1 and the S_2, when presented in motion, exhibited suppressive control. However, when they were presented stationary, neither stimulus exerted such control unless the subject had previously been exposed to it moving.

By exhibiting appropriately differentiated response tendencies to the stimuli when presented stationary, these subjects provide clear evidence of their capacity to discriminate between the familiar and the unfamiliar. A stationary imprinting stimulus suppressed distress vocalization only when it had previously been presented in motion. Clearly, the undifferentiated reactions of very young ducklings to *moving* stimuli occur despite the subjects' ability to discriminate between them. This conclusion is similar to the one reached by Schaffer (1966) in a study in which ability of human infants to discriminate between their mothers and a stranger was examined. Schaffer noted that this ability became evident before the infants displayed fear of the strangers—apparently an "age-gap exists, when the stranger is experienced as different (from the mother), yet not as frightening. It must be concluded that the ability to make the distinction is a necessary but not a sufficient condition . . . [p. 103]" for the emergence of fearlike reactions.

All this indicates that in both the duckling and the human infant, maturational factors must play an important role in the emergence of novelty-induced fear. This would explain the findings reported here, and it would also explain what has been described as "the critical period for imprinting" (Lorenz, 1935, 1937). Prior to the period when strong fear emerges, a duckling will immediately approach and stay nearby any stimulus that exhibits the prerequisite eliciting properties. As the tendency to react fearfully emerges, however, the subject shows an increasing tendency to run away from imprinting stimuli that are unfamiliar. If, as was seen in Figure 6, these efforts lead to complete escape (a condition that might be expected to occur in a natural setting), the duckling will persistently run away. As a result, the innate tendency to react filially will never gain expression, and imprinting as defined here will be precluded. Apparently, in precocial birds the critical period for imprinting corresponds to the relatively brief period that precedes the emergence of strong tendencies to react fearfully to novel stimuli. This, of course, is not to say that imprinting after the emergence of novelty-induced fear is impossible. Rather, it is suggested that

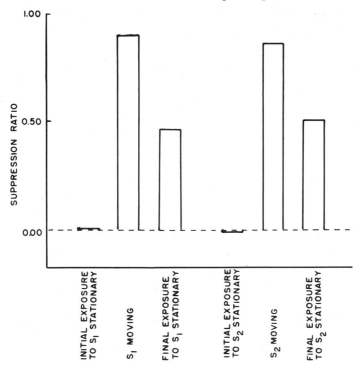

FIGURE 7. The suppression of distress vocalization by each of two imprinting stimuli in 12-hour-old ducklings. (For half of the subjects, S_1 represented the foam rubber stimulus and S_2 the lamp stimulus; for the other subjects, S_1 represented the lamp stimulus and S_2 the foam rubber stimulus. In addition, final exposure to S_1 stationary and initial exposure to S_2 stationary were counterbalanced within each group.) With the index of suppression used here, a ratio of 1 indicates that ongoing distress calling terminated completely during stimulus presentation, whereas a ratio of zero indicates that ongoing distress calling continued unabated throughout stimulus presentation. (From Hoffman & Ratner, in p 1973a, 1973b.)

if a subject is first exposed to a given imprinting stimulus after the tendency to exhibit novelty-induced fear has emerged, special efforts must be employed to prevent successful escape. In this respect, post-critical-period imprinting shares the dominant features of the procedures that are sometimes described as gentling or taming. However, except that the innate tendency to respond filially may weaken somewhat as the subject matures, and that one must take steps to reduce fear, there seems to be no compelling reason for believing that post-critical-period imprinting involves behavioral processes that are basically different from the ones contributing to the imprinting that occurs during the critical period.

THE DEVELOPMENT OF
SEPARATION–INDUCED AVERSIVE REACTIONS

Like infants of many species, including man, when an immature duckling is separated from its mother, distress calling ensues. The evidence presented thus far points to the conclusion that the abrupt termination of distress calling that occurs when the mother returns reflects an innate reaction to what are, initially, certain unconditioned aspects of the total stimulus complex represented by the mother (or her surrogate). This conclusion is supported by the finding illustrated in Figure 2: 17-hour-old ducklings that had never before seen a moving object, terminated ongoing distress calls within a second or so of their first exposure to such stimulation. That finding, however, provides little information about the source of the distress calling that ensued when the imprinting stimulus was subsequently withdrawn. The problem is that stimulus presentation occurred in a setting that was unfamiliar and in which distress calling occurred prior to the initial stimulus presentation. This factor prevents an unambiguous interpretation of the distress vocalization that occurred when the imprinting stimulus was first withdrawn. For example, what part of that vocalization reflected the ducklings' having previously encountered the imprinting stimulus and what part was produced by the setting, which itself induced distress calling? One way to resolve this issue is to arrange for a given duckling's first exposure to an imprinting stimulus to occur in a setting that is familiar, and hence does not itself induce distress calling.

Figure 8 shows the pattern of distress vocalization that ensues under the conditions just outlined. We monitored the hatching process, and as soon as a given duckling was free of its shell, it was placed in the test apparatus, where it remained, isolated and undisturbed. After 17 hours the duckling received its first exposure to the imprinting stimulus (Figure 1). Stimulus exposure occurred in a sequence of 1-minute presentations, separated by intervals of 1 minute during which the stimulus was withdrawn.

As seen in Figure 8, no distress calls occurred in the minute prior to the initial stimulus presentation; but as the stimulus was repeatedly presented and withdrawn, the ducklings exhibited an increasing tendency to emit distress calls in the periods of stimulus absence. Since monitoring of distress vocalization during the 17-hour period prior to stimulus presentation revealed an almost complete lack of calling, it is apparent that the setting in which imprinting took place was not itself stressful.[3] On this basis, we can conclude that at least a part of the distress vocalization that ensues when an imprinting stimulus is withdrawn is somehow a product of events that transpire during stimulus presen-

---

[3]Only one bird emitted any distress vocalization during hatching, during transfer to the test apparatus, or during the 17-hour period that preceded stimulus presentation. These events were restricted to a total of 4 minutes of calling in the interval between 10 and 12 hours.

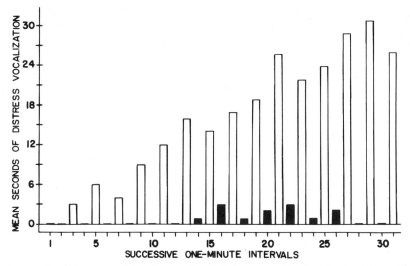

FIGURE 8.   Mean number of seconds of distress vocalization during alternating 1-minute periods of stimulus presentation and withdrawal. Ducklings were placed in the apparatus when they were first free of their shell and remained there undisturbed until testing began (17 hours later). Stimulus presentation occured during even-numbered minutes. (From Hoffman, Eiserer, Ratner, & Pickering, 1974.)

tation and that the effects of these events are cumulative. It might appear (at least at first glance) that this finding could be explained in terms of a simple growth in arousal, but such is not the case. The problem is that stimulus presentation was almost invariably associated with a low rate of distress vocalization, which is the opposite of what one might expect if the stimulus were merely serving to add increments in arousal.

An interesting explanatory system that specifically addresses itself to data of the kind obtained here is the recently developed opponent-process theory of motivation (Solomon & Corbit, 1973; Solomon & Corbit, 1974; Hoffman & Solomon, 1974). According to this theory, the onset and maintenance of any affect-arousing stimulus (whether positive or negative in hedonic quality) creates a primary motivational condition called the a-process. The occurrence of the a-process then automatically arouses an affective process (b-process) having a hedonic quality opposite to that generated by the a-process. When the affect-arousing stimulus is removed, a-process dies out quickly, whereas b-process dissipates only sluggishly; consequently, a motivational aftereffect occurs that is opposite to the affective state generated by stimulus presentation.

In terms of the imprinting situation, suppression of distress calls during stimulus presence is assumed to represent the predomination of the a-process, and the inducement of distress calls after stimulus withdrawal is assumed to mirror the perseveration of the b-process unopposed by the a-process that elicits it. Importantly, Solomon and Corbit postulate that although the a-process is an unconditioned reaction independent of prior stimulus presentations, the b-process is increased through use in that it acquires strength if frequently elicited. These assumptions fit well the findings that suppression of distress calls is immediate on the initial stimulus presentation, whereas occurrence of distress calls after stimulus withdrawal increases with more and more stimulus presentations.

The results depicted in Figure 8 are also relevant to Bateson's (1971) assertion that a naïve newly hatched duckling, under certain conditions, emits "appetitive behavior" that terminates only when the bird makes visual contact with an imprinting stimulus. This behavior—which, according to Bateson, includes the emission of distress calls—might be taken to reflect an aversive "need" for an imprinting stimulus. The finding that ducklings tested in a novel environment (see Figure 2) emit distress calls prior to the initial presentation of an imprinting stimulus is in accord with Bateson's assertion. The performance of the subjects that were reared in the testing apparatus, on the other hand, reveals that ducklings can be reared for at least 17 hours without their displaying any aversive reactions to the complete absence of an imprinting stimulus. Of course it is possible that ducklings tested in a familiar environment would display appetitive behavior reflecting an aversive "need" for an imprinting stimulus if deprivation of that stimulus were prolonged beyond 17 hours. However, regardless of whether such a need could develop independently of exposure to an imprinting stimulus, the present data make it clear that this exposure is sufficient to generate considerable distress calling in circumstances under which it would not otherwise occur. Apparently, independently of any extrinsically determined needs, exposing a duckling to a potential object of filial attachment (e.g., an imprinting stimulus) serves to create its own need.

FEAR–MEDIATED AGGRESSION IN THE CONTEXT OF IMPRINTING

According to the preceding discussion, two distinct behavioral stages occur when a bird older than the age defined by the critical period is forcibly exposed to an unfamiliar imprinting stimulus. Initially, the subject shows strong fearlike reactions such as flight and crouching. These behaviors gradually wane as the fear elicited by the stimulus is reduced, and the bird's tendency to emit filial reactions toward the stimulus becomes increasingly apparent.

A recent series of studies in my laboratory (Hoffman & Boskoff, 1972; Hoffman, Ratner, Eiserer, & Grossman, 1974) has revealed that older ducklings, regardless of their prior history of imprinting, also go through a third distinct stage during exposure to a novel imprinting stimulus. As illustrated in Figure 9, this stage is characterized by aggressive behavior and occurs just prior to the emergence of filial reactions toward the stimulus. Further experiments revealed

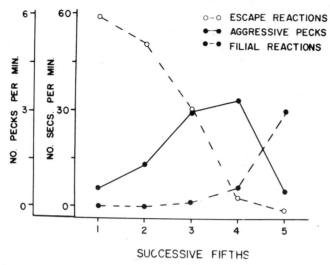

FIGURE 9. Mean number of aggressive pecks and the mean amount of time that 5-day-old ducklings exhibited escape and filial reactions when first exposed to a novel moving object that was in their compartment and consistently approached and stayed nearby. Testing occurred in a single, long session that terminated when a given duckling failed to emit an aggressive peck for approximately 15 minutes. (From Hoffman, Ratner, Eiserer, & Grossman, 1974.)

that this transient stage of aggression was largely dependent on the duckling's being somewhat fearful of the stimulus and being kept in close proximity to it despite an initial tendency to flee; if the subject's fear was either too high (as it was during the early part of the exposure—see Figure 9) or too low (as it was by the end of the exposure), or if the subject was able to flee from the stimulus, little aggression was observed.[4]

This relationship between fear and aggression during post-critical-period imprinting strongly resembles the processes that occur when previously isolated monkeys are placed in an unfamiliar colony. Harlow, Harlow, and Suomi (1971), for example, have noted that "the only social behaviors [shown by such monkeys] were fear and aggression. . . . Before, during and after aggressive attacks, they were frozen in fear [p. 544]."

The studies of aggression in my laboratory have also revealed that if a duckling has a prior history of imprinting to a given stimulus, the presence of that stimulus has complex effects on the subject's aggression toward a novel stimulus. If, in the absence of the imprinting stimulus, the subject's fear of the nov-

---

[4]It is important to note that the aggression obtained in these circumstances is probably only one of several kinds of aggression that can occur in the context of imprinting. Clearly, there is no reason to believe that all instances of aggression in ducklings represent occasions on which the aggressor would flee if given the opportunity.

el stimulus was too high for aggression, presenting the imprinting stimulus increased the amount of aggression. However, if the subject's fear of the novel stimulus was appropriate for aggression in the absence of the imprinting stimulus, its presentation, rather than increasing aggression, reduced the aggressive behavior and tended to increase the amount of filial behavior that was directed toward the novel stimulus. We interpreted this pattern of results as indicating that the imprinting stimulus modulates a duckling's aggression and emission of filial behavior toward a novel stimulus by lowering its fear of the stimulus. Similar calming properties have been attributed to imprinting stimuli before (Moltz, Rosenblum, & Halikas, 1959; Moltz, 1960) and have also been used to describe a mother surrogate's control over an infant monkey's exploration of novel, fear-eliciting stimuli (Harlow, 1958).

THE EFFECT OF AVERSIVE STIMULATION

Aversive stimulation appears to facilitate the formation of social attachments by newly hatched precocial birds. Kovach and Hess (1963), for example, came to this conclusion on the basis of their finding that the tendency of a bird to follow an imprinting stimulus is significantly increased if the subject is periodically given electrical shock in the presence of the stimulus.

Prior work in our laboratory has replicated this effect (Barrett, Hoffman, Stratton, & Newby, 1971), and similar observations have been made with a variety of other animals. Scott (1962), for example, has noted that with dogs and monkeys, "any sort of emotion, whether hunger, fear, pain or loneliness, will speed up the process of socialization [p. 951]." Considering the generality of the effect, it appears that such stimulation facilitates imprinting and socialization by increasing the subject's attention and reaction to an appropriate, arousal-reducing stimulus. Such a motivational interpretation is reminiscent of the earlier arguments of Moltz (1960) and is consistent with the present view of imprinting in that aversive stimulation would be expected to enhance the motivational background against which the reinforcing properties of an imprinting stimulus can operate.

The effects of aversive stimulation on imprinting and on socialization in nonprecocial animals are also similar in that if the stimulation is made contingent on a specific response, the subject's tendency to make that response, even if it is a filial reaction usually directed at the surrogate mother, is reduced. If a duckling is punished for following an imprinting stimulus, for example, it quickly stops following until the contingency is removed (Barrett, Hoffman, Stratton, & Newby, 1971). Similarly, infant monkeys raised by a "motherless mother" or by a surrogate designed to provide aversive as well as tactile stimulation eventually learn to keep their distance during periods when clinging is punished. When, however, the contingency terminates and contact no longer has aversive consequences, clinging resumes (Seay, Alexander, & Harlow, 1964).

Such findings are indicative of the multiple effects engendered by aversive stimulation in the context of imprinting. The occurrence of aversive stimulation *per se* tends to enhance the motivational substrate that supports filial behavior. When, however, the occurrence of the aversive stimulation is response contingent, the response in question is suppressed.

Aversive stimulation can influence the behavior that characterizes imprinting in other ways. For example, Barrett (1972) found that if newly hatched ducklings receive response-independent shock in the presence of a given imprinting stimulus (e.g., the foam rubber object in Figure 1), they follow it more closely than subjects that are not shocked. This, of course, is consistent with the previously described finding that shock *per se* enhances the motivational background for the expression of filial behavior. Barrett also found, however, that if subsequently given a choice between the original imprinting stimulus and a *simultaneously presented* identical object that has been rendered perceptually distinctive (by painting vertical black stripes on its surface), the ducklings approach and follow the new stimulus and eschew their original imprinting stimulus. Since Barrett's study included controls for any difference in preference that the two stimuli may have afforded, it is apparent that when electrical shock consistently occurs in the presence of an imprinting stimulus that stimulus acquires discriminative properties in that it signals the possible occurrence of shock. If the duckling has no alternative, its filial reaction will continue to focus on such a stimulus and may even be enhanced; but given an alternative stimulus that is not too novel, the alternative stimulus will be chosen.

There is at least one more way in which aversive stimulation can function in the context of imprinting. When newly hatched (17-hour-old) ducklings receive an occasional electrical shock in the course of their initial exposure to a given imprinting stimulus (e.g., the moving object in Figure 1), they exhibit relatively little fear of a completely novel imprinting stimulus (e.g., a rotating lamp), when tested several days later.[5] Since this effect is obtained even when the delivery of shock is restricted to periods when the original imprinting stimulus is withdrawn, it seems clear that it is due to early shock *per se* and not to any associations that might develop between shock and the original imprinting stimulus.

This finding is of special interest because it points to an effect that has not previously been seen in work on imprinting, although it has been extensively studied in a variety of other contexts. Denenberg, Carlson, and Stephens (1962), for example, reported that when rats are exposed to electrical shock at an early age, they are subsequently less emotional than nonshocked controls, as

---

[5] This important effect was only recently uncovered by Alan M. Ratner in the course of his doctoral dissertation research.

measured by their behavior in an open field test. Since open field behavior in rats can be assumed to reflect at least in part reactions that are mediated by novelty-induced fear, it is reasonable to suppose that among its many other effects, aversive stimulation delivered at an early age can raise a subject's threshold for the expression of novelty-induced fear.

This consideration underscores the similarity between the present findings and the early stimulation effects investigated by Denenberg and his associates, but it is clear that much more empirical work will be necessary before the implications of this phenomenon for imprinting are fully elaborated.[6] In the meantime, it is relevant to note that the mere detection of such effects in precocial birds goes a long way toward confirming the mounting conviction that rather than being a unique phenomenon, limited to a few species such as ducks, chick-

---

[6] After the present manuscript was completed, Ratner ran another study designed to examine more closely the effects of early shock. Three groups of ducklings were tested. Upon hatching, each duckling was placed in an individual container where it remained for 6 days. Ducklings in one group received a series of 75 brief (0.30 msec) shocks (intensity 1 mA) twice a day during days 1 and 2. Ducklings in the second group also received the same series of shocks while in their home containers, but these occurred on days 5 and 6. The third group of ducklings served as controls and never received shock.

On day 7 all birds received an open field type of test; they were placed in the *empty* imprinting apparatus, and their tendency to emit distress calls or to crouch was assessed. On the next day and on each of several days thereafter, the birds were again placed in the apparatus, but this time the moving foam rubber object was visible throughout the entire session.

When first placed in the empty apparatus (on day 7), ducklings in all groups either emitted distress calls or crouched. But as the 15-minute session proceeded, the ducklings that had received shocks on days 1 and 2 gradually terminated both these behaviors and by the end of the session were actively exploring the apparatus. Ducklings in the other groups showed no decline in their initially high tendency either to crouch or to emit distress calls. When subsequently exposed to the imprinting stimulus (beginning on day 8), ducklings that had received shock on days 1 and 2 rapidly came to spend their time in the immediate vicinity of the stimulus. Ducklings in the other two groups also came to spend their time in the vicinity of the stimulus, but for these birds the process was quite slow.

These findings have several important implications. By including a late shock control, they reveal that the effect is due to *early* shock and not merely to shock *per se*. By revealing that the early shock birds were initially fearful when exposed to the novel empty apparatus for the first time, they indicate that early shock somehow enhanced the subjects' accommodation to a fear-inducing situation rather than merely interfering with their capacity to exhibit fear. And finally, by revealing rapid development of attachment behavior in the early shock subjects, the findings indicate that early shock does not interfere with the capacity to exhibit sustained positive emotional reactions. In short, these findings suggest that in the present context, the effects of the early shocks were directed to those processes involved in *accommodation* to fear-inducing circumstances.

Of course, this conclusion does not necessarily mean that early shock is the only way to facilitate a bird's accommodation to fear-eliciting stimulation. The early stimulation literature indicates that handling (presumably a form of positively reinforcing stimulation) can also produce this kind of effect, and it is conceivable, in light of those findings, that the early positively reinforcing stimulation involved in standard imprinting procedures may also facilitate a bird's accommodation to fearful circumstances.

ens, and turkeys, imprinting represents a complex interaction among several basic behavioral processes that characterize most, if not all, of the higher social organisms.

CONCLUSIONS

According to the view of imprinting elaborated here, some aspect of an appropriate imprinting stimulus provides stimulation that innately elicits filial behavior and is reinforcing. When a newly hatched precocial bird has extended exposure to an imprinting stimulus, the initially neutral features of that stimulus come to elicit filial behavior through a classical conditioning process. While this is happening, the stimulus is rendered familiar, and this condition serves to maintain the subject's tendency to respond filially after the tendency to respond fearfully to unfamiliar stimuli emerges. Accordingly, imprinting is a means of preventing the future suppression of an innately given filial tendency. When viewed in this way, imprinting is seen to encompass a number of basic and in some respects independent behavioral processes that interact in a variety of complex ways. Certain of these processes, such as those responsible for the innate tendency to respond filially, must ultimately depend on the presence or absence of appropriate genetic factors. Others, such as those responsible for the development of familiarity and for certain effects of aversive stimulation, must depend primarily on experience. Still other processes, such as the emergence of novelty-induced fear, are heavily based on an interaction between maturational and experiential factors.

When one considers the convergence of such a variety of processes, it is no wonder that the attachment phenomenon should exhibit so many complex ramifications. Indeed, when viewed from the present perspective, the possibilities for variations and for individual differences are absolutely enormous.

For example, a given organism might be more or less sensitive to a given form of eliciting stimulation. In terms of the opponent-process theory outlined earlier, a given organism might exhibit a strong or a weak a-process. Moreover, even if the a-process is strong, the linkage between a- and b-processes in a given organism might be strong or weak, and this factor could have a profound influence on the behavior generated. There must be individual differences in rate of classical conditioning, just as there must be individual differences in the maturational factors that contribute to novelty-induced fear. In short, the opportunity for individual differences in attachment behavior seem to be almost limitless.

Perhaps, after all, Moore and Shiek (1971) were correct in implicating imprinting in autism. There can be little doubt that this dreadful syndrome represents a distortion of the attachment process, but in view of the considerations outlined here, it is surely wrong to ascribe autism to a simple matter of timing.

This, of course, does not mean that the present view of imprinting and the fear-mediated processes it entails will ultimately provide an explanation of autism or of any other distortion of the attachment process. However, the potentiality is there, and one may hope that this view will serve as a source of interesting hypotheses and methods for future work on these important issues.

References

Barrett, J. E. Schedules of electric shock presentation in the behavioral control of imprinted ducklings. *Journal of the Experimental Analysis of Behavior*, 1972, **18**, 305–321.

Barrett, J. E., Hoffman, H. S., Stratton, J. W., & Newby, V. Aversive control of following in imprinted ducklings. *Learning and Motivation*, 1971, **2**, 202–213.

Bateson, P. P. G. Imprinting. In H. Moltz (Ed.), *The ontogeny of vertebrate behavior*. New York: Academic Press, 1971.

Bateson, P. P. G., & Reese, E. P. Reinforcing properties of conspicuous objects before imprinting has occurred. *Psychonomic Science*, 1968, **10**, 379–380.

Denenberg, V. H., Carlson, P. V., & Stephens, M. W. Effects of infantile shock upon emotionality at weaning. *Journal of Comparative and Physiological Psychology*, 1962, **56**, 877–888.

Dimond, S. J. Visual experience and early social behavior in chicks. In J. H. Crook (Ed.), *Social behaviour in birds and mammals: Essays on the social ethology of animals and man*. New York: Academic Press, 1970.

Gottlieb, G. Imprinting in relation to parental and species identification by avian neonates. *Journal of Comparative and Physiological Psychology*, 1965, **59**, 354–356.

Gottlieb, G., & Simner, M. L. Auditory vs. visual flicker in directing the approach response of domestic chicks. *Journal of Comparative and Physiological Psychology*, 1969, **67**, 58–63.

Harlow, H. F. The nature of love. *American Psychologist*, 1958, **13**, 673–685.

Harlow, H. F., Harlow, M. K., & Suomi, S. J. From thought to therapy: Lessons from a primate laboratory. *American Scientist*, 1971, **59**, 538–549.

Hess, E. H. Imprinting. *Science*, 1959, **130**, 133–141.

Hess, E. H. "Imprinting" in a natural laboratory. *Scientific American*, 1972, **227**, 24–31.

Hess, E. H., & Schaefer, H. H. Innate behavior patterns as indications of the "critical period." *Zeitschrift für Tierpsychologie*, 1959, **16**, 155–160.

Hoffman, H. S., & Boskoff, K. J. Control of aggressive behavior by an imprinted stimulus. *Psychonomic Science*, 1972, **29**, 305–306.

Hoffman, H. S., Eiserer, L. A., Ratner, A. M., & Pickering, V. L. The development of distress vocalization during withdrawal of an imprinting stimulus. *Journal of Comparative and Physiological Psychology*, 1974, **86**, 563–568.

Hoffman, H. S., Eiserer, L. A., & Singer, D. Acquisition of behavioral control by a stationary imprinting stimulus. *Psychonomic Science*, 1972, **26**, 146–148.

Hoffman, H. S., & Ratner, A. M. A reinforcement model of imprinting. *Psychological Review*, 1973, **80**, 527–544(a).

Hoffman, H. S., & Ratner, A. M. The effects of stimulus and environmental familiarity on visual imprinting in newly-hatched ducklings. *Journal of Comparative and Physiological Psychology*, 1973, **85**, 11–19(b).

Hoffman, H. S., Ratner, A. M., & Eiserer, L. A. Role of visual imprinting in the emergence of specific filial attachments in ducklings. *Journal of Comparative and Physiological Psychology*, 1972, **81**, 399–409.

Hoffman, H. S., Ratner, A. M., Eiserer, L. A., & Grossman, D. J. Aggressive behavior of immature ducklings. *Journal of Comparative and Physiological Psychology*, 1974, **86**, 569–580.

Hoffman, H. S., & Solomon, R. L. An opponent-process theory of motivation: III. Some affective dynamics in imprinting. *Learning and Motivation*, 1974, **5**, 149–164.

Hoffman, H. S., Stratton, J. W., Newby, V., & Barrett, J. E. Development of behavioral control by an imprinting stimulus. *Journal of Comparative and Physiological Psychology*, 1970, **71**, 229–236.

James, H. Flicker: An unconditioned stimulus for imprinting. *Canadian Journal of Psychology*, 1959, **13**, 59–67.

James, H. Imprinting with visual flicker: Evidence for a critical period. *Canadian Journal of Psychology*, 1960, **14**, 13–20.

Kovach, J. K., & Hess, E. H. Imprinting: Effects of painful stimulation upon the following response. *Journal of Comparative and Physiological Psychology*, 1963, **56**, 461–464.

Lorenz, K. Der Kumpan in der Umvelt des Vogels, der Artgenosse als auslosendes Moment sozialer Verhaltungsweisen. *Journal of Ornithology*, 1935, **83**, 137–213, 289–413.

Lorenz, K. The companion in the bird's world. *Auk*, 1937, **54**, 245–273.

Mason, W. A., Hill, S. D., & Thompson, C. E. Perceptual factors in the development of filial attachment. *Proceedings of the Third International Primatological Congress*, 1971.

McIlwain, T. Central vision: Visual cortex and superior colliculus. In J. H. Camroe, Jr. (Ed.), *Annual review of physiology*. Vol. 34. Palo Alto, Calif.: Annual Reviews Inc., 1972.

Moltz, H. Imprinting: Empirical basis and theoretical significance. *Psychological Bulletin*, 1960, **57**, 291–314.

Moltz, H., Rosenblum, L., & Halikas, N. Imprinting and level of anxiety. *Journal of Comparative and Physiological Psychology*, 1959, **52**, 240–244.

Montevecchi, W. A., Gallup, G. G., Jr., & Dunlap, W. P. The peep vocalization in group reared chicks *(Gallus domesticus)*: Its relation to fear. *Animal Behaviour*, 1973, **21**, 116–123.

Moore, D. J., & Shiek, D. A. Toward a theory of early infantile autism. *Psychological Review*, 1971, **78**, 451–456.

Rajecki, D. W. Imprinting in precocial birds: Interpretation, evidence, and evaluation. *Psychological Bulletin*, 1973, **79**, 48–58.

Ratner, A. M., & Hoffman, H. S. Evidence for a critical period for imprinting in Khaki Campbell ducklings *(Anas platyrhyncos domesticus)*. *Animal Behaviour*, in press.

Salzen, E. A. Imprinting and environmental learning. In L. R. Aronson, E. Tobach, D. S. Lehrman, & J. S. Rosenblatt (Eds.), *Development and evolution of behavior*. San Francisco: Freeman, 1970.

Schaffer, H. R. The onset of fear of strangers and the incongruity hypothesis. *Journal of Child Psychology and Psychiatry*, 1966, **7**, 95–106.

Scott, J. P. Critical periods in behavioral development. *Science*, 1962, **138**, 949–958.

Seay, B., Alexander, B. K., & Harlow, H. F. Maternal behavior of socially deprived rhesus monkeys. *Journal of Abnormal and Social Psychology*. 1964, **69**, 345–354.

Solomon, R. L., & Corbit, J. D. An opponent-process theory of motivation: I. Temporal dynamics of affect. *Psychological Review*, 1974, **81**, 119–145.

Solomon, R. L., & Corbit, J. D. An opponent-process theory of motivation: II. Cigarette addiction. *Journal of Abnormal Psychology*, 1973, **81**, 158–171.

CHAPTER 3

Contextual Determinants of Infant Affective Response[1]

L. ALAN SROUFE, EVERETT WATERS, AND LEAH MATAS

Institute of Child Development, University of Minnesota

CONTEXTUAL DETERMINANTS OF INFANT AFFECTIVE RESPONSE

Something inside is telling me
That I've got your secret. . . .
Fear is the lock and laughter the key
To your heart

Stephen Stills*

An intimate relationship between fear and laughter has been suggested in the writings of poets and philosophers and in the theories of psychologists. It has been argued, for example, that laughter results from the realization that some apparent evil is harmless (Descartes, 1649), from a "sudden transformation of a strained expectation into nothing" (Kant, 1790), from pleasure at the elimination of something alarming (Hartley, 1749), and from conflict between "the impulse to proceed and the impulse to draw back" (Menon, 1931) (all cited by Berlyne, 1969). The striking similarity between psychological theories of fear and humor also implies a close relationship between strong negative and strong positive affect. Smiling, laughter, wariness, and fear have all been suggested to result from incongruity or discrepancy (Berlyne, 1960, 1969; Hebb,

[1]This research was supported in part by a program project grant from the National Institute of Child Health and Human Development, University of Minnesota (5 PO1 HD05027). Everett Waters is a trainee in the Behavior and Development of Pre-school Children (NICHD, 5 T02 HD00105).

Aspects of this research program were discussed at the second Ethology Workshop (Percha, West Germany; London, England) sponsored by the Grant Foundation, Inc. The authors wish to express their appreciation to the Foundation and to the hosts of the Workshop, Dr. Irenaeus Eibl-Eibesfeldt, Dr. N. G. Blurton-Jones, and Dr. William Charlesworth.

*"Suite Judy Blue Eyes" on *Crosby, Stills and Nash;* recorded on Atlantic Records.

1946; Kagan, 1971; McGhee, 1971; Schaffer, Greenwood, & Parry, 1972; Willman, 1940). Typically, it is posited that encountering an event that violates expectation or fails to match available schemata produces "arousal," and fear (or laughter) is directly or indirectly in response to this change in internal state.

A laughter–fear tie is clearly indicated by previous work on the development of laughter in the first year of life (Sroufe & Wunsch, 1972). In particular, these studies indicated that many items potent in producing laughter (loud sounds, jiggling the baby in the air, and mother's face covered with a mask) were similar to situations previously reported to produce fear (Hebb, 1946; Scarr & Salapatek, 1970; Watson & Rayner, 1920). Moreover, age changes uncovered were consistent with an incongruity–tension-reduction hypothesis. Investigators found developmental changes in both the number and type of stimuli eliciting laughter across the 4- to 12-month age range which were consistent with knowledge concerning cognitive development. In brief, strong auditory and tactile stimulation was most potent for younger infants, whereas "social" and visual stimulation was most potent toward the end of the first year. That is, stimuli that more directly impinged on the infant (e.g., jiggling baby, BOOM, BOOM, BOOM) were displaced by situations that required object permanence (peek-a-boo), those in which the infant was involved in producing the "stimulus" (i.e., assimilating the game), or those which required sustained processing of the input (e.g., watching mother crawl across the floor). On the basis of the total set of findings, including relationships between ratings of "required cognitive sophistication" and age of maximal item potency, we were persuaded that cognitive discrepancy is an important determinant of infant laughter, as well as infant fear.

To explain the apparently paradoxical relationship between laughter and fear, the hypothesis advanced differed somewhat from that of Ambrose (1963). Ambrose reasoned that laughter is an expression of simultaneous stimulus-maintaining and stimulus-terminating tendencies (i.e., of smiling and crying). This ambivalence hypothesis was consistent with many features of our data, such as laughter to loud sounds, to the mock attack of "I'm gonna get you" (looming approach with tickling), and to the approach of mother wearing a full-face mask. However, it did not seem to handle the absence of behavioral ambivalence, the infant's efforts to reproduce the situation, laughter to such items as pulling a cloth from mother's mouth, or trial-by-trial results in which laughter ("ambivalence") routinely built from smiling and faded again to smiling.

In our view, laughter is at the positive pole of an affective response dimension rather than being a simultaneous expression of crying and smiling. When the infant is confronted with a novel, incongruous situation, appropriate to its cognitive-developmental level, behavioral fixation occurs and "tension" develops. Within a positive context—for example, in the home with mother as stimulus agent—the infant will smile or laugh, perhaps reach, and seek to reproduce the situation. Within a negative context the same "stimulus" will produce crying or behavioral avoidance. That is, infants have *both* a strong disposition to approach *and* to avoid novel stimulation, but neither crying nor laughter is an expression of ambivalence. Rather, both crying and laughter occur following the resolution of indeterminancy, with laughter occurring when there is a positive "evaluation" as well as considerable "tension" due to discrepancy.

The results with the mask were especially compelling with regard to the hypothesized interaction between context and discrepancy. While others (Scarr & Salapatek, 1970) have shown that a mask can be an adequate fear stimulus, we routinely found approach by mother-with-mask to elicit positive affect, with between 50 and 80% of the 10- to 12-month-olds *laughing* at this stimulus; smiling was virtually universal. In the absence of mother, *the same mask* on a stranger elicited crying. We also found that positive affect in response to mother-with-mask was suppressed in the laboratory as compared with home testing.

To understand the relationship between fear and laughter and their mutual tie to incongruity, one must consider that affect is characterized by both an intensity and a direction. As Stechler and Carpenter (1967) have pointed out, discrepancy is a quantitative term and as such can only be related to intensity of affect:

"Discrepancy and its various synonyms are quantitative terms and provide no implication of directionality. Further information, beyond the fact of discrepancy, is required to predict whether the arousal will have a positive or negative hedonic quality. It is predominantly the qualitative aspects of affect which are most difficult to explain via the informational model [p. 173]."

"In short, the incoming information must be described not only in quantitative terms of the level of information-processing load imposed on the organism; it must also be described in terms of the more complex qualitative issue, viz., what is the meaning of the information for that organism at that time [p. 172]."

Loud sounds, mock attack, and the masked face are sufficiently tension producing or "arousing" (in Berlyne's sense) to induce either strong fear *or* laughter; the direction of the affect is determined in a complex manner by other factors, certainly including context.

The present program of research was designed to explore the extent to which differential affective, behavioral, and autonomic reactions can be activated by the same "stimulus" (stranger approach, mother-with-mask, stranger-with-mask) through manipulation of the testing environment, familiarization time, sequence of events, and other contextual factors. Although we began by studying the development of positive affect, stranger fear is the focus of several studies presented below. This reflects our view that contextual factors influencing the expression of negative and positive affect are identical, the task for the developmental psychologist being to discover ways in which these contextual factors interact with stimulation and developmental level to produce the specific affective response.

THE ROLE OF CONTEXT IN DETERMINING AFFECTIVE EXPRESSION

The belief that contextual factors influence affective expression is certainly not unique to us and has been the subject of major statements by Bowlby (1973) and Stechler and Carpenter (1967). In both these writings the active role played by the infant in processing stimulation-within-context has been stressed, and familiarity with the background in which stimulation occurs is viewed as a factor of special importance. So important are contextual factors that even isolating a familiar "stimulus" (e.g., mother's face) from a varying background can produce distress (Stechler & Carpenter, 1967).

In addition to setting, familiarization time, sequence of events, and agent, which were manipulated in our studies, a key factor in studies of infant affective expression is presence or absence of the infant's attachment figure (Bowlby, 1973; Spitz, 1965). A number of studies with humans and animals have shown an increased likelihood of negative affect during separation from an attachment figure (Bronson, 1972; Campos et al., 1973; Cox & Campbell, 1968; Escalona, 1953; Harlow & Zimmerman, 1959; Morgan, 1973; Rheingold, 1968). For example, the classic Harlow studies showed that although initially frightened, infant macaques would approach highly novel stimuli when in the presence of their surrogate mother but not in its absence. Similarly, Campos et al. (1973) found significant heart rate acceleration by age 9 months to stranger approach, but only in mother's absence. Mother separation was only episodic in our studies; therefore, the amount of negative affect generated by our situations was attenuated. Nonetheless, variations utilized were sufficient to produce the entire range of infant affective responses.

Setting

The work of numerous investigators suggests that the tendency toward positive affect will be increased and that toward negative affect decreased when an infant is studied in his own home rather than in an unfamiliar setting (Bowlby, 1973; Castell, 1972; Freedman, 1961; Greenacre, 1952; Stechler & Carpenter, 1967). Although most of the evidence is anecdotal, Castell (1972) has shown a statistically reliable increase in proximity seeking to mother when the child is in an unfamiliar home.

In the typical fear study, not only is the stimulus agent a stranger but the test setting itself is unfamiliar to the infant. Thus our report of consistent positive affect to the masked face (Sroufe & Wunsch, 1972) may have been due partly to the familiar home setting as well as to testing by the infant's mother. This setting effect was suggested by a subsequent finding of suppressed laughter in the laboratory, even with mother as agent. The experiment described below was primarily a study of the infant's behavior during approach by an unfamiliar person; however, it was explicitly formulated as a test of setting influences on affective expression.

Procedure

Twenty-two 10-month-old infants participated in a repeated measures experiment with home–laboratory order counterbalanced.[2] Whenever possible, each infant was tested at home and in the laboratory at the same time of day, with one week separating the tests. A fixed sequence of events was adopted, partly to promote contrast with our previous laughter studies. First, there were two stranger approach trials in a standard stepwise fashion (e.g., Scarr & Salapatek, 1970). With mother seated 4 feet to the side of the baby, the female stranger called the baby's name from 8 feet away, waited 4 seconds, called again, and walked slowly to within 3 feet. After a 3-second delay, she extended her arms, palms up, in a pickup gesture. Then she actually lifted the infant several inches out of the high chair, replaced the infant, and withdrew from the room. Following a second stranger approach trial, mother separation was carried out by having mother call her infant's name, turn, and walk from the room. For 10 seconds the infant was left with the stranger who was standing next to where mother had been. Finally, there were four trials in which mother called to the infant, covered her face with a human-looking mask, and leaned to within 1 foot of the infant's face. (See Sroufe & Wunsch, 1972.)

The principal dependent measure was heart rate (HR) change, recorded in standard fashion in the laboratory and by way of FM telemetry in the home. In addition, behavior ratings were made by two independent observers. Since substantial fear was expected in the laboratory, where no efforts were made to simulate a homelike atmosphere, a crude 3-point rating scale was used: (1) crying, (2) distress (including behavioral avoidance), and (3) neutral. In this first study only, we deliberately avoided what we thought might be an ambiguous "sobering" or "wary" category. Within the positive affective responses we distinguished between smiles, active smiles, and laughter. Heart rate was recorded on Beckman type R or RS polygraphs, with cardiotachometer coupler for beat-to-beat recording. To allow HR recovery, intervals between trials (e.g., stranger approach 1 and 2) were 30 seconds (1 minute or longer if the infant had been upset). Events were marked on the polygraph by an observer with a hand switch; for example, during stranger approach, marks were made at calls name 1, calls name 2, closest point, arms out, pickup and out of room.

To ensure stability of initial HR, 10 minutes was allowed for electrode at-

[2]The infants, fourteen males and eight females, were recruited by telephone from a volunteer pool established at the Institute of Child Development, University of Minnesota. Parents of infants born in the Twin Cities area receive a general letter inviting them to participate in infant research. Those returning a card are then called and recruited for specific experiments. The families contacted span the middle and lower-middle socioeconomic classes.

tachment and adaptation. During this time the infant had some exposure to the experimenters, including the "stranger" who attached the electrodes. Even though the infant was seated on the mother's lap and the stranger avoided eye contact, it is to be expected that such a procedure would ameliorate the stranger reaction to some extent.

Results • The heart rate data revealed important home–lab differences in response to stranger approach, even within our relatively innocuous procedure. Although there was no difference in resting HR level *prior* to the test sequence (home $\bar{x}$ = 134.2 BPM; lab $\bar{x}$ = 131.6 BPM; $t(4)$ = .638, p > .25), there was *significantly greater HR acceleration in the laboratory* in response to the approaching stranger. The mean differences between the peak HR at pickup and both the basal HR (taken during 1 minute of rest prior to the procedure) and the HR level immediately prior to the first stranger approach episode were greater in the lab than in the homes $(t(40)$ = 3.514 and 3.740, respectively; p < .01).[3] Initially, the infants watched the stranger closely, stilled, and showed HR deceleration in both home and lab on first visual fixation on the stranger. By arms-out, modest acceleration above the basal HR occurred, but this was not significantly greater in the lab ($\bar{x}$ = 6.3 BPM) than in the home ($\bar{x}$ = 3.3 BPM; $t(40)$ = 1.380, p < .10, one-tailed test, first stranger approach). However, seven (of 22) infants showed pre-to-peak accelerations of more than 18 BPM at arms-out in the lab, whereas only one infant (of 18) showed such a large magnitude acceleration at home (see Table 1).

In contrast to our expectations from the previously published literature, behavior ratings revealed little *frank* fear during stranger approach either at home (1 of 18) or in the lab (4 of 22).[4] In fact, we were impressed with the robustness of these babies. It was far more common for infants to show an initial smile to the stranger and to extend their arms at pickup than for them to cry. Since videotapes were made only in the laboratory, it was not possible to utilize a more refined coding system to assess home–lab differences in overt behavior. (Such a system was developed from laboratory tapes. The utility of this system and the relationship of "wary" behavior to HR is discussed in the section on Familiarization.)

Home–lab differences in HR acceleration to mother separation were largely qualitative. Although the overall pre-to-peak t value was not significant $(t(39)$

---

[3]Since home–lab correlations were routinely modest (.04 to .31, never significant), and since HR records were poor for four home tests, independent t tests were used throughout. Only the first stranger approach trial is discussed in the text; however, preliminary analyses of variance indicated no significant interactions with trials.

[4]Data are reported only for cases in which usable HR recordings were obtained. Records of four infants were inadequate in the home, typically due to interference in FM reception because of local radio stations.

TABLE 1. Heart Rate in Beats per Minute (BPM) During First Stranger Approach

Subject	Base	Pre	Arms Out	Pickup	Base to Arms Out	Base to Pickup	Pre to Arms Out	Pre to Pickup
				In Lab				
1	138	138	145	148	7	10	7	10
2	146	133	148	152	2	6	15	19
3	140	136	153	145	13	5	17	9
4	141	142	148	147	7	6	6	5
5	138	137	135	138	−3	0	−2	1
6	124	122	132	137	8	13	10	15
7	116	112	115	119	−1	3	3	7
8	128	117	121	130	−7	2	4	13
9	130	142	143	144	13	14	1	2
10	128	121	128	141	0	13	7	20
11	119	115	106	126	−13	7	−9	11
12	125	124	137	139	12	14	13	15
13	148	139	168	167	20	19	29	28
14	132	133	158	158	26	26	25	25
15	146	145	142	147	−4	1	−3	2
16	129	143	140	146	11	17	−3	3
17	116	110	126	134	10	18	16	24
18	125	125	128	138	3	13	3	13
19	132	122	137	144	5	12	15	22
20	134	127	142	139	8	5	15	12
21	136	138	145	142	9	6	7	4
22	138	132	151	160	13	22	19	28
				In Home				
1	142	137	145	144	3	2	8	7
2								
3	126	137	129	149	3	23	−8	12
4	150	147	162	147	12	−3	15	0
5	147	147	139	146	−8	−1	−8	−1
6								
7	120	107	114	119	−6	−1	7	12
8	120	128	127	130	7	10	−1	2
9	126	123	131	126	5	0	8	3
10	136	120	118	125	−18	−11	−2	5
11	128	127	133	126	5	−2	6	−1
12	129	126	153	131	24	2	27	5
13	128	134	137	138	9	10	3	4
14	142	142	141	149	−1	7	−1	7
15								
16	159	157	152	149	−7	−10	−5	−8
17								
18	134	122	132	137	−2	3	10	15
19	131	143	147	148	16	17	4	5
20	128	115	132	121	4	−7	17	6
21	132	119	131	123	−1	−9	12	4
22	138	136	152	136	14	−2	16	0

$= 1.511, p > .05$), the five greatest pre-to-peak accelerations (all > 20 BPM) occurred in the laboratory. Perhaps most important, the seven infants showing the greatest acceleration to the first stranger approach in the lab showed an average acceleration of 18 BPM to mother separation, which is significantly greater than the mean acceleration (10.7 BPM) of the other 15 infants $(t(20) = 2.731, p < .02)$. Thus large magnitude acceleration to stranger approach in the laboratory predicted acceleration to separation, even though HR completely recovered to basal level between trials—only two of the seven infants showed base-to-preseparation differences greater than 4 BPM $(\bar{x} = 1.4$ BPM). Taken with the failure to find home–lab differences in basal HR during rest, this suggests that state differences (simple arousal level) may not be essential determinants of the infants' reactions.

Review of videotapes suggested an absence of stress in the lab prior to the test sequence, but additional physiological measures would be required to rule out initial or between-trials differences in arousal level. It is also difficult to determine whether the predictability of extreme reaction to mother separation from pronounced acceleration to stranger approach was due to sequence effects (i.e., a lowered threshold of fear in infants previously frightened) or to individual differences in reactivity. In this regard, the overall correlation in the laboratory between acceleration to stranger approach and acceleration to mother separation was a modest .378 $(p > .05)$.

Familiarization Time

If familiarity with the setting in which stimulation occurs is important in inducing positive or negative affect, familiarization time should be a highly relevant manipulation. As Stechler and Carpenter (1967) have argued:

"The way in which a new piece of information is received and handled may be highly dependent on whether it occurs against the familiar *habituated background,* or against a background which is in a sense no longer a background, but has itself become a situation for alerting and attentiveness because it does not conform to expectations [p. 169, italics added]."

Despite the plausibility of such a hypothesis, there seem to be few data based on a systematic investigation of habituation time.

Development of the Coding System ● Videotapes made in the laboratory portion of the preceding experiment were used to develop a refined coding system for this study. The need for such a system became apparent when inspection of the tapes revealed that several infants categorized as "neutral" during stranger approach engaged in persistent gaze aversion (usually looking down at the high chair tray) and were muscularly stiff. In addition, several of these infants showed dramatic heart rate accelerations. Since the gaze aversion typically occurred only after close initial scrutiny (i.e., during stranger approach or at the closest point), and since the stranger's retreat from the room was also closely watched, it was apparent that these examples of gaze aversion reflected avoidance rather than disinterest. Thus a category was defined in addition to "distressed" and was designated as "wariness" (cf. Schaffer, Greenwood, & Parry, 1972). Two raters were trained on another set of tapes before applying this revised coding system (crying, distressed, wary, neutral) to the 22 infants in the stranger approach study. Interrater reliability was .89. Using this new classification, 50% of the laboratory-tested infants were judged to have shown at least some fear. These fearful (wary, distressed, or crying) infants showed significantly greater base-to-base pickup HR acceleration during stranger approach ($t(20) = 2.37, p < .05$) than the "no fear" infants. A significant difference also was found with mother separation, even when the "wary" infants alone were compared to "no fear" babies ($t(13) = 2.62, p < .05$).

Procedure for the Familiarization Experiment • Concurrently with the home–lab stranger fear study, two other groups of 10-month-olds were tested in the laboratory. Infants in one group were in the laboratory high chair for 3 minutes prior to the testing sequence ($N = 17$; 7 females); the other infants were tested after only 30 seconds ($N = 15$; 10 females). Neither group experienced electrode attachment or contact with the stranger prior to the approaches.

Results • Only 50% of the infants in the original 10-minute familiarization group were classed as fearful; however, 65% of the infants in the 3-minute group were fearful, and 93% of the 30-second group showed fear. One-third (5 of 15) in the latter group exhibited frank distress. The 30-second familiarization group is significantly different from the other two groups.

As expected, analysis of positive behaviors to the "stranger" (e.g., smiling, reaching) showed parallel significant effects in the opposite direction, with significantly more positive behaviors in the original 10-minute group and virtually none in the 30-second group (Table 2). In addition, 7 of 22 (32%) of the infants laughed at mother with mask in the 10-minute familiarization group, and 19 of 22 (86%) smiled. This compares with averages of 5% laughter and 58% smiling in the other conditions.

In a longitudinal study currently in progress, we are also investigating the effect of a play experience on the infant's response to the stranger-with-mask. In the experimental condition mother *and* stranger play with the infant for 3 minutes with the stranger's involvement gradually increasing (cf. Tinbergen & Tinbergen, 1972).

Sequence Effects

In our previous cross-sectional and longitudinal studies of laughter (Sroufe & Wunsch, 1972), between 50 and 80% of the 10-month-olds tested laughed at mother-with-mask in the home, and smiling was nearly universal. Subsequently,

TABLE 2. Affiliative Responses to the Stranger in the Familiarization Experiment

Group	10 minutes (n = 18)	3 minutes (n = 17)	30 seconds (n = 15)
	Percent Smiling		
Arms out	11	29	0
Pickup	0	0	0
Entire sequence	56	53	20
	Percent Any Positive Response[a]		
Arms out	11	35	10
Pickup	0	12	0
Entire sequence	56	59	33

[a]"*Any* positive response" includes smiling, reaching, offering toy, and extending arms.

we found that in a number of *laboratory* studies only between 18 and 33% laughed. These differential percentages have been interpreted as setting effects. Finally, in a recent study, when mother-with-mask *followed* stranger approach and mother separation, laughter *in the home* was suppressed to 33%. This finding suggests that sequence of events, as well as setting, influences affective expression in infants. Moreover, the occasional infants who actually showed distress at mother-with-mask in the laboratory have been those showing dramatic HR acceleration and clear behavioral distress during stranger approach. Others (e.g., Kagan, 1971; Stechler & Caprenter, 1967) have also assumed sequence effects to be important in studies of affective expression, but systematic experiments with infants have not been reported.

An Experiment ● An explicit test of the importance of sequence effects has been carried out.[5] In this study 6- and 10-month-old infant males experienced either two trials of stranger-with-mask or mother-with-mask first, then the opposite condition. In each case the infant had first experienced two trials of stranger approach and a mother separation as in study 1. All testing was done in the laboratory. A clear sequence effect was obtained for the 10-month-olds; for example, 67% (of 9) infants smiled at mother-with-mask when mother preceded stranger in this procedure, but only 12.5% (of 8) smiled when she followed stranger-with-mask. Moreover, 50% of this small sample cried or showed clear distress to mother following stranger, as compared with 22% when mother was first. These results with mother following stranger contrast dramatically with our original findings of universal smiling to mother-with-mask in a playful home context. There was also some carryover from mother to stranger (56% smiled to masked stranger following mother, but only 25% smiled to stranger preceding mother), although the small sample size did not yield statistically significant results. Analysis of reaching responses supports these results; 56% *reached for the mask when mother-with-mask preceded stranger-with-mask, 12.5%* when she followed stranger-with-mask. Most interesting from a develop-

[5]This project was an undergraduate honors thesis conducted by Mark DeWolff.

mental perspective, these effects were not found for the 6-month-old infants; as a group they tended to show neutral affect, with reaching, regardless of agent or order. These results are now being replicated in a longitudinal study of 23 infants from the sixth to the twelfth month of life. Concurrently, performance on the Uzgiris-Hunt scales is also being obtained.

THE RELATION BETWEEN FEAR AND LAUGHTER

This set of studies illustrates the intimate relationship between strong negative and strong positive affect and the influence of contextual factors on these response systems. Previously, we had reported that procedures exceptionally potent for eliciting fear are often the best elicitors of laughter under other circumstances; for example, stranger-with-mask versus mother with the same mask. Now these findings have been extended considerably. Even mother-with-mask can occasion fear in the laboratory, although this procedure universally elicits smiling in a playful home setting. Similarly, stranger-with-mask can activate the range of affective expression from crying through smiling and laughter, depending on contextual factors. Moreover, the same factors—setting, familiarization time, sequence, and agent—have been shown to effect the expression of positive and negative affect in a reciprocal manner. When such analysis was possible, orderings of treatment groups based on measures of positive or negative affect produced strikingly parallel results.[6] Such findings with regard to contextual influences on affective expression have numerous implications for the study of affect.

The Discrepancy Hypothesis

It is well established that a novel stimulus elicits attention (Berlyne, 1960; Kagan, 1971; Kagan & Lewis, 1965; Lewis, Goldberg, & Campbell, 1969; McCall & Melson, 1970; Sokolov, 1963). Most commonly, it is posited that attention is elicited because the input to the perceptual apparatus is discrepant from schemata available to the subject. The relationship between discrepancy and attention is assumed to be curvilinear, with moderately discrepant stimuli producing the greatest attention.

Not only attention but also smiling, laughter, and fear have been explained by invoking the principle of discrepancy or incongruity (Berlyne, 1960, 1969; Hebb, 1946; Kagan, 1971; Zelazo & Komer, 1971; Schaffer, 1966; Sroufe & Wunsch, 1972; Stechler & Carpenter, 1967). In its most elaborated form, the discrepancy hypothesis has been extended to cover the range of affect, assuming that as amount of discrepancy increases, affect shifts from neutral through positive to negative (Hunt, 1965; Stern, 1974).

---

[6]Kagan (personal communication) has also found that both crying and inhibition of play differentiated between separation responses of one-year-olds in the home versus the laboratory.

It is clear, however, that explanations of differential affect in terms of different amounts of discrepancy is untenable. In the first place, specifying amount of discrepancy or incongruity is "operationally slippery," even according to one of the proponents of this concept (Hunt, 1965). Given such difficulties of quantification and measurement, there is a serious risk of circular definitions, based on affect expressed rather than features of the event. And now in our studies it has been shown that the *same* "stimulus" event can occasion the entire range of affective response, depending on context. It is difficult to imagine that mother-with-mask becomes more or less discrepant from an internalized model depending on setting or preceding events, or that an approaching stranger becomes less discrepant as laboratory familiarization time increases. Explanations based on amount of discrepancy, although always possible, become increasingly post hoc and cumbersome as such findings continue to emerge.

Kagan's (1971) influential formulation based on the discrepancy principle is more plausible but still places heavy emphasis on the "stimulus" (e.g., the mask). He suggests that smiling occurs when the infant successfully assimilates the discrepant stimulus, fear when the infant attempts to assimilate the stimulus but fails. Amount of discrepancy need not be assumed to vary in Kagan's explanation of affective response; yet without elaboration, this formulation presents several difficulties.

First, there is the problem of the *same* "stimulus" varying in ease of assimilation. Groups of age-matched infants will predominantly laugh, smile, sober, or cry in response to a given stimulus event when context is varied, and contagion effects are demonstrable in series testing of stimuli for potency in producing positive or negative affect. Such effects can be shown *even within the same infant* across very short time intervals. For example, the mother of a 15-month-old infant picked the baby up by her heels, producing squeals of laughter. Moments later the baby was upset by the intrusion of a stranger. When, after calming, mother again lifted the baby by her heels, the infant cried. Thus it would have to be argued that an event just assimilated was no longer assimilable. Although Kagan's formulation could be elaborated to handle such observations, the result is a fundamental transformation; that is, the same stimulus is not the same stimulus because the event includes context. The inseparability of an event from its immediate background and context is reminiscent of the position taken by Stechler and Carpenter (1967) and is integral to the formulation developed below.

A second problem associated with the notion that failure of attempted assimilation leads to fear is partly intuitive. Failure to assimilate must be a common occurrence as the infant actively seeks *aliment* for its developing schemata and, in fact, plays an important role in cognitive development (Piaget, 1953). Accommodation following incomplete assimilation of novel events promotes the elaboration of available schemata. An automatic fear reaction when assimilation fails would thus be maladaptive. Perhaps in certain cases of "forced assimilation," when the infant is motivated to press his perceptual experience into an existing schema at all costs, failure might result in frustration and negative affect. But failure of attempted assimilation cannot routinely lead to fear. If this were so, considerable evidence of distress would have been expected in our studies of laughter (Sroufe & Wunsch, 1972). It is unreasonable to assume that across age, situations, and individuals, the wide range of items utilized either failed to induce attempts at assimilation or led to successful assimilation in every instance; nor can we suppose that with development individuals always passed from not trying to assimilate (neutral affect) to successful assimilation of each item eliciting smiling or laughter.[7]

It seems more reasonable to assume that in a secure context, typically including the presence of mother, the tension produced in association with attempted assimilation is not necessarily aversive. Even when efforts to assimilate are not successful, an infant may express positive affect. There is little a mother can do within a playful context to evoke fear in her infant (Sroufe & Wunsch, 1972).

A Hypothesis Based on Evaluation

In agreement with Stechler and Carpenter (1967) we believe that stimulus discrepancy plays only a partial role in determining affective expression. Discrepancy of the "stimulus" from available schemata, and related factors such as such as incongruity, novelty, salience, and complexity (cf. Berlyne, 1960), primarily establish the degree of attention and "tension" production, thereby influencing the *magnitude* of the affective response. The positive or negative *direction* of the affect expressed seems largely to be a function of context. Both crying and laughter, for example, are responses to the increased tension produced by a discrepant stimulus event. The infant's "evaluation" of the stimulus event determines which response will occur.

Based on our hypothesis, Kagan's presumed relationship between affective expression and assimilation might be turned around. We have argued (Sroufe & Wunsch, 1972) that positive affect may function to reduce "tension" while still enabling the infant to maintain an approach orientation toward the "stimulus."[8] With repetition, the stimulus can be assimilated. Negative affect,

[7]In this regard, there is reason to question whether all smiling indicates assimilation. More likely, some smiling reflects involvement with the event, that is, the *process of assimilating*. Thus we find that laughter, which may reflect assimilation of the stimulus, builds from smiling and fades again to smiles. The second smiles may reflect what Piaget called "recognitory assimilation."

[8]One bit of evidence concerning the tension-reducing function of laughter comes from our replotting of the data from the original longitudinal laughter study. When we collapsed our "laughter" and "active smile" (a physically vigorous response) categories, developmental trends emerged identical to those seen when percentage of laughter responses was plotted (Sroufe & Wunsch, 1972). However, when we further collapsed our data to include "smiling," the developmental trends washed out entirely.

the other hand, may prevent assimilation of the novel stimulus. This is suggested by our trial-by-trial observations with the mask, which revealed that avoidance occurred earlier in the sequence with repetition.

In our working model the infant brings to the stimulus situation a positive or negative set; that is, a disposition to react positively or negatively or, stated differently, a particular threshold for threat. Set is a function of the infant's immediate state (e.g., fatigue), aspects of context such as setting and preceding events, and, it may be presumed, relatively stable features of the individual and/or the quality of his attachment relationship. This set, *which is continually being updated*, plays some role in determining the magnitude of the orienting response (OR) on presentation of the "stimulus." However, the OR is largely determined by features of the "stimulus" itself (the event in its immediate background). Set plays a more crucial role in the "evaluation" of the "stimulus." As evaluation is the final aspect of the orienting process, affect is the final aspect and result of the evaluation. Our model, emphasizing both set and evaluation, is supported by the finding that home–lab differences in HR and observed behavior emerged only after the introduction of threat, not during initial adaptation. The model also predicts and therefore is partly confirmed by the place of affect expression in the sequence of events from orienting through overt behavior (see below).

Other investigators have also assigned concepts such as evaluation, plans, and thresholds a crucial role in the expression of affect (e.g., Bowlby, 1969; Hinde, 1970; Lazarus, 1966; Lewin, 1936; Schacter, 1964; Spitz, 1965; Stechler & Carpenter, 1967). Ethologists have suggested that an animal's behavioral response repertoire is organized around a complex of set points or thresholds for activation of response systems, and plans governing the selection of responses (e.g., Tinbergen, 1951; Hinde, 1970). Following their lead, Bowlby (1969) stresses that the "sorting of input into pleasurable and unpleasurable" derives from a comparison between internal "set points or standards" and the event, and that these set points vary "to reflect the current state of the organism" (p. 112). Stechler and Carpenter (1967) describe a similar process in discussing the "set goals" and "plans" of the animal. Bowlby (1969) has also stressed the role of evaluation. In fact, in Bowlby's view affect is an indication of how a situation has been "appraised":

"All, or at least most, of what are termed . . . affects, feelings or emotions are phases of an individual's intuitive appraisals either of his own organismic states and urges to act or of the succession of environmental situations in which he finds himself [p. 104]."

Schaffer (1966) has similarly concluded that an appraisal process, rather than mere discrepancy, is at the root of fear responses to strangers. The sight of the nonsmiling, immobile stranger did not produce fear; rather, fear was induced by the active, physical intrusion of the stranger:

"Thus, the very type of stimulation which, when it emanates from familiar individuals, will give rise to positive social responses, resulted in proximity avoidance when offered by unfamiliar individuals. Moreover, it was repeatedly observed that, even when the stranger began to approach the infant, the latter would not immediately withdraw or cry . . . but *would first several times look to and fro between the stranger and the mother—as though comparing one with the other* [p. 100, italics added]."

Although the term "evaluation" seems to be overly interpretive and unparsimonious, to us it is a concise working metaphor, descriptive of what occurs in our experiments. In the absence of differences in heart rate basal values or overt behavior prior to the stimulus events, we cannot conclude, for example, that the infant is more "aroused" in the laboratory than in the home. Rather, we are comfortable saying that the infant is more likely to "judge" a novel, incongruous stimulus as threatening in the laboratory context, with minimal familiarization time, or following some other threatening (aversive) event.

Such a cognitive interpretation seems to be consistent with the total set of findings from our studies and with developmental trends uncovered thus far. In contrast to 10-month-olds, 6-month-olds apparently are not sensitive to the setting, familiarization, and sequence effects discussed previously. Nor do they as a group exhibit HR acceleration during our brief stranger approach procedure. Such data, which are currently being expanded in a longitudinal study, suggest that the cognitive sophistication of the older infants underlies the results obtained in our studies. This interpretation is well substantiated by the work of other investigators, discussed in a later section.

The notion of "evaluation" is also supported by a molecular analysis of the infant's behavior in our situations. For example, in the experiment demonstrating sequence effects, virtually all infants initially showed behavioral freezing, visual fixation on the mask, and dramatic HR deceleration, regardless of age, agent, or order. That is, infants initially attend carefully, with affect uniformly judged "neutral." During this period (of orienting and evaluation) it is not possible to foretell the outcome of the episode from observed behavior or autonomic responses, although age and condition allow very reliable predictions. Following this initial inspection, infants who were to become afraid typically showed a change of facial expression, HR acceleration, and finally behavioral indications of fear and/or crying. (A brief smile at the stranger early in this sequence and a second orienting response is not incompatible with the subsequent emergence of fear.) With positive affect the initial HR deceleration typically was sustained to the point of smiling or laughter. Of special note, smiling as the end point of the "evaluative" process preceded or was concurrent with the reach toward the mask, never subsequent to it. This suggests a possible role for smiling in the release of overt behavior in the face of novel stimulation. The precise timing of these changes is important and will be reported with our current longitudinal study (Matas, Waters, & Sroufe, in preparation).

The Role of the Stimulus and Arousal Level

Presentation of the same mask can occasion either positive or negative affect, and pilot work suggests that variations in the mask per se have relatively little effect. Still, we do not view the "stimulus" event as inconsequential in the activation of affective responses.[9] In particular, the tension-producing function is essential. For example, mother-with-mask is clearly more potent for positive affect than mother approaching without mask, and although order has always been confounded, it seems that stranger-with-mask is more aversive than stranger-without-mask. (A direct comparison of these conditions is planned.) Moreover, we are not prepared to dismiss the possibility that certain stimuli may be prepotent for fear. (See also Bowlby's, 1973, discussion of natural cues to danger.)

Similarly, we do not dismiss the importance of absolute arousal level in our cognitive formulation. It seems plausible to us that at some critical point very high arousal will lead to negative affect regardless of context. We predict that mother-with-mask would produce negative affect even in the home if this were accompanied by intense auditory stimulation, for example. In this regard, Wolff (1969) has reported that tickling produces crying in irritable infants, and we have observed a change from laughing to crying within a single test episode, especially toward the end of a test session. In addition, the extreme physiological arousal (tachycardia) experienced by some babies during stranger approach in the laboratory may have contributed to the infants' negative "evaluation" of the situation. Such an updating of an infant's set to respond with negative affect was suggested because extreme tachycardias were predictive of negative affect to subsequent separation and mask episodes.

Finally, even positing that at some critical level of arousal the infant will shift from positive to negative affect (cf. Berlyne, 1969), a clear role for "evaluation" remains. Similar stimulus events may produce the same level of arousal, but contextual factors may influence the degree of arousal that is tolerable. This notion of a shifting critical arousal threshold is an alternative to the hypothesis that playful aspects of the situation serve to keep arousal within normally tolerable limits (Berlyne, 1969; Greenacre, 1952). To restate our posi-

---

[9]The stimulus is, of course, best thought of as the masking of the mother within a total context, rather than as the mask alone, or even as the mask plus mother. Here, however, we are referring to a particular event in time.

tion: *within certain contexts, even relatively high levels of tension are not aversive for the infant and may occasion positive affect.* As Stern (1973) has suggested, one function of mother–infant play may be to maintain near-maximal levels of arousal through variations in stimulation, thereby increasing the degree of arousal that can be tolerated.

THE DEVELOPMENT OF FEAR

Development in the Second Half-Year of Life

The developmental trends revealed in our work are consistent with an emerging picture of development in the second half-year of life. In two separate studies Campos has found that 9-month-old infants show cardiac acceleration, a possible indicator of stress, both to the "deep" side of the visual cliff (Schwartz Campos, & Baisel, 1973) and to the approach of a stranger in mother's absence (Campos et al., 1973). Five-month-olds show HR deceleration, the pattern typically associated with attentiveness. Yonas and Hruska (1971) reported a similar developmental shift in HR response in the case of a visual looming stimulus. Interestingly, the younger infants in these studies do discriminate between conditions (e.g., 5-month-olds show greater deceleration to the "deep" than the "shallow" side of the visual cliff), but they apparently do not extract the meaning of these perceptual experiences until the later age. Elsewhere in this volume, Ricciuti (Chapter 4) and Kagan (Chapter 9) also discuss data suggesting a discontinuity in development following age 6 months, and Schaffer (Chapter 1) presents a review of his work and that of others pointing clearly to the emergence of cognitive capacities sufficient for fear only in the second half-year of life.

In this regard, two discontinuities in our longitudinal data on the development of laughter should be noted. The first occurred at age 7 months, at which time there was a significant increase in responsivity to "social" items; that is, items that more clearly involved anticipation and interactive play (peek-a-boo; I'm gonna get you). The second occurred at 10 months, when items requiring cognitive elaboration or "interpretation" became dominant (mother crawling on floor, sucking baby's bottle, approaching with mask). The response of the infants to one item dramatically summarizes these data. When a 6-month-old is confronted with mother dangling a cloth from her mouth, typically it watches the cloth closely, pulls it from mother's mouth, inspects it briefly, and then sticks it in its own mouth. Affect is neutral. In sharp contrast, the typical 10-month-old brightens, grins, and frequently laughs. The infant *grabs* the cloth and then, laughing, vigorously attempts to stuff it back into the mother's mouth. There are many ways to describe this developmental change; the older infant assimilates the game, comprehends the meaning of the event, and so on.

What seems clear, however, is that a *qualitative* change in behavior is being described.

Discontinuities in development, such as those described in the preceding paragraphs, are central to the developmental theory of René Spitz (1965). According to Spitz, development proceeds in a smooth, though accelerated fashion until converging lines of rapid development necessitate the emergence of a new plan for growth. The emergence of a "developmental organizer," in Spitz's terminology, hails a new "modus operandi" for the continued unfolding of development. The first developmental organizer becomes apparent at about age 3 months and is marked by the emergence of the exogenous (social) smile, the waning of endogenous smiling and infantile fussiness, and qualitative changes in EEG and sleep patterns (Spitz, Emde, & Metcalf, 1970). This transition marks the end of "objectless narcissism"; the infant no longer responds primarily to internal stimuli but begins to respond to stimuli from the environment (thus the "social" smile). However rapid the pace of physical maturation, such commerce with the surroundings is essential to accelerate both cognitive and social development. This is indeed a qualitative turn in development with "awareness continuing into anticipation." In a real sense, the psyche has become organized, and the ego, with its implications for adaptive functioning, has formed.

The emergence of the second developmental organizer, the second major discontinuity in development, has implications no less dramatic than those of the first organizer. The infant now not only responds to and, in a primitive way, anticipates input from the surround, it can also respond to environmental events in terms of internalized models. The infant is now capable of comparisons, judgments, and decisions. It has a memory and the capacity for categorization. Stimuli can be responded to as members of a class. With these capacities, differentiation of schemata will now occur at a greatly accelerated pace. In Spitz's theory the emergence of the second organizer of the psyche is marked by, though not equivalent to, the onset of genuine stranger anxiety, the expression of which requires that the infant be able to compare the stranger's face with an internal representation of the face of mother. Spitz called this "8-month anxiety."

Spitz's term "8-month anxiety" suggests an unfortunate precision and universality in the onset of stranger fear, and his notion that the sight of the stranger signifies maternal loss is difficult to substantiate. Still, the essence of his developmental perspective is well supported by the literature reviewed earlier. Moreover, the capacities ascribed to infants by Spitz and others in the second half-year are sufficient to account for the onset of stranger fear at this time. As Bronson (1972) has argued, genuine fear, as opposed to wariness concerning the unfamiliar, emerges with the capacity to respond to stimuli in a categorical manner.

Implications for Developmental Research

In addition to supporting an emerging picture of development in the second half-year of life, our results are pertinent to a number of conceptual and methodological issues in the developmental literature on fear. They have special relevance to inconsistencies in the literature on stranger fear and the validation of the construct of "wariness." The results also are suggestive concerning the appropriate level of complexity for behavioral analysis in studies of infant affective response. Finally, our observations underscore the utility of a developmental perspective in studies of infant affective expression and the need for concurrent studies of affective and cognitive development.

The literature concerning the infant's reaction to unfamiliar persons has been plagued by inconsistencies. At least there is much to contradict the assumption that a fearful reaction to strangers is essentially fear of the stranger per se, and the notion that the onset of the reaction occurs with sufficient reliability to serve as a developmental milestone (cf. head raising, eye blink, etc.). Rheingold and Eckerman (in press) have drawn broadly on the literature reporting reactions to strangers in infancy and on considerable laboratory experience to issue a provocative critique of these assumptions. Pointing to the infrequency and unreliability of crying and fussing to strangers and to the inconsistencies in reported age of onset, they have challenged the notion that infants reliably exhibit frank fear of strangers at any age and have questioned the importance of the milder "wary" responses.

In their own laboratory, Rheingold and Eckerman introduced two dozen 8-, 10-, and 12-month-old infants to an unfamiliar person, who first chatted with the infant's mother and then played peek-a-boo and offered the infant a toy. After 10 minutes, mother and infant proceeded to a second unfamiliar room and were greeted by a second stranger. Again mother and stranger chatted while the infant was given the chance to play on the floor. After 5 minutes the stranger placed a toy near the infant and chatted with mother for an additional 5 minutes. The stranger then picked the infant up and walked it around the room, talking and pointing to various interesting sights. Thus the only potential threat introduced was the presence of the stranger qua stranger. The behavior of the infants was outlined in terms of frequency of visual regard of the stranger, smile to stranger, contented vocalization, fuss and cry, and length of contact with a toy or with mother.[10]

Far from showing frank fear, the infants in Rheingold and Eckerman's study

[10]No attempts were made to utilize codings of facial expression or other indices sensitive to mild distress. "No measures were made of quality of visual regard (i.e., whether "staring" or otherwise) or of facial expression except for smiling. Activity rather than cessation of activity was measured" (Rheingold & Eckerman). Nor was there any report of sequences of behavior which would reflect the structure of the situation.

accepted the stranger's presence and often made friendly overtures. In mother's presence they played freely with toys, explored, looked and smiled repeatedly at the stranger, and participated in peek-a-boo. Most of the infants eventually allowed the stranger to hold them in mother's presence and when she left the room briefly. The absence of *strong* persistent fear of the stranger per se in these studies confirms the wisdom of experienced mothers, if not that of developmental psychologists. It also supports our findings concerning familiarization effects.

We agree with Rheingold and Eckerman that unfamiliar persons do not automatically elicit aversive reactions; however, we are not compelled to discard the construct of "wariness" or the notion that negative reactions to strangers exhibit a reliable course of development. Our results demonstrate that affiliative responses toward strangers do not in themselves permit generalizations about the expression of wariness of unfamiliar persons.

Much of the disarray in the stranger fear literature has resulted from the use of intuitive criteria without objective validation, from inadequate attention to behavioral detail, and from insufficient regard for contextual variables in research design. Our own ratings of wariness allowed us to reliably differentiate age groups on the basis of behavioral responses and were validated against the criterion of HR acceleration. In addition, the proportion of infants designated "wary" was responsive to experimental manipulations in a logical manner (e.g., the familiarization time experiment). Far from requiring simply the relaxation of criteria for fearful responses, attention to wariness calls for elaboration of the concept of fear and for an appreciation of the complexity of the train of affect into behavior.

At the methodological level, greater attention to behavioral detail and the use of physiological measures promise to yield useful results. Only the most detailed analysis of the infant's behavior (including visual regard, facial expression, and posture) is appropriate to the complexity and subtlety of the entire range of fearful reactions. For example, we have found that initial fixation and greeting of the stranger with a "simple smile" is very common and is not predictive of the outcome of an encounter. Similarly, attention to temporal dimensions and to outcome suggests that looks away from the stranger at different points in an approach sequence bear a complex relationship to physiological indices of stress and cannot be considered to be functionally equivalent (Waters, 1973).

Physiological measures are useful in distinguishing attentive (orienting) behavior (visual fixation, stilling, "open" facial expression, and HR deceleration) from patterns of fearful, wary response (visual fixation, stilling, "open" facial expression, HR acceleration).[11] Campos et al. (1973) have also reported age

---

[11]Subsequent behavior, especially facial expression and gaze behavior, confirms this distinction.

changes in HR acceleration to stranger approach. In the absence of mother, 9-month-olds showed significant acceleration to intrusion by the stranger, whereas 5-month-olds did not. As we have found also, both groups showed stilling and significant HR deceleration (orienting) early in the approach sequence. Failure to distinguish attentive (orienting) behavior from wariness or fear may be at the heart of many exaggerated reports of fearful reactions to strangers. Autonomic measures may also be useful in combination with detailed analysis of facial expressions (cf. Brannigan & Humphries, 1972) in establishing objective behavioral criteria on which such distinctions can be made.

At the conceptual level, a behavioral systems approach (Hinde, 1970; Bowlby, 1969; Chance, 1962) seems to be advantageous. Fearful responses have most commonly been approached as a set of behaviors that often co-occur and are thought to bear a simple relationship to degree of underlying arousal. This approach can be elaborated to include behaviors that have a common motivational basis or behavioral indices of fear that are mutually incompatible (e.g., freezing and flight) but share common goals or outcomes, common releasers, or terminating conditions. A corollary of the study of behavioral systems is that a specific behavioral/affective response is complexly determined and involves both inhibition *and* activation of available responses; thus the a priori validity and importance of studying such behaviors as coyness, reserve, passive acceptance, and gaze aversion, as well as crying and overt avoidance.

CONCLUSION

Rheingold and Eckerman (in press), Sroufe and Wunsch (1972), and others have shown that infants may be *intrigued* by the unfamiliar, perhaps especially new persons. Bronson (1972), Bretherton and Ainsworth (Chapter 6), and Morgan and Ricciuti (1967) similarly observed a great deal of affiliative behavior in their studies of wariness and fear. We too were struck by the robustness of our infants and the high frequency of affiliative responses toward the stranger. In our original stranger approach study, smiling and offering a toy to the stranger were much more common than crying, although such affiliative responses dropped off sharply when infants experienced only 30 seconds of familiarization to the laboratory. Rather than inducing negative *or* positive affect, it is clear that novel situations and strange persons activate *both* strong approach and strong avoidance tendencies, with the affective outcome being determined by factors such as setting, sequence of events, and familiarization. Bronson (1972) has pointed out the reasonableness of such a duality for adaptation and survival, noting that the organism extends the boundaries of what it knows while avoiding hazards in the environment.

Increasingly, we conceive of our experiments as studies of infant emotional development rather than as studies of fear or humor. Typically, plots of smiling or reaching order conditions in the same way as plots of crying or avoidance, and focusing on *either* the infant's fear behavior *or* its affiliative behavior alone yields a distorted view of the infant's development. The time has come to begin formulating an integrated view of infant emotional development, which will encompass parallels in the emergence of affiliative and avoidance behaviors, and positive and negative affect. Such an integration begins with an understanding of the complexity of motivation related to the unfamiliar.

We need not restrict our aim to formulating an integration of infant emotional development. Studying determinants of infant affective expression is clearly relevant for understanding cognitive-affective relationships as well. We previously suggested that the nature of stimuli eliciting laughter was related to cognitive-developmental factors. Now we are tracing the development of sensitivity to contextual factors as determinants of emotional response. One is uneasy about attributing "thought" or evaluative ability to the "sensorimotor" infant, yet it is clear that considerable evolution toward thought is occurring in the first year of life. The study of infant affective expression may be integral for understanding emerging cognitive capacities.

References

Ambrose, A. The age of onset of ambivalence in early infancy: Indications from the study of laughing. *Journal of Child Psychology and Psychiatry*, 1963, **4**, 167–181.

Berlyne, D.E. *Conflict, arousal and curiosity.* New York: McGraw-Hill, 1960.

Berlyne, D. E. Laughter, humor and play. In G. Lindzey & E. Aronson (Eds.), *Handbook of social psychology.* (2nd ed.) Vol. 3. Reading, Mass.: Addison-Wesley, 1969. Pp. 795–852.

Bowlby, J. *Attachment and loss.* Vol. 1, *Attachment.* London: Hogarth; New York: Basic Books, 1969.

Bowlby, J. *Attachment and loss.* Vol. 2, *Separation: Anxiety and anger.* London: Hogarth; New York: Basic Books, 1973.

Brannigan, C. R., & Humphries, D. A. Human non-verbal behaviour, a means of communication. In N. Blurton-Jones (Ed.), *Ethological studies of child behaviour.* London: Cambridge University Press, 1972.

Bretherton, I., & Ainsworth, M. D. S. Responses of one-year-olds to a stranger in a strange situation. Chapter 6, this volume.

Bronson, G. W. Infants' reactions to unfamiliar persons and novel objects. *Monographs of the Society for Research in Child Development*, 1972, **37** (3, Serial No. 148).

Castell, R. Effect of familiar and unfamiliar environments on proximity behavior of young children. *Journal of Experimental Child Psychology*, 1970, **9**, 342–347.

Campos, J., Emde, R. N., Gaensbauer, T., & Sorce, J. Cardiac and behavioral responses of human infants to stranger: Effects of mother's absence and of experimental sequence. Paper presented at the meeting of the Society for Research in Child Development, Philadelphia, March 1973.

Chance, M. R. A. An interpretation of some agonistic postures; the role of "cut-off" acts and postures. *Symposium of the Zoological Society of London*, 1962, **8**, 71–89.

Cox, F. N., & Campbell, D. Young children in a new situation with and without their mothers. *Child Development*, 1968, **39**, 123–131.

Escalona, S. K. Emotional development in the First year of life. In Senn M. J. E. (Ed.), *Problems of Infancy and childhood, 6th conference*. New York: Josiah Macey Jr. Foundation, 1953.

Freedman, D. G. The infant's fear of strangers and the flight response. *Journal of Child Psychology and Psychiatry*, 1961, **2**, 242–248.

Greenacre, P. Panel on the theory of affects. *Bulletin of the American Psychoanalytical Association*, 1952, **8**, 312–313.

Harlow, H. F., & Zimmerman, R. R. Affectionate responses in the infant monkey. *Science*, 1959, **130**, 421–432.

Hebb, D. O. On the nature of fear. *Psychological Review*, 1946, **53**, 259–275.

Hinde, R. A. *Animal behaviour*. New York: McGraw-Hill, 1970.

Hunt, J. McV. Intrinsic motivation and its role in psychological development. *Nebraska Symposium on Motivation*, 1965.

Kagan, J. The origins of fear. Chapter 9, this volume.

Kagan, J., & Lewis, M. Studies of attention in the human infant. *Merrill-Palmer Quarterly*, 1965, **11**, 95–127.

Lazarus, R. S. *Psychological stress and the coping process*. New York: McGraw-Hill, 1966.

Lewin, K. *Principles of topological psychology*. F. Herder & G. Herder, Transls. New York: McGraw-Hill, 1936.

Lewis, M., Goldberg, S., & Campbell, H. A. A developmental study of information processing in the first three years of life: Response decrement to a redundant signal. *Monographs of the Society for Research in Child Development*, 1969, **34** (9, Serial No. 133), 1–41.

McCall, R. B., & Melson, W. H. Amount of short-term familiarization and the response to auditory discrepancies. *Child Development*, 1970, **41**, 861–869.

McGhee, P. E. Development of the humor response: A review of the literature. *Psychological Bulletin*, 1971, **76**, 328–348.

Morgan, G. A. Determinants of infants' reactions to strangers. Paper presented at the biennial meeting of the Society for Research in Child Development, Philadelphia, March 1973.

Morgan, G. A., & Ricciuti, H. N. Infants' responses to strangers during the first year. In B. M. Foss (Ed.), *Determinants of infant behavior*. Vol. 4. London: Methuen; New York: Wiley, 1969.

Piaget, J. *The origins of intelligence in the child*. London: Routledge & Kegan Paul, 1953.

Rheingold, H., & Eckerman, C. O. Fear of the stranger: A critical examination. In H. W. Reese (Ed.), *Advances in child development and behavior*. New York: Academic Press, in press.

Ricciuti, H. N. Fear and the development of social attachments in the first year of life. Chapter 4, this volume.

Scarr, S., & Salapatek, P. Patterns of fear development during infancy. *Merrill-Palmer Quarterly*, 1970, **16**, 53–87.

Schacter, S. The interaction of cognitive and physiological determinants of emotional state. In L. Berkowitz (Ed.), *Advances in experimental social psychology*. Vol. 1. New York: Academic Press, 1964.

Schaffer, H. R. The onset of fear of strangers and the incongruity hypothesis. *Journal of Child Psychology and Psychiatry*, 1966, **7**, 95–106.

Schaffer, H. R. Cognitive components of the infant's response to strangers. Chapter 1, this volume.

Schaffer, H. R., Greenwood, A., & Parry, M. H. The onset of wariness. *Child Development*, 1972, **43**, 165–175.

Schwartz, A. N., Campos, J. J., & Baisel, E. The visual cliff: Cardiac and behavioral correlates on the deep and shallow sides at five and nine months of age. *Journal of Experimental Child Psychology*, 1973, **15**, 85–99.

Sokolov, E. N. *Perception and the conditioned reflex*. New York: Macmillan, 1963.

Spitz, R. A. *The first year of life*. New York: International Universities Press, 1965.

Spitz, R. A., Emde, R. N., & Metcalf, D. R. Further prototypes of ego formation. *Psychoanalytic Study of the Child*, 1970, **25**, 417–444.

Sroufe, L. A., & Wunsch, J. P. The development of laughter in the first year of life. *Child Development*, 1972, **43**, 1326–1344.

Stechler, G., & Carpenter, F. A viewpoint on early affective development. In J. Hellmuth (Ed.), *Exceptional infant*. Vol. 1. Seattle: Special Child Publications, 1967. Pp. 163–189.

Stern, D. A micro-analysis of mother–infant interaction. In M. Lewis & L. Rosenblum (Eds.), *The effect of the infant on its caregiver*. New York: Wiley, 1974.

Tinbergen, N. *The study of instinct*. Oxford: Clarendon Press, 1951.

Tinbergen, E. A., & Tinbergen, N. Early childhood autism—An ethological approach. *Zeitschrift für Tierpsychologie*, Suppl. 10, 1972.

Waters, E. Patterns of smiling and gaze aversion during brief encounters with a stranger. Ethology Workshop, Max Planck Institute for Behavioral Physiology, Percha, West Germany, July 1973.

Watson, J. B., & Rayner, R. Conditioned emotional reactions. *Journal of Experimental Psychology*, 1920, **3**, 1–14.

Willmann, J. M. An analysis of humor and laughter. *American Journal of Psychology*, 1940, **53**, 72–85.

Wolff, P. H. Crying and vocalization in early infancy. In B. M. Foss (Ed.), *Determinants of infant behavior*. Vol. 4. London: Methuen; New York: Wiley, 1969, Pp. 81–110.

Yonas, A., & Hruska, K. Developmental changes in cardiac responses to the optical stimulus of impending collision. Paper presented at the Eleventh Annual Meeting of the Society for Psychophysiological Research, St. Louis, October 1971.

Zelazo, P. P., & Komer, M. J. Infant smiling to non-social stimuli and the recognition hypothesis. *Child Development*, 1971, **42**, 1327–1339.

CHAPTER 4

Fear and the Development
of Social Attachments
in the First Year of Life[1]

HENRY N. RICCIUTI
Cornell University

This chapter deals with the role of fear or negative affective reactions in the development of early social relationships between the infant and familiar as well as strange adults. The research reported grew out of a concern with the general question of the impact of extended group care experience outside the home early in life on infants' social behavior and developing social attachments. More specifically, the research analyzed infants' changing responses to strangers and to their familiar caregivers in an infant nursery during the first year of life, and the influence of such experience on infants' reactions to new social situations involving brief maternal separations.

Some of the most interesting and important developmental changes occurring during the first 12 or 18 months of life involve the infant's changing responses to various people in his social environment. At a rather gross descriptive level, the course of these changes is quite well known. By 2 or 3 months of age, infants respond readily and positively (smiling, cooing, looking) to virtually any friendly, talking, smiling person. At around 5 or 6 months, these clearly positive responses begin to be more selectively manifested as reactions to familiar persons, and responses to strangers become more cautious, involving a good deal of visual inspection and surveillance. These sober, attentive reactions to strangers become increasingly evident around 9 to 12 months, when many infants respond to the approach of a stranger with considerable distress or fear, particularly if the approach is close and rather abrupt. (There has been considerable recent discussion of the question of how universal such reactions really are, and whether they should all be regarded as representing fear of strangers.)

Paralleling these increasingly differentiated reactions to strangers during the

[1] Preparation of this chapter, and the research reported in it. were supported in part by the National Institute of Education, U.S. Department of Health, Education, and Welfare; and by CEMREL, Inc., a private nonprofit corporation, through funds from the U.S. Office of Education and the National Institute of Education.

second half of the first year, infants' positive affectional responses to particular adults, such as parents, who have become familiar and significant persons in the infants' experience, are more clearly delineated. These specific "attachments" or "focused relationships" are manifested not only by an infant's positive emotional responses shown selectively to such people, but also by reactions of protest and distress, as well as efforts to maintain or regain proximity, on actual or anticipated separation from the parental figure.

It has been well known for some time, based on both human and animal studies, that negative reactions to strangers or strange environments and maternal attachment behavior are interrelated in a number of important ways and that they have roughly parallel developmental "timetables." One proposition of substantial generalizability is that proximity to the mother or attachment object facilitates exploration of a strange environment (Ainsworth & Bell, 1970; Rheingold, 1969) and substantially attenuates fear of strangers or strange stimuli (Bronson, 1972). Morgan and Ricciuti, for example (1969), found that even a distance of 4 feet between mother and infant made quite a difference in infants' responses to strangers, once attachment to mother had developed. At 8, 10 and 12 months of age, infants tended increasingly to respond more positively and/ or less negatively to the approach of a stranger if they were seated on mother's lap rather than 4 feet away. Prior to 8 months, however, infants' responses were generally positive regardless of the distance between infant and mother. This reduction in negative reactions to fear-inducing stimuli as a result of maternal proximity has been found even when the "mother" is a cloth-covered surrogate to which infant rhesus monkeys have been "attached" (Harlow, 1961) or a styrofoam rectangle to which peking ducklings have been "imprinted" (Stettner & Tilds, 1966). (See also Hoffman, Chapter 2, this volume.)

A related generalization, which has been documented somewhat less formally than the one just discussed, involves the proposition that the infant will show more distress when separation from mother involves being left in a strange environment or with a strange person than when the infant is left with a familiar person and/or in a familiar environment (Robertson & Robertson, 1971).

Although the patterns of developmental change just outlined seem to be reasonably clear at a rather gross descriptive level, substantial problems of definition and conceptualization make it difficult to arrive at more precise and confident statements concerning the nature, age of onset, and developmental course of infants' fear of strangers. A number of investigators in recent years, for example, have reported data indicating that fear of strangers in the last quarter of the first year is not as predictable or universal a phenomenon as was formerly thought to be the case (Greenberg, Hillman, & Grice, 1973; Morgan & Ricciuti, 1969; Rheingold & Eckerman, in press), and at least one recent study reports onset of negative reactions to strangers as early as 4 or 5 months (Bronson, 1972). It seems quite clear that such differences in results are attributable largely to variations in the manner in which fear is conceptualized and defined operationally, as well as in the instigating circumstances and situational contexts employed for eliciting responses to strangers.

Several years ago, Ricciuti (1968) and Ricciuti and Poresky (1972) argued that in studying emotional responses such as fear in infants, it was necessary to assess three distinct components of such responses, if possible by independent criteria: *(a)* a behavioral component, in the form of approach, acceptance, or stimulus-maintaining behaviors on the one hand, or withdrawal, avoidance, or stimulus-terminating behaviors on the other; *(b)* an arousal or activation component, indicated by changes in levels of activity, motility, or excitement, revealed by both physiological and behavioral changes; and *(c)* a hedonic or pleasure-displeasure component, as revealed primarily by facial expressions and vocalizations.

We were led to this formulation partly as a result of efforts to describe more precisely infants' responses to strangers or strange stimuli. Such responses often consist primarily of sustained, sober, visual surveillance, along with markedly reduced activity levels, but we preferred not to call this "fear" without further evidence in the way of clear negative affective reactions. This is particularly important because such prolonged visual inspection of a strange stimulus is sometimes followed by pleasure rather than by displeasure reactions. Thus in the present study we have coded the sober, intent, visual surveillance of a stranger or strange object *neutral* affectively, although other investigators have sometimes scored such responses, or frowning, as evidence of negative or fear reactions (Bronson, 1972; Scarr & Salapatek, 1970). Infants' responses to strangers sometimes involve both positive and negative components, either successively in a given response modality, or simultaneously in different response systems (e.g., smiling coyly while turning away from a stranger). The assessment approach just described permits separate coding of such response components to facilitate identification of such ambivalent or conflictful reactions.

Most recent studies of infants' responses to strangers have attempted to go beyond the descriptive level and have focused increasingly on problems of explanation. Attention is being directed both to concurrent situational or contextual determinants of infants' reactions and to earlier antecedents in terms of variations in infant experience (Bretherton & Ainsworth, Chapter 6, this volume; Bronson, 1972; Morgan & Ricciuti, 1969; Rheingold & Eckerman, in press). Similar explanatory issues are being carefully examined in recent studies of attachment and separation behaviors in infants (Ainsworth, Bell, & Stayton, 1972; Corter, Rheingold, & Eckerman, 1972; Messer & Lewis, 1972; Spelke, Zelazo, Kagan, & Kotelchuck, 1973).

More and more investigators are recognizing that to understand more fully infants' responses to strangers and to maternal separation, we need a better understanding of the perceptual-cognitive context in which the infant responds to and attempts to deal with the stimulus situation he confronts in our studies;

moreover, this context must be considered in the light of the infant's cognitive competencies at that point in development, as well as his expectations and prior experience (Benjamin, 1963; Lewis & Brooks, Chapter 8, this volume; Morgan & Ricciuti, 1969; Sroufe, Waters, and Matas, Chapter 3, this volume). It has been frequently suggested, for example, that fear of strangers might be seen as a special instance of the more widely observed negative reactions to incongruity, dissonance, or the unexpected (Freedman, 1961; Hebb, 1946; Schaffer, 1966). Meili (1955) and more recently Kagan (Chapter 9, this volume) have proposed thinking of the negative reaction as a consequence of the infant's inability to assimilate perceptually or cognitively the discrepant or incongruous stimulus event, in the context of prior experience with similar stimuli. On the other hand, it is still difficult to explain why such situations also produce positive reactions and even humor in some instances (Ricciuti & Poresky, 1972; Sroufe et al., Chapter 3, this volume).

Of particular relevance to the research reported in this chapter is the question of the role of previous experience in determining infants' responses to strangers as well as to short-term separations. With regard to responses to strangers, for example, it is well recognized that some home-reared infants are particularly sensitive to and fearful of strangers, perhaps from a relatively early age, whereas others rarely show negative reactions and may be quite positively responsive to strangers even toward the end of the first year. These wide individual differences might be attributable in some measure to temperamental characteristics (Bronson, 1972; Scarr & Salapatek, 1970); however, one would expect them to be accounted for at least partly by variations in previous experience with a variety of adults outside the nuclear family. For the most part, however, it has not been possible to demonstrate systematic relationships of this type empirically. Morgan and Ricciuti (1969), for example, found no significant correlations between infants' responses to strangers over the age range of 3 to 12 months and variations in the frequency of exposure to a variety of strangers and situations outside the home. More recently, Bronson (1972) reported a similar absence of such relationships. On the other hand, Bretherton and Ainsworth (1972) found some evidence of connections between fear of strangers and patterns of mother–infant relationships.

There seems to be considerably more empirical evidence bearing on the question of previous experience and infants' responses to maternal separation. Much of the work in this area (reviewed by Bowlby, 1973) has stressed the disturbing consequences of prolonged or difficult separations, such as those involved in hospitalization, on subsequent mother—child relationships. Some of these consequences are shown in either excessively distressed and angry, or detached and indifferent responses to later brief separations from and reunions with mother. Within the more normal range of variations in experience, Ainsworth, Bell, and Stayton (1971) found that one-year-olds who reacted to brief maternal separation and reunion with active proximity seeking and contact maintenance were likely to be characterized as having "harmonious" interrelationships with mother, as observed on home visits. However, infants who showed little proximity seeking, avoided interaction, or seemed to be ambivalent and conflictful during the experimental separation and reunion, were more likely to have been judged as having experienced disturbed mother–infant interactions.

There is relatively little systematic evidence bearing on the question of whether infants can learn to adapt effectively to relatively frequent separations from mother during the first 12 to 18 months of life, under circumstances that minimize distress, such as being left with a familiar caregiver available as an alternate attachment figure. This is not only a matter of considerable theoretical significance; it is also of great contemporary importance in the formulation of social policy and practices with regard to the issue of day care for infants.

Two recent investigations were addressed to the question of the possible impact of infant day care experience on mother–child attachment relationships. The first study (Caldwell, Wright, Honig, & Tannenbaum, 1970) compared 30-month-old children with and without extended group care experience on a number of child–mother and mother–child attachment variables obtained from a combined interview and observation session. Essentially no differences were found between the groups on such characteristics as affiliation, nurturance, hostility, happiness, and emotionality, and the investigators concluded that the day care experience of this sample, which began between 6 and 15 months of age, had not impaired mother–child attachment relationships. A more recent study by Blehar (1973), on the other hand, includes findings considered to be suggestive of disturbances in the mother—child relationships of 2- and 3-year-old children who had been enrolled in full-time day care for about 5 months. In comparison with control children, children in day care were more distressed during brief maternal separation in a strange situation, and they showed more avoidant and resistant behaviors to mother on her return. Moreover, the older children, who entered day care at 35 months of age, showed a mixture of proximity and contact seeking, as well as resistance and avoidance, which Blehar considers to be indicative of anxious, ambivalent attachment.

The Present Research

The studies reported in this chapter stemmed from an interest in the effect of extended day care experience beginning as early as 2 to 3 months of life on the infant's social development, with particular reference to responses to familiar and strange adults. The investigations were carried out in connection with the operation of a small experimental infant nursery, as part of a research and development program concerned with the articulation of guidelines for providing quality group care environments for infants in the first year. One of our research interests was to analyze the role played by the infants' familiar nursery caregivers as alternate attachment figures. We were also concerned with the impact of this day care experience in the first year of life on the infants' responses to strange social situations and to brief maternal separation.

A major portion of the data presented comes from a longitudinal investigation of the development of infants' recognition of and attachment to their particular nursery caregivers from approximately 3.5 months of age, shortly after enrollment in the program, through the end of the first year (study A, 1971–1972). The study was designed to permit a longitudinal comparison of infants' changing responses to strangers and to their gradually familiar caregivers, as well as their reactions to brief separations from mother and from caregiver. It was also possible to examine the impact of the stranger and the caregiver as inducers or attenuators of infant distress in the context of brief maternal separations.

Because of our interest in the possible developmental effects of daily group care experience beginning early in the first year, several exploratory studies were carried out comparing various social responses of two small groups of infants having been in our nursery during 1971–1972 or 1972–1973 with matched non-day-care controls. One investigation (study B, 1973) compared 12- to 13-month-old day care and control infants' responses to an adult stranger with and without mother present, employing a procedure very similar to that used in the aforementioned longitudinal study. Additional data bearing on the same issues come from a somewhat larger investigation of stranger and separation reactions of 12-month-old infants (primarily non-day care) examined as a function of whether the stranger's initial approach is relatively abrupt or gradual, and whether the mother, infant, and stranger remain together for a short (3-minute) or longer (10-minute) period before maternal separation takes place (study C, 1973). Finally, we compared the behavior of our 1971–1972 and 1972–1973 nursery infants at 12 to 19 months with that of matched controls, when brought by mother into a natural social situation involving a group of 3-year-old preschool children playing with an adult teacher (study D, 1972, 1973). (For convenience, the four studies are identified as A72, B73, C73, and D72, 73.)

STUDY A (1971–1972)[2]

Subjects and Setting

The subjects of the longitudinal study were ten infants in the Cornell Infant Nursery (eight boys, two girls), five enrolled in a morning group and five in an afternoon group, attending daily sessions of about 4 hours' duration. The in-

[2]Dr. Robert H. Poresky had major responsibility for the observations, data collection, and preliminary steps of data analysis in this study. Lucille Atkin assisted with observations and carried out much of the later data analyses, along with Alice Kopan, Marilyn Kaufman, and Jeanette Valentine. For a preliminary report on part of this study, see Ricciuti and Poresky (1973).

fants entered the program between September and November 1971, when they were between 2 and 3.5 months of age. (One entered at 4 months, 3 days.) They remained in the nursery program until late July 1972, when most of them were 12 to 13 months old. For the most part, the infants came from middle-class families, and their mothers worked part time in nearby settings. Also, the infants generally spent the remaining half-day at home, rather than in a different day care setting.

The Infant Nursery provided daily care for five or six infants in a morning group and the same number in an afternoon group. Each group of infants was cared for by two female caregivers, each of whom had primary responsibility for two or three infants, although there was relatively frequent interchanging of caretaking roles. From time to time, other adults associated with the program came into the nursery to provide temporary assistance or to visit briefly; thus the infants had ample opportunity to see other adults besides the two caregivers. The two caregivers responsible for each group remained in that role throughout the program year, since it was desired to have a sufficiently small number of different adults responsible for the care of five or six infants, with sufficient stability and continuity to enable us to facilitate the infants' gradual recognition of their respective caregivers in the nursery, as well as the development of appropriate feelings of confidence, trust, and perhaps even affection for them.

Experimental Procedure

Beginning when each infant was 3 to 4 months old, once a month on arrival at the nursery at the usual time, the mother took the baby to a special playroom where carefully structured procedures were employed for eliciting and measuring the infant's affective and approach–withdrawal responses to his caregiver, to a stranger, and to brief maternal as well as caregiver separation. These monthly assessments took approximately 10 minutes, and were carried out on two successive days.

The experimental procedure is described briefly in the following paragraphs and is outlined in Table 1.

(a) Mother and infant were allowed 2 to 3 minutes by themselves to become adapted to the testing room; toward the end of the time the mother placed the baby in an infant seat or "Baby-Tenda," while she sat in a chair close by at the infant's right, within a distance of 2 to 3 feet. This arrangement placed the person next coming into the room at about a 30° angle to the infant's left, with the door about 8 feet away.

(b) At this point, on day C, the infant's principal caregiver entered the room, smiled silently for a few seconds, greeted the baby gently but warmly from 5 or 6 feet away, then approached closer to the infant while continuing to chat naturally, finally reaching out and touching the baby while talking. (This approach sequence, modeled after Morgan & Ricciuti, 1969, was carefully struc-

TABLE 1. Experimental Procedure

Approximate Time Intervals	Day C (Caregiver First)	Comparisons	Day S (Stranger First)	
2½ minutes (a)	Mother and infant in playroom		Mother and infant in playroom	(a)
50 seconds (b)	Caregiver enters, approaches infant	1	Stranger enters, approaches infant	(b)
30 seconds	CG & MO chat	4	STR & MO chat	
15 seconds (c)	Mother leaves,	2	Mother leaves,	(c)
30 seconds	CG & INF alone	5	STR & INF alone	
50 seconds (d)	Stranger enters, approaches infant	3 6	Caregiver enters, approaches infant	(d)
30 seconds	STR & CG chat		CG & STR chat	
15 seconds (e)	Caregiver leaves infant with stranger		Stranger leaves infant with caregiver	(e)
30 seconds	STR & INF alone		CG & INF alone	
50 seconds (f)	Mother returns, approaches infant		Mother returns, approaches infant	(f)

tured but quite naturalistic and took about 50 seconds.) The caregiver then sat down and chatted with the mother for about half a minute.

(c) The mother then told the baby: "I'm going to have to go out for a few minutes now, but I'll be back." She then walked to the door, called goodbye, and left the room, closing the door as she went.

(d) After half a minute or so, a trained female stranger[3] entered the room, greeted the baby from a distance, and in approaching followed the same sequence previously used by the caregiver. The stranger then sat down and chatted with the caregiver for about half a minute.

(e) At this time, the caregiver said goodbye to the baby and left the room, leaving the infant with the stranger.

(f) After another half-minute, the mother reentered the room and greeted the baby, saying "Hi, honey—I told you I'd be back after a little while, and here I am," generally following the same approach sequence as previously indicated.

The general procedure just described was repeated on a second day (day S), but with the stranger approaching the infant first, instead of the caregiver. Thus on day S when the mother departed temporarily she left the infant with the

[3] The same stranger was used on the two days of each monthly assessment, and six different female strangers were used throughout the study. A stranger did not reappear to an infant on subsequent monthly tests except after an interval of at least 3 months; thus there was minimal likelihood of the stranger being recognized.

stranger, rather than with the familiar caregiver as on day C. At each monthly assessment, half the infants had day C first, followed by day S; half had the reverse order. Also, for each infant the order of days C and S was alternated on successive monthly sessions. It should be mentioned, finally, that detailed instructions were prepared for mother, caregiver, and stranger to obtain standardization of the procedures followed.

Observation and Measurement

Throughout the experimental sequence, two observers behind an observation mirror independently rated the infants' visual and manipulative–postural responses on an approach–withdrawal continuum, as well as their affective responses on a pleasure–displeasure continuum. Ratings on each of these three dimensions were dictated into a tape recorder approximately every 10 to 12 seconds, during designated segments of the approach and departure sequence being followed by the caregiver, the stranger, and the mother. Interobserver reliability was satisfactorily high (typically $> .90$ for the various subscores used in the analyses), and ratings from the two observers were averaged for each coding unit in the experimental sequence. (When a second observer was not available, videotapes of the session were employed to confirm the "live" observational ratings.)

The three rating scales, which were used extensively in a previous study of emotional behavior and development in the first year of life (Ricciuti & Poresky, 1972), can be described briefly as follows.

Visual (V) and Manipulative–Postural (M–P) Directionality ● The V and M–P scales are both 9-point scales, indicating the extent to which the infant's responses in the particular modality reflect stimulus maintaining, stimulus seeking, or "approach" behaviors on the one hand, or stimulus terminating, stimulus avoiding, or "withdrawal" behaviors on the other. Scale values run from $+4$ for maximum approach behavior, through a midpoint of O, to -4 for maximum withdrawal or avoidance. Thus a rating of $+4$ would indicate sustained visual fixation directed to the target person for essentially the entire segmental unit of observation (V), or sustained reaching and definite postural inclination toward the target person (M–P). A -4 rating (V) would indicate sustained visual avoidance (rarely observed), or pronounced, persistent withdrawal of hands or arms, and postural inclination of body away from target person (M–P). A zero rating would indicate an absence of any approach or withdrawal behaviors.

Affectivity ● Another 9-point scale, affectivity, reflects the intensity of the infant's pleasure–displeasure or hedonic responses, based primarily on facial expression and vocalizations, with visual and manipulative–postural approach and withdrawal responses given some consideration as secondary cues. Since major emphasis is on affective responses, this scale is described in more detail:

+4 Sustained smiling accompanied by positive vocalizations (coos, gurgles, squeals), or activity bursts, or strong postural or reaching (M–P) responses, while visually oriented toward person (V).

+3 Sustained, broad smiling and visual orientation, without positive vocalizations or activity increases; or sustained positive vocalizations and visual orientation without sustained smiling; or sustained M–P approach behavior accompanied by intermittent smiling or positive vocalizations.

+2 Intermittent broad smiling or sustained moderate smiling, without positive vocalizations or M–P responses; or intermittent moderate smiling and occasional positive vocalizations or M–P responses.

+1 Occasional or infrequent smiling; or occasional positive vocalizations (unaccompanied by other positive responses in each case).

0 Neutral affectivity—absence of clear positive or negative cues in facial expression or vocalizations; facial expression may be neutral, sober-attentive, or animated (not smiling).

−1 Occasional distress (precry) face; or infrequent whimper (in each case without other negative cues).

−2 Intermittent facial distress or intermittent whimpering, without other negative cues.

−3 Sustained facial distress, with some whimpering or negative M–P response; or intermittent distress face, with some whimpering and mild negative M–P responses.

−4 Sustained crying, with or without other negative cues; or intermittent crying with clear V or M-P avoidance; or strong V or M-P avoidance with intermittent whimpering and facial distress.

It should be noted, for reasons mentioned earlier, that a sober-attentive or serious facial expression was rated as neutral affectivity, rather than negative, as is the case in some studies.

Analytic Comparisons

The present report focuses primarily on the analysis of infants' affective responses, with some attention to visual orientation as well. The first step in the analysis was to obtain for each infant at each age derived scores for each of the major portions of the experimental sequence outlined in Table 1, for day C and day S. These scores were obtained by averaging the ratings for the four short segments included in each of the designated steps of the sequence. Mean scores for the sample as a whole, reflecting affective or visual responses during the various portions of the sequence, were then plotted as a function of age, and the following comparisons of the developmental curves thus obtained were carried out.

1. A comparison was made of the infants' visual and affective responses to the first approach of the *caregiver* and that of the *stranger* (step b, day C vs. day S). It was anticipated that some time after 4 months of age, the infant should begin showing differential responses to the stranger and the caregiver, perhaps through more positive greeting responses to the caregiver, as she gradually became recognized as familiar. It was not expected that fearful responses to the stranger would be particularly common or marked in this context toward the end of the first year, although it seemed reasonable to anticipate less positive reactions to the stranger than the caregiver at that point in development.

2. Visual and affective responses to mother's departure when the infant was left with the *caregiver* were compared with responses to being left with the *stranger* (step c, day C vs. day S). The expectation here was that when infants reached the point at which some distress at separation from mother might be anticipated, this distress should be substantially less, if present at all, when the infant is left with a person who has become familiar to him as a significant caregiver.

3. To examine additional evidence concerning the familiar caregiver's role as a significant attachment figure, the infant's visual and affective responses to being left alone with the stranger by the *caregiver's departure* were compared with the previously mentioned reactions to being left with the stranger by *mother's departure* (step e, day C vs. step c, day S).

4. In the first comparison in this list, responses to the stranger's approach were observed while the infant was in the *mother's presence*. These behaviors were also compared with reactions to the approach of the stranger in *mother's absence*, after she had left the infant with the caregiver. It was anticipated that in the latter case the reactions might be more negative, or less positive (step b, day S vs. step d, day C).

5. To achieve a more precise assessment of the impact of the stranger's approach in mother's absence, the responses just mentioned were also examined in relation to the prior affective state of the infant during the last two segments of the preceding interval (about 30 seconds) when infant and caregiver were alone after mother had departed (step d vs. last two segments of step c, day C).

6. For comparative purposes, an equivalent analysis was made of the impact of the caregiver's approach after mother had left the infant alone with the stranger (step d vs. last two segments of step c, day S).

7. Finally, developmental curves were plotted for the change scores derivable from comparisons 5 and 6 above, indicating the direction and magnitude of the changes in affective state brought about by the approach of the caregiver or the stranger, when each entered the room after mother had left the infant in the presence of the other.

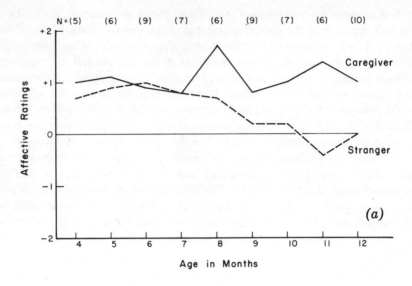

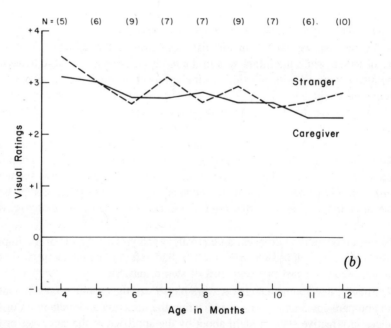

FIGURE 1.   Responses to first approach of caregiver and stranger (mother present): *(a)* affective, *(b)* visual.

Results

1. The results of the first analytic comparison are presented in Figure 1*a*, in terms of the mean ratings of the infants' affective responses to the first approach of the caregiver and the stranger, plotted longitudinally over the period from 4 to 12 months of age. It is quite clear that up to 7 months the infants showed the same level of moderately positive responses, on the average, to both caregiver and stranger. Beginning at 8 months, however, although average responses to the caregiver continued at the same generally positive level, responses to the stranger's approach became increasingly less positive, moving gradually into the affectively neutral to slightly negative range. (Differences between the two curves are significant, $p <$ .001, when the 8- to 12-month data are pooled; $p <$ .05 for monthly comparisons except at 9 months.)

It should be noted that mean responses to the stranger never became clearly negative; thus there is little or no evidence in these data for fearful reactions to strangers as a modal response toward the end of the first year of life. On the other hand, there is considerable variability within the group, particularly after 7 months, and at each age level from 6 months on there were one or two infants who showed mild or moderate negative reactions to the stranger (eleven in all). Only once did such negative ratings reach a value greater than -1.4 (-3.1 at 11 months). It should also be noted that there were only four negative reactions to the caregiver, one each occurring at 7 and 9 months, two at 10 months. At every monthly level except 6 months, the maximum positive response to the caregiver was greater than the maximum positive response to the stranger, and these differences became especially pronounced from 9 months on.

Visual responses to the first approach of the stranger and caregiver are shown in Figure 1*b*. There was considerable looking toward both persons throughout the age span covered, with the ratings being at virtually the same levels for both caregiver and stranger. At 11 and 12 months, however, the curves begin to separate slightly, with somewhat more visual fixation being directed toward the stranger than the caregiver (significant at 12 months and for both ages combined, $p <$ .05). There were no individual negative ratings suggesting consistent visual avoidance of either person.

2. The second analysis (Figure 2*a*) compares average affective responses to mother's departure when the infant was left with the *caregiver* or with the *stranger*. As one would expect, from 4 through 6 months of age infants' affective reactions to brief maternal separation were essentially neutral under both conditions. Beginning at 7 months, however, the infants began to show increasing evidence of distress when left with the stranger, with these reactions becoming most pronounced at 10, 11, and 12 months (-1.1, -1.2, -1.3). On the other hand, when left with the caregiver their responses continued to remain in the generally neutral range during this period, except at 12 months, when the infants showed a moderately negative reaction ($-.70$). (Pooling the 8- to 12-

month data indicates a highly significant difference between the two conditions—$p < .005$; only the 10-month individual comparison was significant, however—$p < .025$.)

Considering the data displayed in both Figures 1a and 2a, it is quite clear that substantially greater distress was produced when the infant was left alone with the stranger as mother departed briefly than when the stranger approached the infant in mother's presence. In the former case, of course, the infants' responses were influenced both by maternal separation and by the presence of the stranger. An examination of individual differences in infants' reactions indicates that some of the most pronounced negative responses occurred under this condition of "dual stress." Ratings between -3 and -4 occurred in three infants at 12 months, and one each at 11, 10, and 8 months under those circumstances. At the same time, some of the earliest negative reactions of rather substantial magnitude were also produced in this condition (e.g., ratings between -2 and -3 appearing at 6 and 7 months).

Ratings of the infants' visual orientation toward the mother as she leaves the child with the *stranger* or the *caregiver* are plotted in Figure 2b. (It should be noted that these ratings are based on observations during the first two segments of *step c* in the experimental sequence, as the mother moved to the doorway and left the room.) The infants showed only a moderate amount of looking toward the mother and her point of departure, particularly from 4 to 6 months of age. Although one might expect minimal looking behavior at these early ages, it is somewhat puzzling that more sustained visual orientation toward the mother was not observed in the later months, when considerable distress at mother's departure was manifested, particularly in the stranger condition. It is interesting to note, further, that the two curves in Figure 2b are virtually indistinguishable, although at 11 and 12 months there is some tendency for the infants to show more sustained visual orientation toward the mother as she leaves them with the stranger than with the caregiver (significant only for the two ages combined, $p < .025$).

3. The next analysis dealt with the question of whether the infants showed separation distress when the familiar caregiver left them alone with a stranger, as was previously shown to occur when the mother did so. Figure 3a presents mean affective responses to caregiver separation, and the data can be compared with responses shown when mother left the infant alone with a stranger (as previously depicted in Figure 2a). It is readily apparent that these two curves are essentially indistinguishable. Starting at 6 to 7 months of age, the infants began to show increasingly negative separation reactions, which were generally equivalent whether the familiar caregiver or the mother left them with a stranger. These negative responses were most marked toward the end of the first year.

Ratings of visual orientation toward the caregiver and mother as each left the infant with a stranger are shown in Figure 3b. These two curves are also remarkably similar throughout the entire age range. Thus whether the infant was left

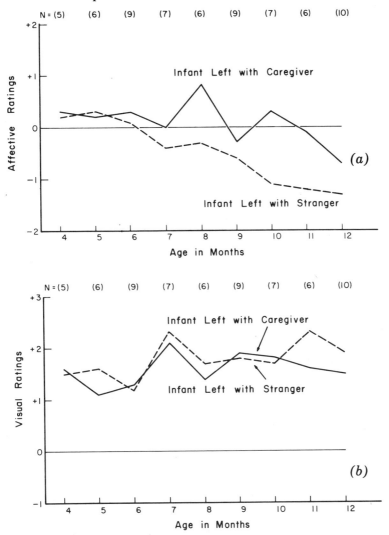

FIGURE 2. Responses to mother's departure, infant left with caregiver or stranger: *(a)* affective, *(b)* visual.

with a stranger by the mother or the caregiver, the affective as well as the visual responses to separation exhibited virtually identical developmental courses for the two conditions over the period from 4 to 12 months.

4. It will be recalled that the first analysis of infants' affective responses to the stranger compared these reactions with those shown to the caregiver, and in both instances the mother was seated close by. The next analysis (Figure 4) involves a comparison of these reactions to the stranger in mother's presence

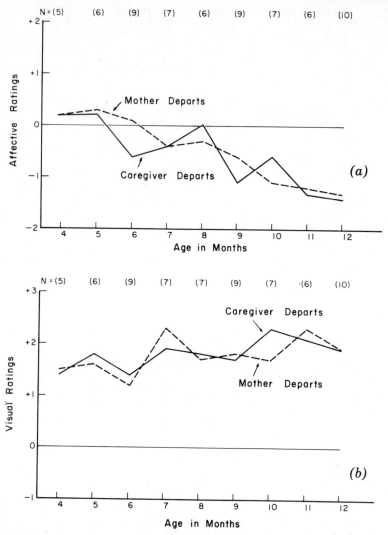

FIGURE 3.   Responses to mother's departure and caregiver's departure, infant left with stranger: *(a)* affective, *(b)* visual.

(as previously depicted in Figure 1*a*) and those shown when the stranger approached the infant in mother's absence, just after she had left the infant with the caregiver. Although the differences in the two curves portrayed in Figure 4 are for the most part rather slight, there was clearly a tendency throughout the age range studied for responses to the stranger in mother's absence to be somewhat less positive, or more negative, than reactions shown in mother's presence. It is also interesting to note that the shift in affective reactions from

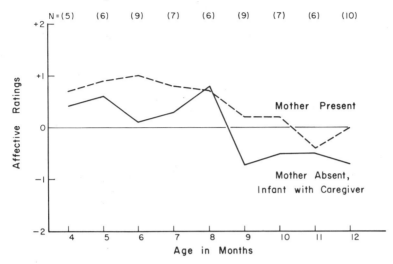

FIGURE 4.   Affective responses to approach of stranger in presence of mother and after mother has left infant with caregiver.

positive to negative occurred earlier (9 months) and more sharply in the mother-absent condition than when mother was present. (Difference between the two conditions is significant when data are pooled for all ages, $p < .001$.)

5. It is apparent that responses to the stranger's approach in mother's absence are influenced partly by the stranger as such, partly by the immediately preceding departure of mother, and most importantly, by an interaction of these two sources of influence. In an attempt to shed further light on this issue, responses to the stranger in the mother-absent condition are again plotted in Figure 5, along with ratings of the infants' affective state during the immediately preceding 30 seconds or so, after mother's departure and just before the stranger's entrance. Thus a "baseline" is provided, permitting the examination of the impact of the stranger's approach as a function of the infant's prior affective state.

From 4 through 7 months, the entrance of the stranger produced no consistent shift from the prior neutral-to-positive state of the infants as they remained with the caregiver after mother's departure. Beginning at 8 months, however, although the differences between the curves are neither uniformly large nor significant, the mean response to the stranger is consistently less positive, or more negative, than the immediately preceding state of the infant during mother's absence. At 10 and 11 months the negative reactions to the stranger represent a substantial (but not significant) shift from the previously positive response state. However, at 9 and at 12 months particularly, the infants were already in a somewhat negative state, and the approach of the stranger produced only minimal increments of added distress. In short, reactions to the stranger were generally more negative in the mother-absent than in the mother-present condition

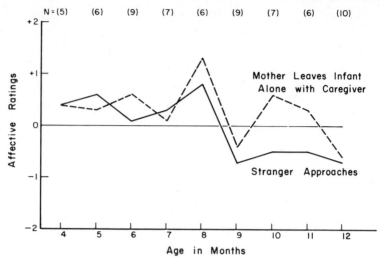

FIGURE 5. Affective responses to stranger compared with preceding affective state after mother has left infant with caregiver.

(Figure 4), but a substantial portion of the more negative reaction seems to have been induced, at least at some ages, by the preceding maternal departure.

6. Having examined the impact of the stranger's approach on the behavior of infants who have just been left by mother with the caregiver, an equivalent analysis was carried out to examine the effect of the caregiver's approach to infants whose mothers had just left them alone with the stranger. Figure 6 presents a plot of the infants' affective responses to the caregiver in the mother-absent condition, as compared with their immediately preceding affective state prior to the caregiver's entrance. The graph indicates quite clearly that as early as 7 and 8 months, the caregiver's approach produced a substantial shift in the direction of more positive responses. Moreover, from 9 months on, as the infants' reactions to being left alone with the stranger became increasingly negative, the approach of the caregiver resulted in a substantial reduction of these distress responses. (All monthly comparisons from 7 months on are significant, $p < .05$ or better.)

Thus the functional consequences of the approach of the stranger and the caregiver in mother's absence are quite different. After 6 or 7 months of age, when maternal separation begins to have an impact, the stranger's approach tends to produce moderate shifts in the direction of less positive or more negative responses than those shown when the infant was left alone with the caregiver (Figure 5). On the other hand, the caregiver's approach clearly serves to substantially attenuate infants' distress or to increase positive affect, after they have been left alone with the stranger (Figure 6).

7. The contrasts just summarized are illustrated in Figure 7, which indicates

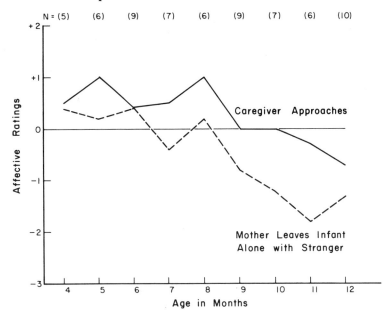

FIGURE 6.   Affective responses to caregiver compared with preceding affective state after mother has left infant with stranger.

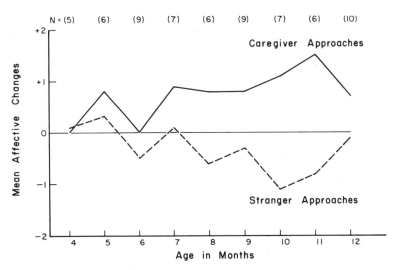

FIGURE 7.   Changes in affective responses when caregiver approaches after infant has been left alone with stranger, and when stranger approaches after infant has been left alone with caregiver.

the magnitude and direction of the shifts in affective responses produced by the stranger and the caregiver under the conditions discussed. Essentially, each curve in Figure 7 is a plot of the mean changes shown in the differences between the corresponding pairs of curves presented in Figures 5 and 6.

Summary

The principal results of the longitudinal study of infants in group care during the first year of life can be summarized very briefly as follows.

1. When infants were tested in the presence of mother, there was no evidence of a modal tendency for fear of strangers to occur toward the end of the first year, although a few infants did show negative reactions. Reactions to the stranger did become clearly less positive after 7 months, however, whereas responses to the familiar caregiver remained at a substantially more positive level.

2. Affective responses to the stranger's approach in mother's absence were generally less positive (in the early months) or more negative (after 8 months) than those observed in mother's presence. However, there is some evidence to suggest that these shifts may be determined to a considerable degree by similar affective changes having occurred before the stranger's entrance, as a result of mother's departure when she left the infant with the caregiver.

3. The most pronounced distress reactions occurred when the mother left the infant alone with the stranger. These negative responses began to appear clearly at 7 months and became increasingly negative by the end of the first year. Under these circumstances, the approach of the caregiver substantially reduced the infant's distress, while in the early months it increased the infant's positive affect.

4. Being left alone by mother with the caregiver generally produced little or no distress until the 12-month period, when moderately negative reactions occurred, although these were substantially less negative than those observed when the infant was left alone with the stranger.

5. Finally, the developmental progression of increasing distress at being left alone with a stranger by mother is paralleled very closely by the pattern of infants' distress reactions when left alone with the stranger by the caregiver.

Studies B (1973) and C (1973)

Some additional data bearing on the issue of infants' responses to strangers with and without mother present come from two related studies, which also provide preliminary data relevant to the question of the degree to which the behavioral observations just reported from our longitudinal study might have been a function of the extended day care experience of this particular sample (A 72).

Procedure

One study (B 73)[4] involved a comparison of stranger and separation reactions at 12 to 13 months of age for a group of nine infants enrolled in our experimental nursery during 1972–1973 (B_1), and a group of nine control infants, matched for age and sex but without regular group day care experience (B_2). The day care infants entered the nursery between 2 and 6 months of age, with five infants (one boy and four girls) in full day care and four (two boys and two girls) in half-day care. Thus at the time of the behavioral assessments to be described, these infants had had from 7 to 10 months of daily group care experience in our nursery, the general setting of which was as previously described for the A 72 study. The assessment procedure utilized in this study was identical with that employed in the second investigation, described below.

The second study (C 73) was carried out as a doctoral thesis (Trause, 1974), and several parts of it are relevant to the present discussion. Forty 12-month-old infants with little or no regular group care experience were observed in an experimental situation involving three systematic approaches to the infant by a female stranger: (1) shortly after mother and infant had become adapted to the testing room (mother present), (2) shortly after mother had left the infant alone with the stranger, and (3) just before mother returned. The stranger's approach to the infant followed the same general pattern as that described in the longitudinal study (A 72), except that on the first approach or "run" (with mother present), the stranger approached half the infants somewhat more quickly or abruptly, without first pausing silently and greeting the baby from a distance, as was the case in our earlier procedure. This contrast between a "quick" and "slow" initial approach by the stranger was not continued in the subsequent runs, when the more gradual approach was employed. Observations of the infant's affective, manipulative–postural, and visual responses to the systematic approaches of the stranger were rated with the same scales as those used in the longitudinal studies.[5]

Results

Figure 8 and Table 2 summarize comparable data from the two smaller studies just described, and from the 12-month level in the previously discussed longitudinal study, bearing on the question of 1-year-olds' affective responses to the approach of a stranger, with and without mother present. These data also permit

[4]Data collection for this study was primarily the responsibility of Mary Anne Trause, with Jeanette Valentine assisting with data analysis.

[5]This experiment also involved varying the amount of time infant, mother, and stranger were together in the room before maternal separation (i.e., 3 vs. 10 minutes). Only data obtained in the 3-minute condition are reported in the present chapter, however, since this is the condition most comparable to the procedure used in the A 72 study. This accounts for the reduction in number of subjects from 40 to 20 from the first to second run in Table 2, C 73 sample.

some preliminary comparisons of infants with and without extended group care experience.

Considering first infants' responses to the stranger's initial approach while in mother's presence (upper portion of Figure 8), the data from the B 73 and C 73 studies generally confirm the previously reported results of the longitudinal study (A 72), indicating no particular tendency for one-year-old infants to respond negatively to strangers. In fact, the mean responses for the B 73 and C 73 samples are very slightly more positive (means = .17, .10, .42, for slow and quick combined) than for the longitudinal sample (mean = 0.0).

It is interesting to note, further, that there are essentially no differences between the day care and non-day care groups in response to the stranger with

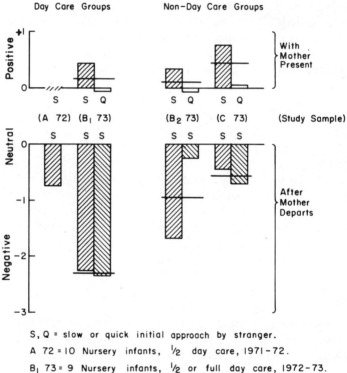

S, Q = slow or quick initial approach by stranger.

A 72 = 10 Nursery infants, 1/2 day care, 1971 - 72.

B₁ 73 = 9 Nursery infants, 1/2 or full day care, 1972 - 73.

B₂ 73 = 9 Matched controls, no regular day care experience.

C 73 = 40 Infants, little or no regular group care experience.

(N = 20 after mother departs)

FIGURE 8. Mean affective responses to stranger's approach with and without mother present (12- to 13-month-old infants in day care and non-day care groups).

TABLE 2. Mean Affective Responses to Stranger's Approach with and without Mother Present (12- to 13-Month-Old Infants in Day Care and Non-Day Care Groups)

Study Samples	Affective Response to First Approach of Stranger, Mother Present		Affective Response to Stranger After Mother's Departure	
Day care				
A (1972)	$(S)^a$	0.0 (10)	(S)	−0.73 (10)
B₁ (1973)	(Q)	−0.06 (5)	(S)	−2.33 (4)
	(S)	0.45 (4)	(S)	−2.25 (4)
	(T)	0.17 (9)	(T)	−2.29 (8)
Non-day care				
B₂ (1973)	(Q)	−0.08 (5)	(S)	−0.25 (4)
	(S)	0.33 (4)	(S)	−1.68 (4)
	(T)	0.10 (9)	(T)	−0.96 (8)
C (1973)	(Q)	0.05 (20)	(S)	−0.70 (10)
	(S)	0.78 (20)	(S)	−0.43 (10)
	(T)	0.42 (40)	(T)	−0.57 (20)

[a] S, Q = slow or quick initial approach by stranger.

mother present, as shown particularly in the matched sample comparisons in the B 73 study. Finally, there is a slight but consistent tendency for infants to respond more positively when the stranger's initial approach is gradual rather than quick, as indicated in all three comparisons shown.

Comparing the upper and lower portions of Figure 8, the general tendency for infants' affective reactions to the stranger to become more negative in mother's absence is quite clear in all four samples, for both day care and non-day care groups, and in both the slow and quick initial approach conditions. The most pronounced shift in the negative direction $(p < .005)$ occurred in the B₁ 73 day care group.

With respect to comparisons of infants with and without extended day care experience, attention is directed first to results from the B 73 study, which involved matched samples tested with the same stranger and identical procedures[9] There was a substantially greater negative reaction to the stranger immediately following mother's departure in the day care sample (-2.29) than in the non-day care group $(-.96)$. Although not statistically significant and based on a very small sample, this is an interesting finding nonetheless. Further evidence of the greater distress at maternal separation for these day care infants is supplied by the behavior of six of these children, in contrast to three in the non-day care group, who were sufficiently upset to require mother's return after 4 or 5 minutes, rather than the planned 10 minutes.

It should be mentioned at this point, however, that when the B_1 73 day care infants were tested, they were brought by mother on her arrival at the university directly to a strange testing room in an adjoining building rather than to the familiar nursery. There, departing from the pattern to which the infants had become accustomed, they were greeted by and left with a stranger rather than their familiar caregiver. Thus one could argue that for the day care infants, the experience of being left with a stranger under these particular circumstances represented a considerably more dissonant or incongruous experience, hence a more distressing one, than was the case for the non-day care infants.

Figure 8 also indicates that in the A 72 day care group, negative reactions to the stranger in mother's absence were substantially lower $(-.73)$ than in the B_1 73 day care group just discussed (-2.29), $(p < .05)$. It may well be that we find this difference in magnitude of the negative reaction because after mother's departure the infants in the A 72 study were still in the presence of the caregiver, who was previously shown to have an attenuating effect on infant distress. In the B 73 and C 73 procedure, on the other hand, infant and stranger were alone during this assessment. If this interpretation is correct, the data provide another example of the importance of the specific social and cognitive context of the situation in which the infant's behavior is observed.

Finally, it is interesting to note that the mean negative response in the A 72 day care sample $(-.73)$ is quite comparable to those of both non-day care groups (B_2 73, mean $= -.96$; C 73, mean $= -.57$). For the reasons just discussed, of course, this is a rather ambiguous finding, since it may be attributable to the apparently more favorable circumstance of the caregiver's presence in the A 72 procedure.

Study D (1972, 1973)

The last set of data to be reported briefly comes from a preliminary and rather informal study[6] of the manner in which infants with substantial and with little or no group care experience in the first year of life approach a new, quite "natural" social situation involving 3-year-old children and an unfamiliar adult. Despite the tentativeness of the findings, they are reported because they shed some additional light on the day care versus non-day care comparisons of stranger and separation reactions just discussed.

The groups included in this study were the A 72 and B 73 samples from our experimental nursery and corresponding control groups matched for age and sex but without regular group care experience. (When tested, A 72 children were mostly 12 to 19 months old, with a mean of 16 months, B 73 children

---

[6]Marilyn Kaufman had primary responsibility for carrying out the experimental procedures, observations (assisted by Anne Willis), and preliminary data analysis for this study.

mostly 12 to 13 months old, with a mean of 12.5 months).[7] The mother took the infant or toddler into a large playroom, where a teacher and three or four preschool children (3-year-olds) were seated around a table. Mother and toddler paused some 8 to 10 feet away, and mother encouraged the child to visit with the older children. After a minute or so, if the toddler was reluctant, mother took him by the hand, guided him closer to the children, and then moved back to her previous location. The teacher and children were naturally friendly, but made no special efforts to encourage the visitor to join them. After another minute, mother indicated she had to leave momentarily, and moved out of sight into an adjoining space, where the toddler could follow her if so inclined. She remained there about one minute.

A number of relevant behaviors were observed and recorded during successive 10-second units of the sequence, leading to the following measures for each toddler: *(a)* distance moved away from mother toward children during first 2 minutes of sequence, *(b)* maintenance of distance from mother when she left the play area during the last portion of the session, *(c)* amount of sustained physical contact with mother' *(d)* visual orientation toward mother and toward children, and *(e)* general affective state (positive, neutral, negative). All but the first two indices were based on observations over the entire sequence.

Cooparisons of the scores on each of the measures just listed for the day care and non-day care groups in both the 72 and 73 samples are presented in Figure 9. In both samples, the day care infants remained farther away from mother and closer to the children during the first 2 minutes of the observation than did the control children (significant only for 72 sample, $p < .005$). Similarly, the day care infants in the 72 sample maintained a significantly greater distance froo mother, rather than following her closely, when she moved into the adjoining space $(p < .01)$. Sustained physical contact with mother was also substantially less for day care infants in both the 72 and 73 samples (but significantly so only in the former, $p < .05$).

Insofar as visual orientation is concerned, infants in the day care groups spent less time looking at mother and more time looking at the children than was the case for the control infants. These differences were consistent in both the 72 and 73 samples (and significant in three of four instances, $p < .001$, $< .10$, $< .01$). Affective state throughout the session was generally rated very close to neutral for both day care and non-day care groups, although means for the latter were slightly (but not significantly) more negative in both the 72 and 73 samples.

[7]Because of scheduling delays, the 1972 children were tested 3 to 6 months after leaving our infant nursery program (although some were still in partial day care), whereas the 1973 infants were tested while still attending our infant nursery. Also, the 1972 sample in the present follow-up study included nine of the ten infants previously included in the A 72 longitudinal study.

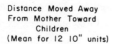

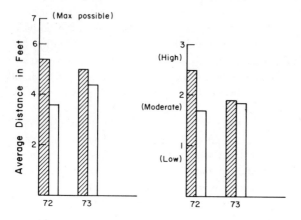

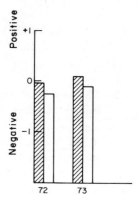

FIGURE 9. Approach of 12- to 19-month-old day care and non-day care infants to strange social situation involving preschool children and teacher.

The pattern of tentative findings just summarized suggests that the extended group care experience of the day care groups may have encouraged greater readiness to move away from mother and toward a new social situation with several somewhat older children and a strange adult. The contrasts were particularly clear in the 72 sample (where the children were somewhat older), but there were generally similar, consistent trends in the 73 sample as well. In the previously discussed B 73 study the day care infants were considerably more distressed by the stranger during maternal separation than were control infants; however, they responded somewhat more positively than controls in the more natural social setting of the present study, and this behavior appears to be understandable in terms of differences in the situational context. In the setting of the present investigation, the infant was never alone with an adult stranger, could move as close to the children and teacher as he wished, and could follow or "check on" mother when she moved into the adjoining space if he wanted to maintain physical or visual contact with her—conditions quite different from those of the B 73 procedure.

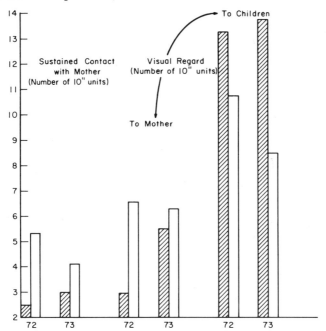

FIGURE 9   (continued).

Discussion

The general findings from three of the studies presented, based on infants with
and without extended day care experience, add to the growing body of recent
literature (Greenberg et al., 1973; Rheingold & Eckerman, in press) indicating
that so-called fear of strangers is not as universal or readily predictable a reaction in infants toward the end of the first year of life as had often been maintained. The data from our longitudinal study, however, clearly indicate a
gradual differentiation of the infants' originally positive responses to both
stranger and caregiver, beginning at 8 months, so that by 9 to 12 months of
age responses to the stranger became clearly less positive and were rated as affectively neutral, on the average, in contrast with the continuing more positive
reactions to the familiar caregiver. This oodal response to the stranger near the
end of the first year can best be characterized as one of sustained, sober visual

orientation and interest, unaccompanied by clear expression of either positive or negative affective responses.

It is obvious that in considering these findings concerning responses to strangers, particularly in our longitudinal study, we must bear in mind that the infants were in a group day care environment beginning at 2 to 3 months of age. Whether an equivalent pattern of gradually differentiated responses to strangers and familiar persons would be found for infants without concurrent group care experience is not directly answerable from these studies.

Our results also need to be reviewed in the light of the experimental procedures employed for eliciting and assessing responses to strangers. It is particularly relevant that the stranger's approach to the infant was a relatively gradual and naturalistic one, and our measures involved averaging the infants' responses to the stranger greeting the infant from a few feet away and coming close and touching the baby. Since infants who tend to be fearful are more likely to show this reaction when the stranger is close (Morgan & Ricciuti, 1969; Lewis & Brooks, Chapter 8, this volume), considering only the latter part of the sequence would probably yield somewhat more negative scores in such instances. Also, our strangers were adult females, to whom infants may respond more positively, or less negatively, than to males (Morgan & Ricciuti, 1969; Greenberg et al., 1973). The importance of these procedural variations is systematically discussed in Décarie's recent monograph (1972).

Clearly, the statement that fear of strangers is not as universal or predictable a characteristic of 9- to 12-month-olds as was once thought to be the case must be qualified by recognition that obviously fearful, negative affective reactions to strangers do indeed occur in some infants at this age. Indeed, such reactions are observed in some instances at rather earlier ages than one would expect even under relatively nonthreatening procedural circumstances such as those employed in the present research. It is interesting to note that most of the negative reactions occurring in our longitudinal sample during the 9- to 12-month period came from the same two or three infants. As mentioned earlier, the problem of accounting for such relatively stable individual differences in responses to strangers is still very much with us and clearly deserves the continued systematic inquiry being addressed to it (Bronson, 1972; Kagan, Chapter 9, this volume). The problem is even more intriguing because we found substantial individual differences in our sample despite the partial "homogenization" of experience provided through long-term enrollment in our group day care program, and it is not entirely satisfying simply to attribute such variations to temperamental differences.

The findings of substantially greater distress reactions to strangers in mother's absence than in mother's presence were very consistent across our three studies, for day care as well as non-day care infants (A 72, B 73, C 73). These results were certainly predictable, and they add further confirmation of the well-documented generalization (even across species) that presence of the imprinted or attached object attenuates fear of the strange (Bowlby, 1973; Bronson, 1972; Morgan & Ricciuti, 1969). Although the validity of this broad generalization is quite clear, the ways in which the stranger's presence and the mother's presence or absence interact as joint influences on the infant's behavior are not yet fully understood, and more detailed examination of this issue is certainly necessary (e.g., Ainsworth & Bell, 1970)9 Several points of interest in our studies bear on this general problem. First, although the stranger'e approach did not induce distress reactions in the early months of our longitudinal study even in mother's absence, the infants' responses to the stranger were generally less positive under this condition than with mother present (Figure 4), suggesting that the mother's presence facilitates a somewhat more positive response to the stranger during this early period.

In addition, we found it very helpful to examine reactions to the stranger in the mother-absent condition as they related to the immediately preceding affective state of the infant who had been left alone with the caregiver. This longitudinal analysis suggested that at least in sooe instances the stranger's approach added very little increment to the moderate distress already present after mother's departure. Of course, this result might be attributable in part to the tension-reducing role played by the familiar caregiver, since data from our B 73 cross-sectional study indicate a considerably more negative reaction to the stranger's approach at 12 months when stranger and infant were alone, than was the case in our longitudinal study when the caregiver remained in the mother-absent condition (Figure 8). Nevertheless, this finding, suggesting that the apparently greater negative reaction to the stranger in mother's absence is largely a continuing response to separation rather than a heightened negative reaction to the stranger as such, is consistent with recent results reported by Ainsworth and Bell (1970). These investigators found that being in a strange situation with a stranger produced very little crying in most one-year-olds when mother was present, but crying increased sharply when stranger and baby were alone after mother's departure and declined on mother's return.

Turning next to the question of infants' negative reactions to separation, one of the general problems that confronts us is the difficulty of specifying the nature of these distress responses and related behaviors, which may involve components of anger as well as fear especially in the older infants (Ainsworth & Bell, 1970; Bowlby, 1973). Moreover, these responses may be primarily expressive, primarily instrumental, or a mixture of both. Our procedures did not permit the important but difficult qualitative distinctions among behavioral responses to separation indicative of anxious or ambivalent attachment as contrasted with defensive detachment, for example, as done by Ainsworth, Bell, and Stayton (1971).

The data from our studies indicate that just as the stranger's approach produces more negative reactions when the infant is alone than when he is with the caregiver, and least when with the mother, so the reactions to maternal .separation depend very much on whom the baby is left with. The most negative reactions clearly occurred when mother left the infant with the stranger, while very little distress was shown when the infant was left with the familiar caregiver, except at 12 months. This finding is not only of theoretical interest, it also supports the view that providing stable, familiar caregivers in day care programs facilitates the daily transitions from home to the group care environment by reducing the separation distress normally associated with being left with strangers in a strange environment. Our results here are very consistent with recent reports from Robertson and Robertson (1971), indicating that separation distress can be substantially reduced by providing skilled care from a familiar substitute caregiver, and from Spelke et al. (1973) who reported little or no maternal separation protest when 1-year-olds were left in a strange room in the presence of father. Although our procedure did not provide a condition in which mother left the infant alone in a strange room, Ainsworth and Bell (1970) found the greatest distress occurring under these circumstances, following mother's second departure.

The moderate negative separation reactions shown at 12 months when the infant was left with the familiar caregiver suggest that the onset of separation distress as one manifestation of an emerging affectional tie to the mother or primary caregiver follows a relatively stable developmental course, even under the relatively favorable circumstances of separation to a familiar caregiver. The appearance of separation protest at about the same age, even in groups with highly contrasting social experience, was reported recently (Stevens, 1971) in a comparison of infants reared in nuclear families and in institutions, where a variety of individuals were responsible for the infants' care. Similarly, in a recent unpublished study reported by Kagan (this volume, Chapter 9), no differences were found between day care and home-reared infants in distress responses following maternal separation. The regularity of the appearance of separation protest in these groups with disparate experience may indeed be determined partly by a regularity in the emergence of the cognitive competencies required to perceive and assimilate the discrepancy or incongruity represented by the separation event, as Kagan suggests. At the same time, our data indicating the appearance of some distress at 12 months when the infant is left with the same caregiver he has been left with repeatedly, suggests that we must also consider the developmental regularity of the emergence of an affectional bond between mother and infant, which the infant may perceive as threatened or interrupted even when left with a familiar substitute caregiver.

Even the aforementioned observations of moderate distress reactions at being left with the caregiver, however, need to be considered in the light of the context in which such separation observations were made. The findings just referred to came from observations of mother leaving the infant with the caregiver in the course of a structured experimental situation in a playroom. In our 1972–1973 nursery sample, we found considerably less frequent and less marked negative reactions when weekly observations were made of mother's leaving the infant with the caregiver at the entry hall to the nurserz, under more natural circircumstances (Willis & Ricciuti, 1974).

The comparisons of infants with and without extended day care experience provide some preliminary findings relevant to the broader question of the impact of variations in previous experience on infants' responses to strangers and to maternal separation. At the same time, however, these findings illustrate the difficulty of interpreting such comparisons of infants with markedly different prior experience, because of the difficulty of specifying salient characteristics of the social and cognitive cotext of the situations in which our observations are made, as viewed from the perspective of the infant and the expectations he has developed.

Thus, for example, the somewhat more negative reactions of our B 73 day care infants to the stranger's approach in mother's absence are considered to be a function, at least in part, of the greater perceived incongruity or dissonance of the stranger–maternal-separation experience presented by our experimental conditions for the day care infants, given their expectations, than was the case for the non-day care group. This seems a more reasonable and parsimonious interpretation than to assume that the daily separations of the day care group had rendered them more susceptible to separation distress, perhaps through the development of an insecure or ambivalent attachment relationship. This was essentially Blehar's (1973) interpretation of her findings with children entering day care at 26 and 35 months of age, which the results of our B 73 study resemble somewhat, insofar as reactions to the stranger in mother's absence are concerned. Such an interpretation in the case of our more limited observational data seems less plausible, in part, because our infants entered day care before 6 months of age and were attended by the same caregivers throughout their participation, such that there was little or no distress associated with daily separations from mother.

The view that our B 73 day care infants' more negative reactions to the stranger in mother's absence were largely determined by contextual or situational factors (as opposed to an insecure maternal attachment relationship) is compatible with the findings of Caldwell et al. (1970) of essentially normal mother–infant attachment relationships in 30-month-old children who had entered day care between 6 and 15 months of age. This conservative interpretation is also supported by the generally more positive approaches made by the day care, rather than non-day care infants to the more naturalistic social situation involving a small group of preschool children and a teacher, with mother close by and accessible, even though out of view part of the time. Clearly this issue needs a great deal of further systematic investigation, with larger samples than those represented in the studies discussed this far.

Although a good part of the discussion to this point has dealt with infants' responses to maternal separation, one of the most interesting results of our longitudinal study was the finding that with increasing age, infants showed the same pattern of increasing distress reactions at separation from the familiar caregiver that was exhibited at separation from mother. This finding of course should not be construed as suggesting that mother and caregiver are in any sense equivalent with respect to the infant.[8] It does, however, provide some evidence that the familiar caregiver begins to play a significant role as an alternate attachment figure for the infant in the extended day care situation, particularly after 7 months or so. The persuasiveness of this inference is supported by the other data indicating continued positive greeting responses to the caregiver through the end of the first year, very limited distress reactions shown by infants when they are left by mother with the caregiver, and the caregiver's role in reducing distress (or increasing positive affect) when the infant has been left with a stranger. The overall pattern of results suggests that fearfulness and distress are least prevalent when the infant is with the mother, next when with the familiar caregiver, and most prevalent when alone with the stranger.

References

Ainsworth, M. D., & Bell, S. M. Attachment, exploration and separation: Illustrated by the behavior of one-year-olds in a strange situation. *Child Development,* 1970, **41,** 49–67.

Ainsworth, M. D., Bell, S. M., & Stayton, D. J. Individual differences in strange-situation behavior of one-year-olds. In H. R. Schaffer (Ed.), *The origins of human social relations.* London: Academic Press, 1971.

Ainsworth, M. D., Bell, S. M., & Stayton, D. J. Individual differences in the development of some attachment behaviors. *Merrill-Palmer Quarterly,* 1972, **18,** 123–143.

Benjamin, J. D. Further comments on some developmental aspects of anxiety. In H. S. Gaskill (Ed.), *Counterpoint.* New York: International University Press, 1963.

Blehar, M. P. Anxious attachment and defensive reactions associated with day care.

---

[8]It would have been interesting, as an additional control, to have a third, unfamiliar person leave the infant with the stranger, to ensure that the infant was not simply responding negatively to the departure of any individual who left him alone with a stranger. It does not seem very likely, however, that the departure of a stranger who has been in the room with the infant for 3 or 4 minutes, leaving the infant alone with a second stranger who has been in the room for 1 or 2 minutes, would produce the type of increased negative reactions resulting when the mother or familiar caregiver leaves the infant with a stranger.

Paper presented to the Society for Research in Child Development, Philadelphia, March 1973.

Bowlby, J. *Attachment and loss.* Vol. 2. *Separation.* London: Hogarth; New York: Basic Books, 1973.

Bretherton, I., & Ainsworth, M. D. Responses of one-year-olds to a stranger in a strange situation. Paper presented to the Eastern Psychological Association, Boston, April 1972.

Bretherton, I., & Ainsworth, M. D. Responses of one-year-olds to a stranger in a strange situation. Chapter 6, this volume.

Bronson, G. W. Infants' reactions to unfamiliar persons and novel objects. *Monographs of the Society for Research in Child Development,* 1972, **37,** (Serial No. 148).

Décarie, T. G. *La réaction du jeune enfant à la personne étrangère.* Montreal: University of Montreal Press, 1972.

Caldwell, B. M., Wright, C. M., Honig, A. S., & Tannenbaum, J. Infant day care and attachment. *American Journal of Orthopsychiatry,* 1970, **40,** 397–412.

Corter, C. M., Rheingold, H. L., & Eckerman, C. O. Toys delay the infant's following of his mother. *Developmental Psychology,* 1972, **6,** 231.

Freedman, D. G. The infant's fear of strangers and the flight response. *Journal of Child Psychology and Psychiatry,* 1961, **2,** 242–248.

Greenberg, D. J., Hillman, D., & Grice, D. Infant and stranger variables related to stranger anxiety in the first year of life. *Developmental Psychology,* 1973, **9,** 207–212.

Harlow, H. F. The development of affectional patterns in infant monkeys. In B. M. Foss (Ed.), *Determinants of infant behavior.* Vol. 1. London: Methuen; New York: Wiley, 1961.

Hebb, D. O. On the nature of fear. *Psychological Review,* 1946, **53,** 259–276.

Hoffman, H. S. Fear-mediated processes in the cotext of imprinting. Chapter 2, this volume.

Kagan, J. The origins of fear. Chapter 9, this volume.

Lewis, M., & Brooks, J. Self, other, and fear: Infants' reactions to people. Chapter 8, this volume.

Meili, R. Angstentstehung bei Kleinkindern. *Schweiz. Z. Psychol. Anwend.,* 1955, **14,** 195–212.

Messer, S., & Lewis, M. Social class and sex differences in the attachment and play behavior of the year-old infant. *Merrill-Palmer Quarterly,* 1972, **18,** 295–306.

Morgan, G., & Ricciuti, H. N. Infants' response to strangers during the first year. In B. M. Foss (Ed.), *Determinants of infant behavior.* Vol. 4. London: Methuen; New York: Wiley, 1969.

Rheingold, H. L. The effect of a strange environment on the behavior of infants. In B. M. Foss (Ed9), *Determinants of infant behavior.* Vol. 4. London: Methuen; New York: Wiley, 1969.

Rheingold, H. L., & Eckerman, C. O. Fear of the stranger: A critical examination.

In H. W. Reese (Ed.), *Advances of child development and behavior*. New York: Academic Press, in press.

Ricciuti, H. N. Social and emotional behavior in infancy: Some developmental issues and problems. *Merrill-Palmer Quarterly,* 1968, 14, 82–100.

Ricciuti, H. N., & Poresky, R. H. Emotional behavior and development in the first year of life: An analysis of arousal, approach–withdrawal, and affective responses. In A. D. Pick (Ed.), *Minnesota symposia on child psychology.* Vol. 6. Minneapolis: University of Minnesota Press, 1972.

Ricciuti, H. N., & Poresky, R. H. Degelopment of attachment to caregivers in an infant nursery during the first year of life. Paper presented at meeting of Society for Research in Child Development, Philadelphia, March 1973.

Robertson, J., & Robertson, J. Young children in bried separation: A fresh look. *Psychoanalytic Study of the Child,7¿* **26,** 264–3159

Scarr, S., & Salapatek, P. Patterns of fear development during infancy. *Merrill-Palmer Çuarterly,* 1970, **16,** 53–90.

Schaffer, H. R. The onset of fear of strangers and the incongruity hypothesis. *Journal of Child Psychology and Psychiatry,* 1966, **7,** 95–106.

Spelke, E., Zelazo, P., Kagan, J., & Kotelchuck, M. Father interaction and separation protest. *Degelopmental Psychology,* 1973, **9,** 83–90.

Sroufe, L. A., Waters, E., & Matas, L. Contextual determinants of infant affective response. Chapter 3, this volume.

Stettner, L. J., & Tilds, B. N. Effect of presence of an imprinted object on response of ducklings in an open field and when exposed to fear stimulus. *Psychonooic Science,* 1966, **4,** 107–108.

Stevens, A. G. Attachment behavior, separation anxiety and stranger anxiety. In H. R. Schaffer (Ed.), *The origins of human social relations.* London: Academic Press, 1971.

Trause, M. A. Effects of duration of mother's stay and stranger's approach on infants' responses to a stranger before and after maternal separation. Unpublished doctoral dissertation, Cornell University, 1974.

Willis, A. E., & Ricciuti, H. N. Longitudinal observations of infants' daily arrivals at a day care center. Technical Report, Cornell Research Program in Early Development and Education. Ithaca, N.Y.: Cornell University, 1974.

CHAPTER 5

Social and Situational Determinants of Fear in the Playgroup[1]

Peter K. Smith
University of Sheffield

This chapter is concerned with signs of fear shown by young children in pre-school playgroups or nurseries. The discussion is pivoted on behavioral indices of fear, and neither physiological measures of fear nor verbal reports by the subjects are considered. The frequency of occurrence of such indices of fear can be used as a measure of how changes in the social and physical environment affect levels of fear, in a relatively natural social situation such as a children's playgroup.

Agreement is incomplete regarding which behaviors are indicative of fear. Animal psychologists have used behavioral measures such as flight, freezing, or defecation, in experimental studies of this topic. Although these are all observable in humans, they are signs of a high degree of fear and are not usually seen at full intensity in playgroup observations. Nor would it be ethical to attempt to bring about the occurrence of such behaviors frequently. Instead, behaviors likely to reflect lower intensities of fear are considered. These include puckered face, crying or screaming; clinging to an adult; sucking thumb, fingers, or an object; holding or fumbling with an object in the hands; shuffling the feet; standing and watching other children without joining in; shifting gaze to avoid visual contact with another child; locomotion away from another child's approach or play invitation; submissive behavior in a conflict over toy or apparatus; stereotyped or automanipulative behaviors such as body rocking or swaying, clothes fumbling or hitching, hair grooming, eye rubbing, ear pulling, nose picking, hand to face, genital manipulation, hand fumbling, mouth fumbling.

It may be debated whether some of these behaviors—such as nose picking or hand fumbling—are related to fear, yet the performance of these various behaviors does involve a common denominator. From a long tradition of work in child psychology (Carmichael, 1954), as well as from recent work on motiva-

[1] The research carried out at Sheffield University was supported by the Social Science Research Council, London.

tional analysis of preschool children (Blurton Jones, 1972; McGrew, 1972; Smith, 1973), it is clear that during the preschool years, and no doubt beyond, several important motivational systems are finding expression. In a secure environment, children are busy manipulating objects, being physically active around the room or on apparatus, and making social contacts with peers and adults. The latter activity involves verbal, visual, and physical contacts, and it may be centered around object use and exchange or rough-and-tumble play. In addition, by 3 or 4 years of age both types of social play may incorporate elements of fantasy or imaginary role-play. Finally, aggression and resistance to aggression are an inevitable feature of repeated social encounters. These are the kinds of behavior observed in a playgroup, given that basic needs—hunger, thirst, sleep—are satisfied. There is ample evidence from developmental and comparative studies that such behaviors are of vital importance for cognitive and social development.

Other behaviors—in particular the kinds listed previously as likely indicators of fear—are to varying degrees incompatible with the successful execution of the behavior patterns of object manipulation, physical activity, and social interaction. This is partly true in a purely physical sense. A child who is sucking two fingers or fumbling his clothes or an object cannot be using his hands for nonstereotyped object manipulation. A child who is shuffling his feet cannot be physically active. A child who only watches other children, avoiding social contacts or conflict situations, cannot be participating in effective social interaction. These are behaviors that, *if continued by a child for substantial periods,* would be likely to interfere greatly with normal social and cognitive development. Factor analytic studies have shown that behaviors such as crying, sucking, watching other children, looking around the room, shuffling, object holding or fumbling, and automanipulating, tend to be more frequent in less socially mature children. In addition, motivational analysis involving temporal association of behaviors over short time periods has confirmed that such behaviors—in particular, puckered face, crying, sucking, submissive behavior—do not usually occur in temporal association with the motivational patterns characteristic of play. This is also true of approaching and leaning against or clinging to an adult, at least in playgroups or day nurseries in which the staff do not greatly interact with the children in play contexts.

In a more general sense, then, one could consider fearful behaviors as being those which, in the long term, would signify a failure to fulfill natural or developmental potential. Fearful behaviors conflict with the other main motivational systems of hunger, sexual activity, exploration, play, and sleep. Although often adaptive in the short term—a crying child fetches its mother, a fleeing child avoids pain or danger—pronounced or prolonged fearful behavior may be maladaptive for the individual. This does not mean, however, that a range of individual responsiveness to fear is maladaptive for the species.

It is quite clear that young children show great individual variation in the readiness with which they manifest fearful behavior. Nevertheless, the types of situation producing fear are probably the same for all children. With some of these—such as physical pain or possible particular stimulus configurations, such as fear of snakes—this discussion is not concerned. Rather, two kinds of situations inherent in the playgroup context are considered. One, the social and environmental novelty of a playgroup to a new child, generally gives rise to some expressions of fear in the short term, followed by social and environmental exploration and play. The second, the crowding of a large number of children together in a condition of fixed physical resources, may cause the elevation of fear responses over a longer term, but the responses will be of lower intensity. The latter issue is the more controversial and is considered in greater detail.

NOVELTY IN THE PLAYGROUP

One main cause of fear responses in children is the presence of novelty or strangeness. Fear of novelty can be observed in preschool children in playgroups, but there is little research to compare with the detailed experimental work carried out on younger infants, in which the effects of different stimulus dimensions have been controlled for. Nevertheless, the playgroup provides a fairly realistic social situation, and it is worth considering in what ways fear of novelty is manifested.

Hutt (1970) distinguishes three kinds of novelty—conspecific novelty, object novelty, and environment novelty. This of course raises several questions. In what ways does a conspecific differ from an object? How does an environment differ from a collection of objects? It certainly seems, however, that responses to these three kinds of novelty differ. We observed differences in response to novel objects, and to a novel environmental feature, in a research playgroup started at Sheffield University. Two groups of children attended playgroups separately, each for two mornings a week; thus we could replicate any findings. Each group consisted of 24 children (12 boys, 12 girls) aged between 2.5 and 4.5 years. The playgroups were set up for a study on crowding (described later), but the present observations were made prior to this, during the third week after formation.

At various times during the third week new toys were introduced to the playgroups, in addition to those already present. Three of each were introduced at a time. The new toys were *(a)* prams *(b)* telephones *(c)* Wendy Houses (play houses). In all cases children very rapidly approached and played with the new toys. In the case of the prams and telephones, latency to manipulation was virtually zero. In the case of the Wendy Houses, latency to manipulation was some 10 seconds, the children looking around and into the Wendy Houses before playing in them. Apart from the slight wariness in approaching the Wendy

Houses, none of the children showed any signs of fear of the objects as such. Some signs of fear were evident, however, in relation to social use of the objects. In the case of the prams and telephones, only one or two children could play with each item, and there were many fights over possession of the new toys. Besides actual fights, several children came and stood near the toys, often thumb sucking or automanipulating, watching the other children and apparently interested in the toys but afraid to attempt to play with them. More boys played with the new toys than girls, initially, but this may have been because more girls lost fights over the toys, or stood around watching.

Introduction of a new environmental feature produced somewhat different results. For the first 2 weeks the children had only played in two-thirds of the total available area of the large room in which the playgroup was held; a curtained partition had hidden the remaining third. During the third week the partition was moved back to the end of the room, making the remaining area available. The new area contained additional toys; the children had not had these toys before, but they were of exactly the same type as those which had been previously available. The extra part of the room itself was no different in design from the original part. The new environmental area was therefore novel, but not particularly strange.

Entries into the new area during the first 10 minutes, for both groups of children, are given in Table 1. For both groups, the first entry was made by a child to get the tricycle (the most popular toy), which was then taken back to the familiar area. Subsequent entries were generally not very prolonged and not very frequent. During the initial period there were usually only two or three children in the area, compared with the seven or eight children who would be expected on a chance basis, and which was indeed the mean occupancy on subsequent occasions. Also a few children seemed definitely wary of the new area—for example, tricycling up to the line marking the new area, then turning back. Most children ignored it at first, playing in the familiar area. There were no signs of fear as such, or of aggression over occupancy of the area. Gradual incorporation of a new area by preschool children has also been observed in the outdoor area of a nursery school by Hutt and McGrew (1967).

The new toys and the new area were similar in that neither produced many overt signs of fear, in themselves, but they differed in the amount of approach behavior. Compared with subsequent occasions, the new toys were overused during the initial period of presentation, whereas the new area was underused. Neither the new toys nor the new area behaved unpredictably, and in both cases the child could control the amount of stimulus salience.

Hutt (1970) argues strongly that object novelty per se does not produce fear in humans, but rather approach and investigation, provided this novelty is not confounded with environment or conspecific novelty. She suggests that the higher primates and particularly man has a "hypertrophy of curiosity" and that

TABLE 1. Entries to and Exits from a New Play Area by Boys (B) and Girls (G) in Two Playgroups, During First 10 Minutes

Time of Entry	Child	Time of Exit
	Group 1	
0:12	G1 gets tricycle	0:30
1:00	G2, G3 to rocking-boat	5:40
4:10	G1, B1 on tricycles	4:25, 4:35
4:50	G4, G5 to jigsaws on table	
6:20	G3, B2 to table toys	6:35, 7:40
	more short entries and exits by G3, B2 and G1	
	Group 2	
0:08	B1 gets tricycle	0:12
0:35	G1 walking	0:40
1:20	B2 on tricycle	1:40
1:35	G2 to slide	2:50
2:20	B1 walking	2:40
2:35	B2 on tricycle	in/out several times
5:30	B3 + mother, G3 to rocking-boat	
7:10	B4 walking, on slide	8:15
	more short entries and exits by B1, B2, and B4	
9:30	B5 walking	

the ready approach and manipulation of new objects is of adaptive significance for flexible development. Environment novelty, by contrast, does lead to fear responses. Even on Hutt's own arguments, however, it is difficult to see why investigation of a new environment should not be just as adaptive as investigation of a new object; and indeed the evidence available fails to support the strength of the distinction made.

First, to say that novel objects do not produce fear overstates the case, if only slightly. Hutt herself (1966) showed that a preschool child presented with a novel object in a familiar room had a lower latency of approach when an adult was present; this would suggest at least a certain wariness of the object, which the adult's presence served to counteract. Second, personal observation indicates that sometimes a new toy will cause a fearful response in a child, if the toy behaves in an unpredictable way—a moving train or a walking robot, for example. Generally, however, a novel object does not move or behave unpredictably, and its stimulus salience is under the control of the child, who can approach and inspect the object as he wishes. Under these conditions children certainly show little or no fear, and rapid approach and investigation.

The reported fear of novel environments seems to be limited to cases in which the child is placed into the situation (Arsenian, 1943), when again he lacks control over the situation. When a child has free entry to a new environment, few signs of fear are observed. The difference in these two conditions, for 10-month-old infants, has been shown by Rheingold (Rheingold, 1969; Rheingold & Eckerman, 1969). Children still seem to be much slower or more cautious in exploring a new environment than a new object, but it can be argued that this is simply a matter of the size or amount of stimulus novelty involved, or of the balance of novel to familiar stimuli of which the child is aware.

One could conceptualize a continuum of situational (nonsocial) novelty, varying from object novelty—the introduction of a single, small, novel object in familiar surroundings—to environment novelty—the total nonsocial environment being new to the child. A similar continuum could be postulated for social novelty, and differing degrees of this can be observed in the playgroup. A low degree of social novelty would be represented by a child encountering a strange child or adult while in the presence of known person or persons. A high degree of social novelty would be represented by a child alone being put into a group of strangers. Both these extremes occur simultaneously in the case of the introduction of a new child to an established playgroup, in the one case from the point of view of a child already in the group, in the other from the point of view of the newcomer.

Some data are available on how children in a playgroup react to a strange child and to a strange adult. McGrew (1972) has made systematic observations of the introduction of a new child to a nursery class in Edinburgh, and his observations are closely borne out by our own observations at Sheffield and by Waterhouse and Waterhouse in nursery schools in Reading. Many children ignore a new child introduced to the group or limit themselves to brief visual inspection. Overt aggression to a new child seems to be very rare, although not infrequently a child stares with slight frowning. A few children show low-intensity fear at a newcomer's entry, perhaps sucking thumb or fingers or hitching at clothes. Social contact with newcomers is usually made in common use of toys or apparatus. These contacts are usually investigatory and neutral or friendly, although children may react with hostility if a newcomer is felt to intrude on a game—in a Wendy House, for example, or with a toy.

Connolly and Smith (1972) have reported on the reactions of children in day nurseries to a strange adult visitor (in this case a bearded male). Three predominant patterns of behavior were observed. Some children stared at the visitor from a distance, sometimes thumb sucking. These children were often alone. These or other children might walk up to him, stare, and smile if smiled at. Finally children often playing in a group might walk or run up, laughing or smiling, and talk to the adult, either asking him what he is doing or making some kind of play invitation, showing him toys, or making play noises at him. Similar observations were made in a London nursery school by Blurton Jones

(1967) (also a bearded male). In an experimental situation, Stern and Bender (in press) found signs of fear (often mixed with signs of affiliation or aggression) when preschool children were asked to approach a strange adult. The rather greater evidence of fear or ambivalent behavior in these results probably appears because the child was constrained into making a close approach, instead of being allowed to act under his own volition.

Fear reactions are most common, and sometimes intense, when a child is first introduced to a playgroup. Generally in this case everything is novel—the environment, the toys, the adults, and the children. Often the mother accompanies the child on its first few visits, and while the mother is present the child often stays near her, venturing out to explore and then returning in a way similar to that described by Harlow and Harlow (1965) in monkeys and Rheingold and Eckerman (1969) for 10-month-old infants. Distress reactions are most apparent when the mother tries to leave or a short interval after she has left. At times a child may show quite extreme distress, screaming, clinging to the mother's dress or hugging her legs, beating at the door if she has left, or lying kicking on the floor. However, there are enormous individual variations. Often a mother can leave her child within a quarter of an hour or so, at the first visit, with the child showing only slight signs of distress subsequently.

Blurton Jones and Leach (1972) kept records of whether children cried when their mothers left them at a research nursery in London. The children ranged in age from 21 to 58 months. Crying was common in children of up to 2.5 years, and rare after that, which agrees with the nursery lore about age of readiness for preschool. The presence of a sibling also greatly reduced the likelihood of crying.

A quantitative study of behavioral changes in children during the first days at nursery was made by McGrew at Edinburgh. He found that new children had higher frequencies of sucking, automanipulating, and immobility than experienced children. In one study, in which more than half the children were new to the group, sucking and automanipulating declined over a 7-day period, although immobility did not. In a second study, in which children were introduced singly to an established group, automanipulating and immobility declined rapidly for the new child over a 5-day period and had declined still further after 65 days. Looking also decreased, and running and talking to children increased. Sucking was not monitored in the study. Over a longer time period of 8 months, Smith and Connolly (in preparation) found steady decreases in sucking, pucker face, watching adults and children, clothes fumbling, following an adult, looking around or in the distance, and doing nothing, after initial group formation. The decreases were rapid up to the second term and less noticeable subsequently.

Although by a child's second term at playgroup he is no longer a newcomer and is almost invariably well settled, it is still possible to observe minor signs of fear and distress each morning on arrival and separation from mother. The behavioral manifestations are similar to those seen on first introduction, and changes in behavioral frequency during a morning session parallel those observed over successive visits. McGrew (1972) found that automanipulation and immobility declined significantly during the morning, both during the first 5 days at nursery and on 5 days near the end of term. Averaging over an 8-month period, Smith and Connolly reported significant decreases through the morning in watching adults and children, looking around and in the distance, following an adult, and doing nothing, although no decreases were noted for sucking or automanipulation.

Although the initial settling into a group is potentially the most fearful situation many preschool children have to face, there is little to suggest that boys—supposedly the less fearful sex (Gray, 1971)—cope more easily with this ordeal. Indeed, what evidence there is points in the opposite direction. Blurton Jones and Leach (1972), who observed 27 boys and 46 girls on first visit to the nursery, commented that "boys appear more likely to cry than girls," although the differences did not reach significance. McGrew (1972) in his study of new children remarked that "the six boys observed were more fearful and inhibited than the six girls," with the latter showing significantly more walking, looking, and laughing during first day at nursery. At our research playgroups in Sheffield we have had 98 children to date. Table 2 presents ratings of how well boys and girls settled during the first few days. These were made by myself, based on observations and daily diary records, and independently by one of the playgroup staff from personal experience with the children. Significantly more boys than girls were rated as having settled poorly or having been distressed. Of ten children withdrawn from the playgroup through failure to settle, seven were boys and three girls.

Two other studies from the United States also support this generalization. A monograph by Slater (1939) reported occurrences of emotional disturbance in children introduced to a nursery school at Harvard. Forty children were observed (18 boys, 22 girls). Although overall sex differences were nonsignificant, the trend was in the suggested direction; of the children with clearly high counts for disturbance, four were boys and only one was a girl. Finally a study by Heathers (1954) of 31 children introduced to the Fels nursery school also reported more upset in boys during the first few days, although again the difference did not reach significance. Thus there are five studies showing a sex difference in the same direction. Two remaining studies—(Waterhouse & Waterhouse, 1973; Washburn, 1932) did not report on sex differences.

Assuming that this sex difference remains confirmed (always a dangerous assumption), there are several possible explanations. First, children arriving at playgroup are a nonrandom sample, and Blurton Jones (personal communication) suggests that mothers may be more protective of girls, thus those who do come to playgroup are less fearful. However, this explanation seems to be con-

TABLE 2. Ratings of How Many Children Settled Well During First Week at
Playgroup (A), Were Average (B), or Had Settled Poorly and Shown Distress (C).
Independent Ratings by Observer (a) and Playgroup Staff Member (b)

	A	B	C			A	B	C	
Boys	9	18	23	50	Boys	10	19	21	50
Girls	8	30	10	48	Girls	24	16	8	48
	17	48	33			34	35	29	

(a) $\chi^2 = 8.2$ $p < .02$

(b) $\chi^2 = 11.7$ $p < .005$

traindicated by the fact that our waiting list has many more girls than boys,
and Blurton Jones also received more girls than boys at his London nursery.
Another explanation is that girls more quickly attach themselves to a (female)
member of staff; yet another is that older girls may be more friendly to a new
girl than older boys are to a new boy (Brindley et al., 1973). Finally, a greater
variability in boys than girls might be considered, with more boys showing extreme levels of fear. All these explanations would be interesting from a biological viewpoint. However, there is little evidence to support a decision among
them.

In summary, it is clear that novel persons, objects, or environments may produce fearful responses in preschool children, but these are seldom very marked
when a child has control over his approach to the novelty, hence of the salience
of the novelty to him. Besides eliciting fear responses, they also elicit exploration, and, in the case of novel persons, affiliative and sometimes aggressive responses. Investigation of novel objects is generally rapid, but of novel persons
and environments rather more slow. This difference is probably due to the
greater unpredictability in the behavior of persons; in the case of environments,
perhaps the much higher ratio of novel to familiar stimuli encountered is responsible. Although novel objects elicit rapid exploration, with little fear of their
novelty per se, they (and other attractive objects) may nevertheless increase
behavioral levels of fear in a social situation; this, however, is fear in a situation of social competition, when one child wishes to approach or play with
a toy but is afraid to initiate a dominance encounter with another child in the
process. This is considered further in discussing how crowding may affect fear.

CROWDING IN THE PLAYGROUP

Besides the encountering of novel stimuli, social interaction with conspecifics
is another kind of situation that may give rise to fear responses. In particular,
conflict or competition between two individuals often results in fearful or sub-

missive behavior by one of them. Whereas the adaptive value of fear of novelty lies in the formation of primary social bonds and the avoidance of possible dangers, the adaptive value of fear in social interaction is presumed to lie in the stabilizing of social organization. The number of animals, and the resources available, are assumed to affect the amount of competitive social interaction. This competition is made conventional by social mechanisms such as territorial acquisition or dominance hierarchy; conventional competition provides a less wasteful, more efficient method of resolving disputes than continued intraspecific fighting. However, the more fearful or submissive individuals are less likely to acquire valued resources, and, ultimately, to reproduce. Although disadvantageous for the individual, this tendency is advantageous for the species. Fear, and the antagonism of fear with social assertion and reproductive success, form part of a mechanism for population homeostasis.

This viewpoint, proposed by Wynne-Edwards (1962), has been criticized by Lack (1966) for example, who believes that extrinsic factors such as predation or starvation are more responsible for population control. However, the broad features of the Wynne-Edwards theory have received a considerable measure of support. In particular, experimental studies of population growth or crowding, in which external factors (predation, starvation) are eliminated, have shown that crowding can have significant and generally adverse effects on social behavior. Many of these studies have been on rodents. On the basis of such studies, Christian and Gray (Christian & Davis, 1964; Gray, 1971) have suggested that high population density leads, by way of increased fear and stress responses in competitive social interaction, to overactivation of the pituitary–adrenal–gonadal systems, hence to increased aggression and social withdrawal and to decreased reproductive success. The mechanisms by which the population density operates, however, may vary in different species. For example, Alexander and Roth (1971) have suggested that population controls in Japanese monkeys operate through group fission and dominance hierarchy, rather than through reproductive physiology.

Given the mounting crises of human population and resource levels (Ehrlich & Ehrlich, 1970), it is of practical importance, as well as theoretical interest, to know whether any similar mechanisms are operative in human groups, and if so what form they take. Two kinds of crowding study have been made involving humans—correlational studies of high-density urban living and social illness or breakdown, and experimental studies on relatively small groups. The experimental work has included studies of adults in laboratory settings and of children in playgroups. The studies of children have the advantage of featuring a fairly natural social situation, with much ongoing social behavior. In addition, actual behavior has been observed, rather than verbal reports, checklists of affect, or task performance, the methods usually employed with adults. A disadvantage of course is that the response to crowding of young children cannot be generalized to adults. However, it is only the intention to review studies of crowding in playgroups here (see Freedman, 1973, for a recent review of studies on adults).

First, we examine the meaning of the term "crowding" and the methodology of experimental studies of crowding. Second, the effects of the various parameters of crowding are summarized, insofar as they are known, from the half-dozen studies reported to date. Finally, the possible behavioral mechanisms responsible for these effects are discussed.

What Is Meant by Crowding?

A very wide perspective on crowding is taken by Esser (1972), who regards it as a subjective experience of being put upon or harassed by the presence of others. This could be due to a person's mood or the unfamiliarity of the setting, as well as number of others present and the nature of the environment. By this definition, fear of strangers would be a crowding phenomenon. Although there is some virtue in taking a broad definition, we run the risk of making the terms "crowding" and "fear-arousing" almost synonymous.

Crowding is often referred directly to density, the latter term being defined as number of individuals per unit of space (Freedman, 1973). However, Stokols (1972) and Desor (1972) prefer to regard crowding as a subjective experience that occurs when spatial restrictions are perceived by the individuals exposed to them, and this could depend on mood, partitioning of space, and presence or absence of additional stressors, for example.

In a recent review Zlutnick and Altman (1972) refer more generally to the richness of environmental resources. This can mean much more than various spatial parameters, although it is the latter that have almost always been manipulated in experimental studies. There is increasing evidence from field studies of primates and ungulates that the amount and distribution of resources such as food, water, and sleeping sites, may markedly affect social structure and behavior (Crook & Goss-Custard, 1972), and the availability of these and other resources may well be important in considerations of crowding.

The view taken here is that experimental research on crowding presents two main variables to be manipulated—namely, the number of conspecifics N in an interacting group, and the amount of resources R of which the group makes communal use. The density parameters $D = N/R$ are then dependent variables. An independent parameter is T, the duration of the crowding experience.

Neither of the variables N or R is simple. Besides the actual number of conspecifics N, the heterogeneity of the group is an important consideration. This could include age, sex, personality, and the preconceptions and past experiences of the individuals involved. In addition, the subjects may be strangers, acquaintances, or intimate contacts. The point has already been made that resources R includes the amount and distribution of any valued resource, not just space per se.

In the playgroup research many of these variables are simplified. The groups are of limited age and mixed sex distribution, and the members are not usually strangers. The important resources during free play sessions are space and play equipment, the latter usually being distributed evenly in a nonpartitioned area. Since the experiments are of relatively short duration, they are perhaps best referred to as investigating the effects of changes in crowding.

Two methodological points remain to be made. The first relates to interpretation. Any experiment necessarily varies two main parameters simultaneously. For instance, if you vary numbers, keeping resources constant, you also vary density. This will be called an ND-type experiment, since either N or D might be responsible for any effects. Alternatively, you can vary resources, keeping numbers constant—a DR-type experiment. Finally in an NR-type experiment, numbers and resources are varied together, keeping density constant. Since you have two independent variables, you must do (at least) two different type experiments to reach conclusions about which parameter was responsible for what effect. (Also, of course, interpretation is limited to the range of values over which the parameters have been varied.)

The second point relates to the use of statistics for generalization. Studies of crowding are essentially concerned with group phenomena. Ideally, results should be replicated on a number of groups if generalization to other possible groups is to be made. The appropriate unit for statistical tests would then be group means, not individual means within a group.

These two considerations are brought to attention, since none of the playgroup research carried out to date conforms satisfactorily to both of them. The relevant studies are summarized in Table 3.

The Effects of Different Crowding Parameters

The first study on playgroups was by Hutt and Vaizey (1966), who varied group size in a hospital playroom at Oxford (type ND). The subjects, between 3 and 8 years of age, were five normal children, five autistic children, and five children with gross brain damage. Group size was varied from fewer than six to more than twelve individuals. Results were reported for three kinds of behavior: aggressive/destructive behavior, nonaggressive social encounters, and time spent near periphery of the room. It was found that in larger groups, both the normal and brain-damaged children spent much more time in aggressive behavior, and the normal children spent less time in nonaggressive social encounters. Autistic children spent more time near the boundary of the room.

The results clearly suggest that an increase in either group size or density leads to more aggressive and fearful behavior, and that the reactions of mentally

TABLE 3. Summary of Studies of Crowding in Nurseries and Playgroups

Reference	Type	Statistics	Comments	Group Size	Space (ft^2)	Density
Hutt & Vaizey (1966)	ND	Incorrect	Heterogeneous groups	<6, 7-11, >12	470	79, 53, 39
Bates (in prep.)	ND		Brief report only	10-15, 17-24, 25-30	700	57, 34, 27
P.L. McGrew (1970) W.C. McGrew (1972)	ND, DR	Incorrect	Only space varied	8, 16	780, 590	86, 74, 52, 37
Smith & Connolly (1973)	DR	Incorrect but 2 replicate groups	Space and toys varied	24	1800, 1200, 600	75, 50, 25
Preiser (1972)	DR		Only space varied brief report only	15	600, 400	40, 27
Loo (1972)	DR	Correct 10 groups	Only space varied	6	265, 90	44, 15

disturbed children may differ from those of normal children. Although the work is valuable as a pioneer study, however, it would be inappropriate to rely heavily on the results of this experiment, as one or two subsequent writers have done. It seems from the report that the normal and abnormal children were mixed together, making very heterogeneous groups. Furthermore, group size was varied by using other children in the hospital, and the children may well have been relative strangers. The terms "aggressive/destructive behavior" and "social interaction" were not defined (though see Hutt & Hutt, 1970). Finally, the statistical analysis, based on individuals, was not appropriate for generalization to other groups of children.

A similar ND-type experiment has recently been carried out by Bates (personal communication), in a nursery school in Oregon. Children 2 and 3 years old were observed in free play. Because of fluctuations in attendance on different weekdays, and absences, group size varied from 10 to 30 children. The larger group sizes or densities are reported as having different effects for boys and girls. Girls played more often in smaller groups or alone, whereas boys played more in larger groups and reduced their locomotor activity. Both boys and girls had more conflict interactions in large groups. No statistical analyses are reported in the summary available, but presumably they would be on individuals, since basically only one group was studied.

A study by W. C. McGrew (1972) and P. L. McGrew (1970), performed in a nursery class at Edinbrugh, is the only project to date that has carried out a double experiment (types ND and DR), although space was the only resource considered. The class consisted of 20 children aged 3 to 5 years. Group size was varied by sometimes sending half the children outside, giving mean group sizes (after absences) of 8.4 and 15.8. Space was varied by sometimes reducing available area to 80% of total, using a barrier of chairs and benches. These two kinds of variation were independently manipulated, giving four different density conditions (see Table 3).

One observer (P. L. McGrew, 1970) recorded four measures of proximity at frequent intervals, while the other (W. C. McGrew, 1972) observed the occurrence of 12 different behaviors, including four relevant to levels of fear: weeping, immobility, digit sucking, and automanipulating. Behavior scores were obtained by event-sampling occurrences for the whole group, but no measures of observer reliability were reported. The results for the latter scores especially do not give a very clear pattern. For variations in amount of space, the only results found to be significant for both group size conditions were a decrease in running and an increase in close peer proximity, in the smaller space. For variations in group size, the only results significant for both space conditions were a decrease in negative expletives and an increase in proximity to adults and a decrease in solitary position, in the larger group. There were variations in measures of aggressive and fear behaviors, but they were not generally consistent or significant. Since the results differed for the *ND* and *DR* experiments, the inference is that for the effects found, amount of space and number of children were the important parameters, rather than spatial density per se. Again the proviso must be made that statistical analyses were carried out on individuals, leading to an overestimate of significance levels. Also, despite the double experiment, inferences regarding effects of group size would not be justified, since no resources other than available space were considered. In particular, it seems that the amount of play equipment was not varied in the two group size conditions. Variations in group size involved a simultaneous variation in amounts of space and of play equipment per child. The effects of spatial density only could be estimated and allowed for in the experimental design.

In a recent study carried out at Sheffield University, in collaboration with Professor Kevin Connolly, we decided to investigate the relative importance of spatial density and equipment density on children's behavior in playgroups. We used a large rectangular room, nearly 2000 ft^2 in area. The available space was manipulated, by means of a curtained barrier, so that either one-third, two-thirds, or all the room area was accessible. This gave us the maximum density (25 ft^2/child) allowed by local authority regulations, and both medium- and low-density conditions. To vary the amount of play equipment, we made up a basic set, consisting of climbing frame and slide, Wendy House, table and toys, bookcase, easel, sandpit, toy chest, pram, tricycle, and a few other small items. This basic set was intended to be sufficient for a group of 24 children, only if appreciable sharing of equipment took place. However on some occasions two, and on other occasions three, of these basic sets of equipment were put out together. Under these conditions play equipment was plentiful. In this way the *amount* of equipment was not confounded with the *kinds* of equipment provided.

The amounts of space and equipment were covaried to give nine possible environments. The separate effects of spatial and equipment densities, and any interaction, could then be evaluated over a range of values. At each morning session one environmental condition was presented, and each condition was presented six times in all (partial latin square design). For each session four time samples of behavior were recorded for each child, during free play periods. In each sample, occurrence (or nonoccurrence) of a wide range of behaviors, activities, and companion groupings was recorded (Smith & Connolly, in preparation).

Statistical tests were done using individual totals in the different conditions, which means an overestimate of significance levels. Although likely to be less serious in a large group of 24 children than in a small group, the exact extent of the effect is not known. To guard against accepting results particular to one group, we used two independent groups of children. Each group of children contained twelve boys and twelve girls, attended two mornings a week, and experienced the same environmental variations. Results were only accepted when found for both groups.

In general, the variation of space and equipment appeared to have quite independent effects, with the latter having much the more interesting results on social behavior. In brief, the conditions with fewer toys brought about a decrease in solitary play and an increase in parallel play and in physical contacts between children. Visual contacts increased slightly, but talking between children and cooperative group play were not increased. Both parallel and cooperative groups were larger, however, as more sharing of equipment occurred. There was little change in the amount of object manipulation, but some increase in free motor activity. Finally, there were increases in the frequency of agonistic encounters and of several behavioral indices of fear and social stress. By contrast, conditions with less space available decreased free motor activity, and increased activity on apparatus and physical contacts, but had no effects on fear behaviors or on social and aggressive behaviors generally.

Results for some fearful behaviors and for agonistic encounters appear in Table 4. Both the number of agonistic encounters and occurrences of digit sucking increased steadily and appreciably in the conditions with fewer toys. This is also true, although not quite so clearly, with crying and inactivity. Inactivity was scored when a child made no sustained social interaction or use of toys or apparatus, during a sample period. In general, there seems to be good evidence that levels of anxious or fearful behavior and of social competition were raised moderately but significantly by reductions in play equipment (while remaining unaffected by reductions in available space). An unexpected result was that automanipulative behaviors showed no such variation. This category included eye rubbing, ear pulling, nose picking, hand to face, hair brushing or grooming, genital manipulation, hand fumbling, mouth fumbling, and also clothes fumbling and hitching. Individual analysis of these behaviors yielded no significant effects, apart from an increase in hand fumbling and clothes hitching, in group 2 only, with less equipment. One reservation is that interobserver agreement was low, around 50% for some of these behaviors (as compared with over 70% for most others). In a subsequent experiment, however, all the large apparatus was removed from the playroom and only small toys left; we found under these conditions that object manipulation increased and automanipulations decreased significantly (Smith, in press). This suggested that object manipulation and automanipulation were antagonistic behaviors, and this possibility has also been raised by observations on retarded children and institutionalized defectives (Hollis, 1965; Berkson, 1967). Nevertheless, automanipulation is often observed in conflict situations, and the absence of crowding effects remains surprising.

TABLE 4. Number of Occurrences of Agonistic Encounters and Fearful Behaviors in Different Space and Equipment Conditions, for Two Groups of Children. Main Effects from Analysis of Variance

Occurrence	Group	Space				Equipment			
		1	2	3		1	2	3	
Agonistic encounters	1	165	146	154	n.s.	179	146	140	.05
	2	104	108	100	n.s.	122	103	87	.05
Digit sucking	1	159	170	144	n.s.	188	145	140	.02
	2	172	147	154	n.s.	180	161	132	.02
Pucker, cry, scream	1	41	33	30	n.s.	34	50	20	.01
	2	25	11	20	n.s.	23	17	16	n.s. (.25)
Inactivity	1	221	199	211	n.s.	230	198	203	n.s. (.25)
	2	235	197	223	n.s.	249	231	175	.001
Automanipulation	1	529	526	546	n.s.	551	515	535	n.s.
	2	546	613	606	n.s.	606	577	582	n.s.

Two further *DR* type experiments, involving space variations only, have been reported. Preiser (1972) reduced available space by one-third in a nursery class of fifteen children in Virginia. From the brief report now available, it seems that significant results on social interaction and aggressive behavior were not obtained. A recent report by Loo (1972), however, comes to different conclusions about the importance of space or spatial density. In her study 60 children, aged 4 and 5 years, were split into ten groups of six (three boys, three girls). Each group had 48 minutes in a low-density condition and an equal time in a high-density condition (only one-third of the original area available). Order effects were counterbalanced across groups. Statistical analysis was done, quite correctly, on group means. Six observers were placed behind a one-way-vision screen and, at the end of each session, each observer rated each subject for aggression, dominance, number of interruptions, resistance, submission, nurturance, number of children interacted with, solitary, onlooker, and group involvement.

The results showed that in the higher spatial density condition, children interacted with fewer other children. There were tendencies for less group play and more solitary play, but for more interruptions by others to occur. The boys were *less* aggressive in the high-density condition, but girls increased their level of dominance behavior, and there were no changes in submission or resistance (to dominance and aggression). A reservation concerning the finding on reduced aggression is that play-fighting was scored as aggressive (Loo, personal communication). We found that play-chasing was reduced in a smaller space (Smith & Connolly, in preparation), and it is possible that this was the main effect responsible for Loo's result.

The changes in social and aggressive behavior in this experiment contrast with the lack of such changes in similar experiments by McGrew, Smith and Connolly, and Preiser. However none of these other studies examined spatial densities above 25 ft²/child (Table 3), whereas the highest density in Loo's experiment was 15 ft²/child, a very crowded condition. This is the most likely reason for the discrepancy, although it would be desirable to see whether the results are replicated for larger group sizes and spaces and to sample a wider range of behaviors, including fear indices.

Summarizing the findings of all these experiments (Table 3), it is convenient to consider the *ND* and *DR* types separately. Of the three *ND* experiments, two suggest that crowding increases social conflicts or aggression (Hutt & Vaizey, 1966; Bates, personal communication). The third does not (P. L. McGrew, 1970; W. C. McGrew, 1972). Evidence relating to changes in levels of fear or anxiety is indirect or equivocal. Any results from these studies could be due to group size, spatial density, or equipment density.

However, three of the four *DR* experiments (W. C. McGrew, Smith & Connolly, personal communication; Preiser, 1972) agree that neither spatial density nor amount of space has much effect on levels of fear, social conflict, or social interaction, over a wide range of densities up to 25 ft²/child. The evidence from Loo's report is that at 15 ft²/child there is some social withdrawal, and possibly more behavioral interruptions and changes in aggressive and dominance behavior.

Finally, Smith and Connolly found that decreasing play equipment did raise levels of fear behaviors moderately but significantly; increases in social conflicts and size of groups also occurred, but there was no change in cooperative group play. It would be interesting to know whether results from the *ND* experiments are due to equipment density, or whether group size is an important variable in its own right with regard to levels of fear and social interaction. This could be best done by carrying out an *NR* experiment in which numbers are varied with both spatial and equipment density held constant, and we are now performing such an experiment to clarify the importance of the group size parameter.

Possible Behavioral Mechanisms

Several elements or behavioral processes important in the experience of crowding have been proposed. These have included inability to control interactions with others, frustration in the achievement of some purpose because of the presence of others, overall level of social stimulation, information overload, unpredictability of social interaction, interruption of behavior sequences, and amount of competitive social interaction. These all perhaps reflect different facets of a complex kind of phenomenon.

The previous discussion emphasized the amount of competitive social interaction, in line with a similar emphasis in many studies of animal crowding. It is likely that a decrease in resources per individual will affect the level of competitive social interaction—by increased fighting, perhaps, or by dominance/submission encounters. However, such alternative strategies as social withdrawal, decreased resource use, or increased sharing, might also occur. It is also assumed that the resource is an important one (i.e., that individuals are motivated to obtain it). For children in a playgroup, for example, space does not seem to be an important resource in this way. Reduction in play equipment led both to increased sharing and to increased competitive social interaction.

It seems likely that the effects of certain *density* parameters on fear and stress may be mediated by levels of competitive social interaction; however, the means by which *group size* may affect behavior remains much more speculative. Nevertheless, in reviewing the literature on human crowding, Freedman (1973) concludes that group size is probably a more important parameter than density (although, as we have seen, its importance for crowding in the playgroup situation has not been verified).

An increase in group size is likely to mean an increase in the number of conspecifics with whom an individual will make interactions and with whom some relationship must be formed. (It is assumed here that the term "group" implies that interactions occur among its members; we are considering increases in group size, independently of resources—such as spatial partitions, foci of attention—which might serve to reduce such interactions.) Two main characteristics of social relationships considered in social psychology are dominance and affiliation, the latter being affected both by how well two individuals know each other and by how much they like each other. It may be that considering these characteristics will prove a useful way of examining how group size might have stressful behavioral effects.

Probably a certain element of dominance, or status, enters into any social interaction. Increased group size would then increase the number of status relationships to be defined and redefined. It is certainly a possibility that this in itself, independent of resource conflicts, would increase levels of fear or stress.

The less well known one individual is to another, the more unpredictable his behavior is likely to be (and will be expected to be); as the two become known to each other, behavior becomes more predictable, but never completely so. An important component in social attraction and the development of social affiliation seems to be an optimum amount of unpredictability in behavior, coupled with a contingency of responsiveness between individuals that provides a mutual feeling of efficacy or competence in social encounter (Latané & Hothersall, 1972). Again, increases in group size may, beyond certain levels, increase the unpredictable elements in social interaction beyond an optimum level for the individual concerned. In part this would be because one individual cannot know all the other individuals in a large group so well as others in a small group (given equivalent time in the groups). In a large group, some individuals may be relative strangers.

In the earlier discussion of fear of novel persons and environments, it was suggested that both the amount or degree of novel or unpredictable stimulation, and the presence or absence of contingency or control by the individual over the stimulus salience, would be important in determining the level of fear behavior manifested. From the point of view of degree of unpredictable stimulation, it would be expected that increases in group size would be pleasurable at first, but beyond certain levels aversive. In larger groups, however, individuals might act to restrict the number of social contacts or to maintain them at an optimum level. Nevertheless, the contingency of social contacts, or the degree of control the individual feels he has over partially unpredictable events, may also be adversely affected by certain parameters of crowding. Here physical parameters might be of great importance. For example, in the very high spatial densities of Loo's experiment, the spatial constraints tended to increase the number of behavioral interruptions, and this condition was associated with social withdrawal. For large groups, it might be especially stressful.

In summary, it is suggested that whereas the adaptive value of fear in the individual lies primarily in avoidance of possible dangers, the range of individual variation in fear responses may have adaptive value for the species in terms of allocation of resources, and, ultimately, control of population. Some situations giving rise to fear responses in social groups of children have been discussed. Both unpredictability and lack of contingency or control seem to be important elements in fear of novel persons or environments. It is hypothesized that they may also be important fear-arousing or stressful elements under certain conditions of crowding, such as large group size combined with severe spatial restrictions. In the case of novel objects or toys, which are attractive and evoke little fear in themselves, signs of fear are seen in some children in relation to the social competition that attempts to use the toys would involve. It is hypothesized that circumstances favoring social competition are also likely to increase fear responses, at least in certain individuals, and that crowding (considered as density of desirable resources per individual) would arouse fear in this manner. At present, however, too little evidence is available for firm conclusions to be reached.

References

Alexander, B. K., & Roth, E. M. The effects of acute crowding on aggressive behavior of Japanese monkeys. *Behavior*, 1971, **39**, 73–90.

Arsenian, J. M. Young children in an insecure situation. *Journal of Abnormal and Social Psychology*, 1943, **38**, 235–249.

Berkson, G. Abnormal stereotyped motor acts. In J. Zubin & H. Hunt (Eds.), *Comparative psychopathology*. New York: Grune & Stratton, 1967.

Blurton Jones, N. G. An ethological study of some aspects of social behavior of children in nursery school. In D. Morris (Ed.), *Primate ethology*. London: Weidenfeld & Nicolson, 1967.

Blurton Jones, N. G. Categories of child-child interaction. In N. G. Blurton Jones (Ed.), *Ethological studies of child behavior*. Cambridge, England: Cambridge University Press, 1972.

Blurton Jones, N. G., & Leach, G. M. Behavior of children and their mothers at separation and greeting. In N. G. Blurton Jones (Ed.), *Ethological studies of child behavior*, Cambridge, England: Cambridge University Press, 1972.

Brindley, C., Clarke, P., Hutt, C., Robinson, I., & Wethli, E. Sex differences in the activities and social interactions of nursery school children. In R. P. Michael & J. H. Crook (Eds.), *Comparative ecology and behavior of primates*. London: Academic Press, 1973.

Carmichael, L. (Ed.) *Manual of child psychology*. New York: Wiley, 1954.

Christian, J. J., & Davis, D. E. Endocrines, behavior, and population. *Science*, 1964, **146**, 1550–1560.

Connolly, K., & Smith, P. K. Reactions of pre-school children to a strange observer. In N. G. Blurton Jones (Ed.), *Ethological studies of child behavior.* Cambridge, England: Cambridge University Press, 1972.

Crook, J. H., & Goss-Custard, J. D. Social ethology. *Annual Review of Psychology,* 1972, **23,** 277–312.

Desor, J. A. Towards a psychological theory of crowding. *Journal of Personality and Social Psychology,* 1972, **21,** 79–83.

Ehrlich, P. R., & Ehrlich, A. H. *Population, resources, environment.* San Francisco: Freeman, 1970.

Esser, A. H. A biosocial perspective on crowding. In J. F. Wohlwill & D. H. Carson (Eds.), *Environment and the Social Sciences: Perspectives and Applications.* Washington, D.C.: American Psychological Association, Inc., 1972.

Freedman, J. L. The effects of population density on humans. In J. T. Fawcett (Ed.), *Psychological Perspectives on Population.* New York: Basic Books, 1973.

Gray, J. A. *The Psychology of Fear and Stress.* London: Weidenfeld & Nicolson, 1971.

Gray, J. A., & Buffery, A. W. H. Sex differences in emotional and cognitive behavior in mammals including man: Adaptive and neural bases. *Acta Psychologica,* 1971, **35,** 89–111.

Harlow, H., & Harlow, M. K. The affectional systems. In A. M. Schrier, H. F. Harlow, & F. Stollnitz (Eds.), *Behavior of Nonhuman Primates.* Vol 2. London: Academic Press, 1965.

Heathers, G. The adjustment of two-year-olds in a novel social situation. *Child Development,* 1954, **25,** 147–158.

Hollis, J. H. The effects of social and non-social stimuli on the behavior of profoundly retarded children. Parts I & II. *American Journal of Mental Deficiency,* 1965, **69,** 755–771, 772–789.

Hutt, C. Exploration and play in children. *Symposium of the Zoological Society of London,* 1966, **18,** 61–81.

Hutt, C. Specific and diversive exploration. In H. Reese & L. P. Lipsett (Eds.), *Advances in child development and behavior.* Vol 5. London: Academic Press, 1970.

Hutt, C., & McGrew, W. C. Effects of group density upon social behavior in humans. Unpublished paper presented to Symposium on Changes in Behavior with Population Density, Association for the Study of Animal Behavior, Oxford, 1967.

Hutt, C., & Vaizey, M. J. Differential effects of group density on social behavior. *Nature (London),* 1966, **209,** 1371–1372.

Hutt, S. J., & Hutt, C. *Direct Observation and Measurement of Behavior.* Springfield, Ill.: Thomas, 1970.

Lack, D. *Population Studies of Birds.* Oxford: Oxford University Press, 1966.

Latané, B., & Hothersall, D. Social attraction in animals. In P. C. Dodwell (Ed.), *New horizons in psychology.* Vol 2. Harmondsworth, England: Penguin, 1972.

Loo, C. M. The effects of spatial density on the social behavior of children. *Journal of Applied Social Psychology,* 1972, **2,** 372–381.

McGrew, P. L. Social and spatial density effects on spacing behavior in preschool children. *Journal of Child Psychology and Psychiatry,* 1970, **11,** 197–205.

McGrew, W. C. *An ethological study of children's behavior.* New York: Academic Press, 1972.

Preiser, W. F. E. Work in progress: Behavior of nursery school children under different spatial densities. *Man–Environment Systems,* 1972, **2,** 247–250.

Rheingold, H. L. The effect of a strange environment on the behavior of infants. In B. M. Foss (Ed.), *Determinants of infant behavior.* Vol 4. London: Methuen; New York: Wiley, 1969.

Rheingold, H. L., & Eckerman, C. O. The infant's free entry into a new environment. *Journal of Experimental Child Psychology,* 1969, **8,** 271–283.

Smith, P. K. Temporal clusters and individual differences in the behavior of preschool children. In R. P. Michael & J. H. Crook (Eds.), *Comparative ecology and behavior of primates.* London: Academic Press, 1973.

Smith, P. K. Aspects of the playgroup environment. In D. V. Canter & T. R. Lee (Eds.), *Psychology and the built environment.* London: Architectural Press, in press.

Smith, P. K., & Connolly, K. J. Toys, space, and children. *Bulletin of the British Psychological Society,* 1973, **26,** 167; manuscript in preparation.

Slater, E. Types, levels and irregularities of response to a nursery school situation of 40 children observed with special reference to the home environment. *Monographs of the Society for Research in Child Development,* 1939, **4.**

Stern, O. N., & Bender, E. P. The behavior of preschool children approaching a strange adult: sex differences. In R. Friedman (Ed.), *Sex differences in behavior.* New York: Wiley, in press.

Stokols, D. On the distinction between density and crowding: Some implications for future research. *Psychological Review,* 1972, **79,** 275–277.

Washburn, R. W. A scheme for grading the reactions of children in a new social situation. *Journal of Genetic Psychology,* 1932, **40,** 84–99.

Waterhouse, M. J., & Waterhouse, H. B. Primate ethology and human social behavior. In R. P. Michael & J. H. Crook (Eds.), *Comparative ecology and behavior of primates.* London: Academic Press, 1973.

Wynne-Edwards, V. C. *Animal dispersion in relation to social behavior.* Edinburgh: Oliver & Boyd, 1962.

Zlutnick, S., & Altman, I. Crowding and human behavior. In J. F. Wohlwill and D. H. Carson (Eds.), *Environment and the social sciences: Perspectives and applications.* Washington, D.C.: American Psychological Association, 1972.

CHAPTER 6

Responses of One-year-olds to a Stranger in a Strange Situation[1]

INGE BRETHERTON
AND
MARY D. SALTER AINSWORTH
Johns Hopkins University

The extensive literature on infants' responses to strangers during the last months of the first year of life yields evidence of wide differences among individuals and, for any one individual, substantial variability from one situation to another. Responses range from prompt avoidance with crying to cheerful friendliness, with willingness to approach and to interact with the stranger. The great majority of responses are intermediate between the extremes of avoidance and approach and the extremes of positive and negative affect.

Spitz (1950) held that fear of strangers was the norm in infants approximately 8 months old. Other investigators reported that full-blown fear reactions were far from ubiquitous even toward the end of the first year, and that reactions (or components of reactions) that are positive or affiliative are often to be observed (e.g., Bronson, 1972; Lewis & Brooks, see Chapter 8, this volume; Morgan & Ricciuti, 1969; Scarr & Salapatek, 1970; Schaffer, 1966; Tennes & Lampl, 1964). Nevertheless, these authors, like Spitz, tended to focus their discussions on the fear, anxiety, or wariness activated by strangers. Rheingold and Eckerman (in press) challenged the generally accepted notion that infants fear strangers in the second half of the first year of life, presenting evidence that

[1]An earlier version of this chapter was presented at the meeting of the Eastern Psychological Association, Boston, April 1972. The research that yielded the data has been supported by grants 62-244 of the Foundation's Fund for Research in Psychiatry, R01 HD 01712 of the U.S. Public Health Service, by one from the Grant Foundation, and one from the U.S. Office of Child Development. Mary B. Main's study, whose data we also used, was supported by a grant from the National Science Foundation. This support is gratefully acknowledged. We thank Judy Zyroff and Carol Gore, who consolidated the narrative records. We also wish to thank John Bowlby, Gordon and Wanda Bronson, and Russel Tracy, whose constructive criticisms of a previous version were very helpful to us in preparing the present version.

131

a positive social response is common, whereas fear behavior is indeed rare. They also deplored the paucity of behavioral detail reported by many studies of infants' responses to strangers.

This chapter provides a detailed descriptive account of the variety of responses observed in one-year-olds when they encounter a stranger in one specific unfamiliar situation termed the "strange situation" (Ainsworth & Wittig, 1969). This situation was originally intended to supplement a naturalistic, longitudinal study of the development of infant–mother attachment. It was designed to highlight three aspects of an infant's behavior, one of these being his response to a stranger in an unfamiliar situation. In contrast to Ganda infants (Ainsworth, 1967), few infants in the longitudinal study had shown any striking fear of strangers in the context of their own homes. It was expected that fear of strangers would occur more frequently in an unfamiliar situation.

Since 1964, when strange-situation observations were begun, 106 white, middle-class one-year-olds have been observed in it. Furthermore, this total sample consists of four separate samples observed at different times in conjunction with different studies; thus the observations have been replicated, adding further credence to the findings. Although preliminary reports have been made of behavior in the strange situation (Ainsworth & Wittig, 1969; Ainsworth & Bell, 1970; Ainsworth, Bell, & Stayton, 1971) this chapter presents the first systematic analysis of responses to a stranger in this version of an unfamiliar situation.

The findings reported in this chapter reflect inevitably the behavior of the strangers in our strange-situation procedure. Although their behavior was constrained to some extent by instructions, it did not constitute a standardized experimental approach to the infant; on the contrary, there was substantial opportunity for the stranger to be sensitively responsive to the infant's behavior and to respond to it contingently.

In previous analyses of infants' behavior in the strange situation it had been found useful (e.g., Ainsworth & Bell, 1970; Ainsworth, Bell, & Stayton, 1971) to view behavior as resulting from the arousal of two major behavioral systems—the exploratory system activated especially by a novel assembly of toys, and the attachment system activated in a sequence of episodes involving stress. Bronson (1972) concluded from his investigation of infants' responses to strangers that "reactions to the larger social environment seem to evolve through an interplay between two developing adaptive systems . . . ," which he identified as affiliation with and wariness of other humans. In the present analysis of response to strangers in our strange situation, we suggest that our findings offer evidence of complex interrelationships among *four* behavioral systems when a baby with his mother in an unfamiliar environment encounters a friendly stranger—an affiliative system, a system that we label "fear-wariness," and the attachment and exploratory systems that previous discussions have emphasized.

METHOD

Subjects

The subjects were 106 white, middle-class, family-reared infants whose mothers were contacted through pediatricians in private practice. Sixty were boys and 46 were girls. The total sample was made up of four subsamples:

Sample I: $N = 23$, median age 51 weeks
Sample II: $N = 33$, median age 49 weeks
Sample III: $N = 23$, median age 50 weeks
Sample IV: $N = 27$, median age 52 weeks

Sample I includes 23 of the 26 subjects of our longitudinal project that were observed in the strange situation, one group in 1964–1965 and the other in 1967. Sample II was studied by Bell (1970) in conjunction with her investigation of the development of the concept of the object. Sample III was assembled in 1971 for a test–retest study of strange situation behavior; the first session only is considered here. Sample IV was studied by Main (1973) in the course of a project linking strange-situation behavior to play, exploration, and cognitive functioning at 21 months. Since in each case both the laboratory situation and the stranger were totally unfamiliar, it is assumed that the differential imbedding of the strange situation in four different studies implies no significant order effects.

Procedure

The experimental room, partially furnished as an office, had a 9 × 9 foot area of clear floor space, divided into 16 numbered squares to facilitate recording of the infants' location and locomotion. One wall of the room contained two one-way-vision mirrors through which the situation could be observed. Near the opposite wall stood a child's chair heaped with and surrounded by toys.[2] Near one window in one corner of the room was a chair for the mother and opposite it, near the window and on the same side of the room as the door, a chair for the stranger. Figure 1 sketches the physical arrangements.

The strange situation (Ainsworth & Wittig, 1969) consists of eight episodes, of which only the first four concern us here. The main focus of the study is on episode 3, but behavior in episodes 2 and 4 is considered here for purposes of several comparisons.

Episode 1 ● The introductory episode lasts only 15 to 30 seconds. The mother, guided by an experimenter, carries the baby into the room. The experimenter

[2] An inventory of the toys will be provided in a future publication (Ainsworth, Blehar, & Wall, in preparation). No attempt was made to devise toys entirely novel to all subjects. It was assumed (and later checked) that although some toys might be familiar to an individual infant, there would be enough unfamiliar toys to make the total array reasonably novel, hence exploration eliciting.

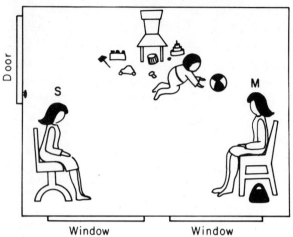

FIGURE 1.   Physical arrangements of the strange situation.

shows the mother where to put the baby down and where to sit, and then leaves.

Episode 2 (3 minutes) ● The mother puts the baby down midway between her own and the stranger's chair (6 feet from the pile of toys) and sits. She has been instructed to read or pretend to read a magazine, to respond if the baby seeks a response from her, but not to try to attract his attention. (A large proportion of the mothers watched the baby rather than reading, although all but a very few heeded the instruction not to intervene.) If after 2 minutes the baby has still not approached the toys, the mother is signaled to interest him in the toys and return to her chair.

Episode 3 (3 minutes) ● The third episode consists of three parts. During the first minute (subepisode 3a) an adult female stranger, whom the baby has not seen before, enters saying "Hello! I'm the stranger," and sits quietly in her chair. During the second minute (subepisode 3b) the stranger engages the mother in conversation. At the beginning of the third minute (subepisode 3c) the stranger is signaled to begin her approach to the baby and to invite him to play with her by enticing him with a toy, while the mother sits quietly. The episode ends when the mother, at a signal, leaves the room unobtrusively.

Episode 4 (3 minutes or less) ● The stranger continues to play with the infant for a few moments. If he seems settled in play she withdraws to her chair, but responds to any overtures he makes. If he is distressed, she tries to distract him or comfort him. If she is unsuccessful the episode is curtailed. The episode ends with the return of the mother.

The stranger's behavior, although controlled by the foregoing instructions, could be more variable than allowed by the procedures of other investigators (e.g., Bronson, 1972; Morgan & Ricciuti, 1969; Shaffer & Emerson, 1964), whose strangers approached and attempted to initiate interaction in a standardized fashion that did not allow the stranger to respond sensitively to the baby's behavior. During subepisodes 3a and 3b the stranger, though nonparticipating, was permitted to respond to a baby's smile or vocalization with a smile and to look away if eye-to-eye contact seemed to make him uneasy. During subepisode 3c the stranger, while approaching and interacting with the baby, attempted to adjust her behavior to his, to cause as little distress as possible. On the other hand, in contrast to the other procedures mentioned, episode 3 was not terminated if the baby withdrew to the mother or began to fuss.

It is perhaps useful to compare our procedure with that of Rheingold and Eckerman (in press), whose strangers were also permitted to respond naturally to the baby. Their tests 2 and 3 were roughly comparable to our subepisode 3b. In their test 1, lasting 10 minutes, the stranger played with the baby, and part of the time the play was mediated by toys. The baby, however, was fastened into a high chair rather than mobile, although his mother sat beside him. In their test 4 the stranger picked the baby up; there was no counterpart for this in our episode 3. They used two strangers; the baby was slightly habituated to both. Our procedure was intended to be minimally disturbing to the infant, and we presume that Rheingold's first three tests were also so intended.

Each of our four samples had a different stranger, but on occasion substitutes were necessary, and there were nine strangers in all. The only noticeable difference among strangers came during subepisode 3c. Although all strangers attempted to interact with the baby by engaging his interest in a toy, the strangers of samples I and II first called to the baby before approaching him, whereas the strangers for samples III and IV approached quickly and quietly and only when close spoke to the baby.[3]

Observation and Data Recording

Two observers, wearing headphones connected to a microphone in the experimental room, dictated two independent narrative accounts of the ongoing events into tape recorders, which also picked up the sound of a buzzer every 15 seconds. (A random spot check revealed that the observers spoke at a mean rate

---

[3]We are convinced that unless one rigidly controls the approach by the stranger, as Morgan and Ricciuti (1969) did, for example, it is very difficult to standardize her approach. Among our strangers, each had her own individual style, and each seemed to be motivated to do her best to allay any anxiety that a baby might feel. Whenever postsession suggestions were made about future modification of behavior in the interest of standardization, these were either resisted or ignored. Maccoby (personal communication) reported similiar attitudes on the part of her strangers when she used the strange-situation technique (Maccoby & Feldman, 1972). We conclude that strangers, like mothers, have their own conceptions of the proper way to behave toward a baby. If one wishes, as we did, to have the behavior of the adults in the strange situation as natural as possible within the limits set by the general structure of the episodes, one cannot expect uniformity of behavior.

of 168 words per minute.) The narrative reports were subsequently transcribed, the typed report showing the descriptions of the two observers side by side for each 15-second interval, thus facilitating comparison.

In all there were 15 observers. Four observers in different pairings, observed sample I. Ten observers were used with sample III, only one of whom had observed any subjects of sample I. A variety of observers were used with sample IV, and all but one had also observed with sample III. Only one observer was used with sample II, however—one who had gained experience with sample I.

The protocols of the two observers were consolidated into one coded record, which retained the 15-second time divisions, in the following manner. The coding sheet had three columns, one for each stranger, baby, and mother. Motor, visual, and vocal behavior, facial expression, and location were entered into the appropriate columns, retaining the language used by the observers. Sequence of behaviors was represented by showing concurrent behavior on the same horizontal line and subsequent behavior on a lower line.

Although discrepancies between observers were few, "rules of thumb" were required to resolve them when preparing the consolidated report. An event was represented as having occurred during the 15-second interval in which it was first mentioned by one observer when the other lagged somewhat behind the first. Since the fields of vision of the two observers differed slightly, it was assumed that a behavior (e.g., a smile or a look) reported by one but not by the other had actually occurred. If one observer used more precise language than the other (such as "the baby gives a huge smile" instead of "the baby smiles"), the more precise expression was used in the consolidated report. The very few instances in which two observers reported discrepant behavior were resolved by the coder in terms of total context, including the positions of the observers relative to the figure observed.

Measures

The measures used in this analysis were calculated for several different time periods. Most of them were calculated for the three minutes of episode 3 (3a, 3b, and 3c), considered separately or together or both. It should be borne in mind that during subepisodes 3a and 3b the stranger's and the mother's roles were comparable—nonparticipant but responsive—whereas in subepisode 3c their roles diverged; the stranger took the initiative in approaching the baby while the mother remained nonparticipant. For some purposes episode 3 (or merely 3a and 3b) was compared with episode 2 or 4. These comparisons were undertaken in full recognition that these three episodes differed substantially in the behaviors they might be expected to instigate; however, it was believed that the comparisons were of value. Finally, the infant's initial reaction to the stranger's entrance at the beginning of subepisode 3a and his initial reaction to the stranger's approach at the beginning of subepisode 3c were considered separately from the more inclusive analyses of 3a, 3b, and 3c.

Three kinds of measure were used: incidence (whether a baby showed a specified behavior), frequency (how often he showed it), and duration or latency of the behavior. In regard to duration and latency, we had the choice between using the 15-second units into which the narrative reports had been divided, or attempting a more precise estimate. We chose the latter course, estimating to the nearest 5 seconds, by dividing the original narrative protocol for the relevant 15-second interval into thirds. Since a spot check had indicated that each observer had a fairly constant rate of dictation, this estimate seemed to be justified.[4] The following measures and classes of measure were used.

Initial Response to the Stranger's Entrance ● The incidence of the following classes of behavior were tallied: visual orientation, facial expression, and locomotor behavior.

The stranger's entrance invariably elicited looking. Two types of *visual behavior* were noted: prolonged gazing and gaze aversion. A look was classified as prolonged if it lasted for 5 seconds or more. Furthermore, the duration of this initial look was estimated to the nearest 5 seconds—an estimate that was usually easy, since the observers regularly noted when a look began and when it either shifted or was averted. The initial look was the criterion for other responses being classed as "initial responses." Thus if a smile, cryface, approach, or withdrawal occurred during or immediately after the initial look, it was classed as an initial response. A gaze was considered to be averted if, after looking at the stranger, the baby looked away, his eyes directed at his lap, at the floor, or at nothing in particular. If he looked at a toy or at his mother or engaged in any locomotor or manipulative behavior, he was considered to have merely shifted his gaze, as opposed to having averted it.

Three types of *facial expression* were identified: *(a)* a cryface, regardless of whether accompanied by vocal crying or fussing, *(b)* a smile, including expressions described by the observers as "little smiles" or "half-smiles," and *(c)* all intermediate expressions. It had originally been intended to differentiate among the intermediate expressions—distinguishing "pleasant" and "open" from "neutral" and neutral from "apprehensive," "sober," "sobering," or "serious." Although some observers described intermediate expressions with some precision, even though they had not been specifically instructed to do so, some did not mention facial expression in the absence of a smile or cryface; thus the expression would have to be classified as "neutral," regardless of whether it was truly neutral. To avoid giving the impression that a large pro-

---

[4]Had we used videotape records, latencies and durations of behaviors could have been measured precisely. On the other hand, it is difficult to judge from video recording whether behavior, such as a look or a smile across a distance, is directed toward a person. We are impressed with the superiority of the human observer as an information-processing system for many aspects of interactive behavior, although videotape is superior for recording facial expression and details of gesture, as well as for timing.

portion of expressions were neutral, any systematic attempt to deal with intermediate expressions was abandoned.

Morgan and Ricciuti (1969), in anchoring points of their effective rating scale, used nuances of facial expression more highly differentiated than those reported here. We agree with their implicit position that facial expression forms an important part of the whole system of nonverbal signals that mediate interaction. Had we the opportunity of beginning afresh, we would either supplement our narrative reports with videotape records to catch facial expression, or we would train observers in the lexicon of human facial expression and gestures developed by ethologists (e.g., Grant, 1969), or both. Fortunately, it was only in regard to nuances of facial expression that any substantial observer differences were encountered.

Two types of *locomotor behavior* were identified: approach to the stranger and approach to the mother.

Initial Response to the Stranger's Approach ● The stranger's approach was considered to have begun when, in response to a signal after 2 minutes, she either called to the baby and showed him a toy before beginning locomotor approach or actually approached him before speaking to him, and then tried to interest him in her toy. The classes of visual behavior and facial expression used were the same as those for classifying response to the stranger's entrance. In regard to other behaviors, however, we did not find it fruitful to distinguish between initial response and subepisode 3c as a whole.

Frequency of Looking[5] ● The number of times a baby looked at the mother and at the stranger was tallied for each subepisode. In this analysis a look was tallied only if the baby looked at the person's face or at the whole figure. Looks at the stranger's hand while she was holding or manipulating a toy (e.g., in subepisode 3c) were not included.

Incidence of Gaze Aversion ● The number of babies who averted their gaze from the stranger in each episode was tallied. (See definition above.)

Incidence and Frequency of Smiling ● The numbers of infants who smiled at the mother and the stranger were ascertained for each subepisode, and also the number of smiles the baby directed toward each figure. Episodes 2 and 3 were compared in regard to incidence of smiling at the mother, and episodes 3 and 4 for incidence of smiling at the stranger.

---

[5]It has been drawn to our attention by Wanda Bronson that our frequency measure of looking is not altogether satisfactory, since the duration of any one look may vary in length from a momentary glance to prolonged gazing. Although we felt it was legitimate to attempt to estimate the duration of an initial gaze to the nearest 5 seconds, since so often this was prolonged, we did not believe it justifiable to estimate the total duration of looking. Therefore, although our frequency measure of looking at the stranger must be a conservative indication of amount of looking, it is of interest to compare this with the frequency of looks at the mother, which tended to be momentary glances, hence conceivably more frequent.

Intensity of Smiling ● Smiles described either as "big" or as "little" or "half-smiles" were distinguished from mere "smiles," which were assumed to be full smiles but not especially intense.

Incidence and Frequency of Vocalization ● Only the incidence and frequency of noncrying vocalization were recorded. The number of infants who vocalized to the mother and to the stranger were tallied, as well as the frequency of those vocalizations for each subepisode. In the case of vocalization, unlike smiling, it is often impossible to ascertain to which person, if either, the vocalization is directed. Therefore, incidence of infants who vocalized was also tallied, as well as the frequency of the vocalizations.

Incidence of Crying ● The number of infants who cried, fussed, or made a cry-face at least once was tallied for each subepisode. Any crying that occurred at the end of subepisode 3c in response to the mother's departure was not included, however.

Incidence of Approach to the Stranger ● The number of infants who made either a full approach or a partial approach to the stranger was ascertained for each subepisode. A full approach was scored only if the baby went close enough to the stranger that he could easily have touched her or clambered up on her, regardless of whether he did so. A partial approach was something short of this, usually a matter of advancing only a few steps or their equivalent in crawling.

Latency of Approach to the Stranger ● We estimated latency to the nearest 5 seconds. Only subepisodes 3a and 3b were considered, because only spontaneous approaches were the focus of interest. Latency of approach to the stranger in episode 3 was then compared with the latency of approach to the toys in the first 2 minutes of episode 2, before any mother was signaled to intervene.

Incidence of Touching the Stranger ● All touches were tallied, no matter how tentative.

Incidence of Approach to the Mother ● Here we were concerned only with full approaches (see above). A separate tally was made of infants who achieved close proximity through the mother's approach to them in response to their signaling behavior, usually crying.

Incidence of Close Proximity to the Mother ● Close proximity was defined as being close enough to the mother to be able to touch her by reaching out, regardless of whether in fact she was touched. Thus a full approach brought an infant into close proximity.

Incidence of Physical Contact with the Mother ● A tally was made of those infants, who having approached their mothers or having been approached by them, achieved physical contact with them. This included all degrees of contact—touching, clambering up to stand, steadied by the mother, being picked up and held, and so on.

Response to the Stranger's Approach ● The analysis of the response to the stranger's approach, which refers to the whole of subepisode 3c, is complicated because the babies were mobile; hence their locations with reference to the mother differed when the stranger approached. The details of the analysis can most conveniently be given in conjunction with the findings, although it is appropriate here to mention that the analysis focuses on the dynamics of approach to and moving away from the mother on one hand and the stranger on the other hand.

Response to the Stranger's Offer of a Toy ● Each stranger attempted to initiate interaction with the baby through the intermediary of a toy, attracting his attention to it by doing something with it before offering it to the baby, either from her hand, by placing it on the floor near him, or rolling it to him, usually accompanying her offer with verbal encouragement.[6] Her choice of mode of presentation was influenced by the baby's behavior, and if he was unresponsive to her first mode or refused the first toys, she tried alternatives.

The incidence of the following responses to the stranger's play invitation was tallied, and in addition the responses are classed as negative, tentative, positive, or no response. The classes of negative response were: *(a)* actively rejects toy by pushing it away or making rejecting motions toward it, and *(b)* mildly snubs toy by first looking at it and then in a seemingly deliberate manner picking up another toy, or by leaning away from it. The classes of tentative response were: *(c)* makes intention movement toward toy, for example, poising for a reach and then not following through; *(d)* reaches for or approaches toy without touching it; and *(e)* touches the toy but does not pick it up. The classes of positive response were: *(f)* picks up the toy but does nothing else with it, *(g)* picks up the toy and plays with it at least briefly, and *(h)* engages in cooperative play with the stranger through a toy—for example, rolling a ball back to the stranger. The classes of no response were: *(i)* merely watching the stranger entertain him with a toy, and *(j)* taking no interest whatsoever in the stranger's efforts to engage him in play.

Assessment of the Balance Between Positive and Negative Responses to a Stranger ● A discussion of the behavior entering into this assessment is best left until after the findings have been presented.

---

[6]Some strangers, especially those of samples I and II, had reserved a toy near their chair, to show the baby across a distance when beginning their intervention. Such a toy was chosen at their discretion as one especially likely to interest babies. Others selected a toy from the array near the child's chair as they approached—either one in which the baby had already shown interest or one that had been popular with other babies. We cannot support our conviction, but we believe that differences in the strangers' initial choice of toy had no consistent effect on babies' responses.

Statistical Tests

Before undertaking the data analysis we had, of course, certain hypotheses, some based on our own impressions after having witnessed many one-year-olds in the strange situation, and some suggested by the work of other investigators. Since this is a descriptive study, however, in which no specific experimental manipulations were undertaken to test specific hypotheses, the statistical tests applied to our data cannot be viewed as tests of hypotheses. On the contrary, they are conceived as checks to any descriptive generalizations we might wish to make.

RESULTS

Intersample Comparisons

Statistical tests were made to ascertain whether the four samples differed significantly from one another in regard to the measures. Such tests seemed to be desirable, since the samples were observed in connection with different studies and used different strangers and different observers. A repeated measures analysis of variance for unequal samples showed that there were no significant differences in frequency of looking at the mother and at the stranger. Incidences of the following behaviors were tested by chi-square: prolonged looking and gaze aversion on the entrance of the stranger and on her approach, smiling at the stranger, smiling at the mother, vocalizing, approaching the mother, crying, gaze aversion, and positive, negative, and tentative responses to the stranger's offer of a toy—and in each case the measures for the four samples showed no significant departures from chance expectations (whenever possible, these intersample comparisons were done for subepisodes as well as for the whole of episode 3). Other behaviors had incidences too low to permit statistical testing of intersample differences; thus they can be assumed not to depart significantly from chance expectations.

Lack of significant intersample differences has at least two important implications. First, and most important, the findings of the original sample—sample I—have been subjected to three replications and have been confirmed thereby. It is suggested that such confirmation invites more confidence in the stability of the findings of this study than do the many successful tests of statistical significance that emerged from the findings of the total sample of 106 subjects. Second, the lack of significant intersample differences justifies combining the four samples for the ensuing data analyses (reported below)—a procedure that simplifies the presentation of results.

Sex Differences

A repeated measures analysis of variance for unequal samples showed that there were no significant sex differences in frequency of looking at mother or at stranger, and no significant sex × subepisode effect in regard to looking behavior. Incidence of the following behaviors was tested by chi-square: gaze aversion from the stranger (at her entrance, in each subepisode, and in the whole of episode 3); coy behavior (whole episode); smiling at the mother and smiling at the stranger (whole episode); vocalizations to the mother, vocalizations to the stranger, and total vocalizations (whole episode); crying (whole episode); close proximity to the mother, clamber on, clutch, or cling to the mother, hold on or touch the mother (whole episode); approach stranger; pick up stranger's toy, play with toy (including cooperative play with stranger), tentative responses to offer of toy, negative responses to offer of toy, and looking at the toy only. In no case was there a significant departure from chance expectations in regard to the incidence shown by boys and girls.

Initial Response to Stranger's Entrance

The entrance of the stranger certainly captured the babies' attention: virtually all infants looked at her with little or no delay. The initial look of 62 infants (58%) was prolonged, lasting at least 5 seconds and in one case continuing as long as 45 seconds. Usually the baby's gaze was directed at the stranger's face, but a few gave her a real "once over," inspecting her from head to foot. After having looked at the stranger, 32 infants (30%) averted their gaze.

Only four infants cried (or made a cryface) when the stranger entered. Substantially more smiled—19 (18%)—although the great majority—83 (78%)—responded to the stranger's entrance with a facial expression intermediate between a smile and a cryface.[7]

Four infants began to approach the stranger within the timespan defined by the initial look at her, two within the first 5 seconds, and two more within 15 seconds, one of whom also touched the stranger. Five infants, two of whom had greeted the stranger with a cry, immediately began a full approach to the mother. Of the ten who were standing near the mother at the beginning of episode 3, four reached for contact whereas four were already in contact.

Table 1 shows the interrelations between length of initial gaze, facial expression, and gaze aversion. Both smiles and cries occurred with looks of varying length. The fact that seven smiled of the eleven whose initial gaze lasted 15 seconds or more suggests that prolonged looking does not necessarily imply sober staring. Similarly, gaze aversion terminated initial looks of varying lengths. On the whole, a baby who smiled at the stranger at some time during his initial gaze did not then avert his gaze. There were six exceptions, and in four of these

---

[7]Merely for the reader's interest, we report here the incidence of expressions described by the observers within this intermediate range. Twenty-three infants were described as sober, serious, or apprehensive, and ten were said to look pleasant, open, or interested on first catching sight of the stranger. Fifty either were described as having a neutral expression or, more frequently, did not have their facial expression described at all.

TABLE 1. Estimated Length of Initial Gaze at the Stranger,
Accompanying Facial Expression, and Gaze Aversion

Length of Initial Gaze	Number of Infants	Cryface	Smile	Gaze Aversion Terminates Gaze
less than 5 seconds	46	3	2	12
5 to 9 seconds	28	0	6	8
10 to 14 seconds	21	1	4	10
15 to 19 seconds	8	0	6	1
20 seconds and over	3	0	1	1
Totals	106	4	19	32

the gaze aversion could be described as coy. This coy response consisted of smiling and averting the gaze, while cocking or ducking the head to the side.

The next five analyses were designed to serve three purposes. First, they compare the infants' behavior toward two figures—one totally unfamiliar, the other an attachment figure. Second, they compare infants' behaviors from one subepisode to the next. Third, they allow a comparison of the babies' initial responses to the stranger's entrance with responses in the whole of subepisode 3a, and later, a comparison of initial responses to the stranger's approach with responses in the whole of subepisode 3c.

Looking

Two repeated measures analyses of variance for unequal samples were undertaken, one for looking at the stranger, the other for looking at the mother. In both, scores from the four separate samples and for three subepisodes of episode 3 were represented. The overall samples effect was not significant for either analysis. The subepisode effect was clearly significant in each case, however. For the stranger analysis $F = 9.438$, $df\ 2/204$, $p < .001$, and for the mother analysis $F = 9.043$, $df\ 2/204$, $p < .001$. There was a significant samples × subepisodes interaction for looking at the mother $(F = 2.285$, $df\ 6/204$, $p < .05)$ because sample III looked at the mother somewhat more often in subepisode 3a—although this affects none of the findings reported below.

Table 2 compares the mean frequencies with which the infants looked at the stranger and at the mother in the three subepisodes of episode 3. It is clear that throughout episode 3 infants looked at the stranger more often than at the mother. The difference was large in subepisode 3a $(t = 12.1$, $df\ 105$, $p = .001)$, during which the stranger entered and both adults sat quietly. This difference cannot be attributed entirely to the fact that the entrance of the stranger attracted a look from all; throughout the rest of subepisode 3a also the babies looked more frequently at the stranger than at the mother. Indeed, the differential in frequency underestimates the difference in the total amount of looking,

TABLE 2. Mean Frequency of Looking at Stranger and at Mother in Episode 3

Figure Looked at	Subepisode 3a, Stranger Silent	Subepisode 3b, Stranger Conversing	Subepisode 3c, Stranger Intervening	Whole Episode
Stranger	4.2	3.2	3.8	11.2
Mother	1.7	2.0	1.2	4.9

since the initial look at the stranger was prolonged in the majority of cases, whereas the looks at the mother tended to be fairly brief.

The difference narrowed substantially during subepisode 3b when the stranger and the mother conversed and indeed behaved in essentially the same way. Although some babies were described as looking back and forth as if they were following a tennis match, there were still significantly more looks at the stranger than at the mother $(t = 5.6, df\ 105, p < .001)$. During subepisode 3c, as might be expected, the now interventive stranger captured most of the infants' interest $(t = 12.0, df\ 105, p < .001)$. Not only did the baby look at the stranger, he also looked at the toy she was holding and manipulating, and he looked at the mother infrequently. Nearly half the looks given to the mother during subepisode 3c occurred at the very end of the episode when the mother was attempting to leave the room unobtrusively, which suggests that the babies were alert to her whereabouts even though their visual attention had been engaged elsewhere.

In summary, even though babies tended to look at the figure whose actions were most salient (stranger entering, stranger approaching and manipulating toys, mother leaving), they still looked more frequently at the stranger than at the mother when both were equivalent in the saliency of their behavior—that is, during most of subepisode 3a and all of 3b.

Gaze Aversion

Babies did not avert their gaze from the mother during episode 3; their looks were invariably terminated by looking either at the stranger, at the toys, or at some other salient feature of the environment, rather than by merely looking away. Consequently this analysis deals only with averting the gaze from the stranger. Table 3 shows that 68 infants averted their gaze at least once in the whole of episode 3. Whereas 32 infants averted their gaze to terminate their initial look at the entering stranger, 19 did so later in subepisode 3a. Clearly fewer infants showed their first gaze aversion in 3b or 3c.

We have already mentioned the coy pattern of gaze aversion. This occurred altogether in thirteen infants—only when the stranger was at a distance and never when the stranger approached in 3c. Other instances of gaze aversion tended to fall into two patterns, but with so many instances intermediate between the extremes that it seemed fruitless to attempt to classify all instances. Therefore, these two patterns are cited wholly for their descriptive interest. One pattern

TABLE 3. Infants Who Show a Behavior for the First Time in
Subepisodes 3a, 3b, and 3c

Behavior	Subepisode 3a, Stranger Silent	Subepisode 3b, Stranger Conversing	Subepisode 3c, Stranger Intervening	Whole Episode
Gaze aversion	51	7	10	68
Smile at stranger	42	11	7	60
Smile at mother	25	7	7	39
Distress	14	5	5	24
Vocalization	46	19	2	67
Approach to or by mother	27[a]	15	5	47
Approach to stranger	8	2	9	19

[a]Includes those near mother when stranger entered.

consisted of glancing at the stranger only briefly, turning away, pausing briefly while not looking at anything in particular, and then returning to play, only to turn around for another look and another gaze aversion. The other pattern was the reverse; the baby took brief respite from a prolonged gaze at the stranger by suddenly but only briefly averting the gaze before another prolonged look. Because a substantial minority did not avert their gaze, we used incidence as the measure rather than frequency.

Smiling

Whereas only 19 babies smiled at the stranger at first sight, an additional 23 mobilized at least one smile during subepisode 3a, while the stranger was sitting silently (see Table 3). This smile, although delayed, occurred without any coaxing from the stranger. During subepisode 3b, while the stranger was conversing with the mother, an additional eleven babies smiled at her for the first time. Thus most babies who smiled at the stranger did so quite spontaneously. Only seven smiled for the first time in response to the stranger's initiation of interaction in subepisode 3c. All the smiles at the mother were unsolicited; most of the babies who smiled at her at any time did so in subepisode 3a.

Smiling was a much less frequent response than looking, both to the stranger and to the mother; indeed 31 infants (28%) did not smile at all. Therefore Table 4 lists the number of infants who smiled at the mother and at the stranger in each subepisode together with the total number of smiles in each, but does not cite mean frequencies. As the table indicates, more babies smiled at the stranger—60 (58%)—than at the mother—39 (37%)—throughout the whole of episode 3 ($x^2 = 10.25$, df 1, $p < .01$).[8] As in the case of looking, the dif-

[8]To avoid the effect of correlated responses, this and subsequent chi-squares omitted infants who smiled at both figures. Similarly, in the comparison of smiling and crying, infants who both cried and smiled were omitted.

ferential was large during subepisode 3a ($x^2 = 7.41$, 1 df, $p < .01$), but narrowed during subepisode 3b, during which more infants still smiled at the stranger than at the mother, although not significantly so. When the stranger attempted to engage the baby in play in subepisode 3c, the differential increased again, almost three times as many infants smiled at the stranger as at the mother ($x^2 = 9.8$, 1 df, $p < .01$). The total number of smiles given by all babies who smiled at mother or stranger follows a similar pattern.

Although smiling took place least frequently in subepisode 3b when the mother and stranger were in interaction with each other, it is notable that fewer babies smiled when the stranger approached in subepisode 3c than had done so when she first entered the room, even though there had been some opportunity to habituate to her before she approached.

Although both incidence and frequency of smiling favored the stranger, intensity of smiling favored the mother, as may be seen in Table 5. A substantial proportion of the smiles given to the stranger (44%) were described as "little smiles" or "half-smiles," but only 14% of the smiles directed toward the mother were so described.

It is of interest to compare episodes 2, 3, and 4 in regard to infant smiling. In episode 2, when the babies were alone with their mothers, only 65 (61%) smiled at the mother. In episode 3, 75 babies (71%) smiled—37% at the mother, 58% at the stranger, and 26% at both figures. In episode 4, even though half the babies were distressed at the mother's absence, 51 (48%) smiled at the stranger.

Crying

Twenty-four infants (23%) cried, fussed, or made a cryface at some time during episode 3, although, as reported earlier, only four did so when the stranger first entered. Ten more did so during the rest of subepisode 3a. Sixteen cried in 3b, five for the first time. Fourteen cried in 3c, five for the first time (see Table 3). No infant cried throughout episode 3, however.

Thus although the minority who expressed distress is not negligible, it is clearly smaller than the number of infants who smiled at the stranger at some point in episode 3 ($x^2 = 18.0$; 1 df, $p < .001$). Six infants both smiled at the stranger and cried at some time during the episode. Only 28 infants (26%) neither smiled at the stranger nor cried.

Vocalization

Whereas more babies smiled in episode 3 when the stranger was present than in episode 2 when the baby was alone with his mother, they vocalized less in episode 3 than previously ($t = 3.82$, $p < .001$). Ainsworth, Blehar, and Wall (in preparation) concluded from these and other cross-episode comparisons that

TABLE 4. Incidence and Frequency of Smiling

Figure Smiled at	Subepisode 3a, Stranger Silent		Subepisode 3b, Stranger Conversing		Subepisode 3c, Stranger Intervening		Whole Episode	
	Inci-dence	Fre-quency	Inci-dence	Fre-quency	Inci-dence	Fre-quency	Inci-dence	Fre-quency
Stranger	42	87	23	36	29	43	60	166
Mother	25	38	15	21	11	12	39	71
Both	14	—	7	—	7	—	28	—

TABLE 5. Intensity of Smiling at Stranger and Mother[a]

Figure Smiled at	Number of Big Smiles	Number of Full Smiles	Number of Little Smiles	Total Number of Smiles
Stranger	22	71	73	166
Mother	12	49	10	71
Totals	34	120	83	237

[a] $\chi^2 = 26.08, df = 4, p < .001$.

TABLE 6. Incidence and Frequency of Vocalization

Figure Vocalized to	Subepisode 3a, Stranger Silent		Subepisode 3b, Stranger Conversing		Subepisode 3c, Stranger Intervening		Whole Episode	
	Inci-dence	Fre-quency	Inci-dence	Fre-quency	Inci-dence	Fre-quency	Inci-dence	Fre-quency
Stranger	19	25	14	14	8	8	30	47
Mother	18	25	14	15	4	4	23	44
All vocali-zations	46	99	44	92	28	34	67	225

the presence of the stranger tends to suppress vocalization.

Table 6 shows both the incidence and frequency of vocalizations to the stranger and to the mother. The total incidence and frequency includes not only these directed vocalizations but also vocalizations that were apparently not so directed. It is clear from Table 6 that approximately the same number of babies vocalize to the stranger as to the mother, and they do so with approximately equal frequency. It also may be seen that vocalization is more likely to occur in subepisodes 3a and 3b, when the stranger is at a distance, than in 3c, when she approaches closely and attempts to initiate interaction.

Close Proximity to the Mother

As shown in Table 7, 47 infants (44%) achieved close proximity to the mother at some time during episode 3. Ten babies were already close to her when the episode began, having approached toward the end of episode 2. Thirty-six (34%) spontaneously approached the mother at some time during episode 3, including four who had begun the episode near to her but had subsequently moved away. Five babies elicited an approach from the mother through crying. Most of the approaches to the mother occurred in subepisode 3a or 3b, with only six infants approaching the mother in 3c, presumably in response to the stranger's approach. We interpret approaches to the mother in this episode as constituting a retreat to the mother coincident with withdrawal from the stranger. Few infants seemed to be seeking mere friendly interaction with the mother; only two approached her offering a toy. In eighteen cases the baby cried before going to the mother. In nine instances the baby had just previously approached the stranger, then hurried back to the mother.

Once close to the mother, 32 infants made contact with her; 16 clambered up, clutched, or clung to her (of these, 3 were picked up); 16 merely held onto her knee or touched her; only 15 sat or stood near her without actually achieving contact. Of the 47 who achieved close proximity to the mother by whatever means, 35 turned to look at the stranger, usually then remaining oriented toward the stranger. Only five smiled at the stranger after having reached the mother. Therefore, even though not all of these infants seemed distressed or obviously anxious, they seemed to be retreating from the stranger to the mother rather than merely approaching the mother.

Once having gained close proximity to or contact with the mother, a baby did not necessarily remain by her side. Twenty-two babies voluntarily left their mothers at some time during the episode, two doing so more than once. Eight did so in subepisode 3a, eight in 3b, and nine did so in 3c in response to the stranger's enticement. In addition, the mothers of five babies took them back to the toys.

Approach to the Stranger

Only ten babies (9%) spontaneously approached the stranger in subepisode 3a or 3b (i.e., before the stranger specifically invited an approach). Five of these approaches were full and five partial. Nine of the babies retreated to mother immediately afterward, as though they had become somewhat alarmed at their own temerity in approaching the stranger and needed to return to mother for reassurance. Fourteen babies (13%) approached the stranger partially or fully in subepisode 3c, nine for the first time. Of the nineteen infants (18%) who approached the stranger in the whole of episode 3, all but two belonged to the group that retreated to the mother. Thus a tendency to retreat to the mother when feeling uneasy and a tendency actively to approach an unfamiliar adult are not mutually exclusive.

TABLE 7. Number of Infants Who Achieved Close Proximity to the
Mother at Least Once in Episode 3

Mode of Achieving Close Proximity	Subepisode 3a, Stranger Silent	Subepisode 3b, Stranger Conversing	Subepisode 3c, Stranger Intervening	Whole Episode
Already close when episode begins	10	—	—	10
Baby approaches mother	17	20	6	36
Mother approaches baby	1	3	2	5
Close in proximity in subepisode	28	33[a]	28[a]	47

[a]Includes infants who achieved close proximity in the previous subepisode and remained there.

Approach behavior directed toward the stranger tended to be hesitant when it appeared at all. Partial approaches were terminated abruptly. No infant approached his mother in a hesitant fashion or terminated a partial approach in the same abrupt manner. Furthermore, only three infants touched the stranger after approaching her, in contrast to the 32 who made contact with the mother after a full approach.

Whereas 82% of the sample made no approach to the stranger in episode 3, a similar proportion (80%) spontaneously approached the toys in episode 2. It is clear that an unfamiliar person and an unfamiliar array of toys offer very different instigations to approach behavior. As Figure 2 indicates, the most common response after having been put down at the beginning of episode 2 was to move toward the toys with relatively little delay. Twenty-six percent made a beeline for the toys immediately, whereas the great majority (76%) began to move toward the toys within one minute. Only two babies explored other aspects of the room first, and a few (13%) made a trip to the mother first. Only 20% failed to approach within the first 2 minutes of the episode, before the mother was signaled to intervene. Furthermore, within the first 2 minutes of episode 2, 78% had actually touched or, more usually, picked up a toy, whereas within the first 2 minutes of episode 3, only 3% touched the stranger.

Initial Response to the Stranger's Approach

The first time the stranger especially drew the baby's attention to herself was by entering the room; the second time was when she initiated overtures to the baby at the beginning of subepisode 3c. For convenience, this initiative is called "approach," although it was much more complex than a mere locomotor approach.

Nine infants cried or made a cryface in response to the stranger's approach, slightly but not significantly more than those who did so in initial response to

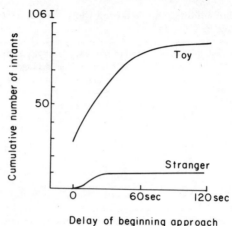

FIGURE 2.   Latencies of approach to toys in episode 2 and approach to the stranger in episode 3.

her entrance.[9] Fourteen (13%) smiled when the stranger approached, slightly but not significantly fewer than the number who had smiled when she entered. The great majority (78%) responded to the approach with facial expressions intermediate between the cryface and the smile. Twenty-two (21%) averted their gaze initially when the stranger approached them—somewhat fewer than the 31 (29%) who did so when she first entered.

Later Response to the Stranger's Approach

A description of responses to the stranger's approach and attempts to engage the baby in interaction is complicated by the mobility of the babies and their consequently varying locations relative to the mother. To facilitate this account a diagram is offered (Figure 3). Two groups of infants are considered separately: those who were near the toys and those who were in close proximity to the mother when the stranger approached. Figure 3 reveals that of the 85 infants who were near the toys, only 9 withdrew from the stranger. Thus although few infants had been willing to take the initiative in approaching the stranger themselves, the majority were willing to have the stranger approach them.

Those who were in close proximity to the mother but not in contact with her, as well as those who sought mere proximity when the stranger approached, either accepted the stranger's overtures from that place of vantage or approached

---

[9]All but two of the infants who cried when the stranger approached were in either sample I or sample II. Although the numbers are too small for a test of significance of intersample differences, our hunch is that the sudden initiation of interaction across a distance by the strangers in the first two samples was more disturbing than the interaction initiated when close at hand by the strangers in samples III and IV. One of us (I.B.) is currently investigating this hypothesis.

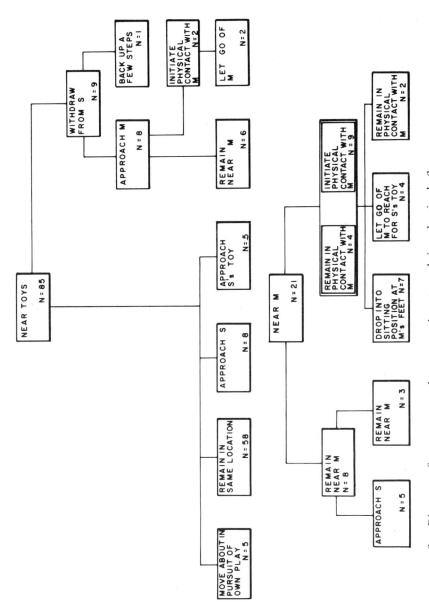

FIGURE 3. Diagram of responses to the stranger's approach in subepisode 3c.

the stranger after spending a short time near mother. Most of those who were in contact with the mother at the beginning of 3c, as well as those who then sought contact with her, were eventually willing to break the contact as the stranger entertained them. At the end of episode 3 only two infants remained in physical contact with their mothers.

Response to Stranger's Offer of a Toy

When the stranger attempted to engage the infant in play in subepisode 3c, she tried to entice him with a second toy if the baby did not accept the first one she offered. The number of toys offered by the stranger ranged from one to four $(\overline{X} = 2.4)$. Table 8 displays the range of responses the infants made. In the first column the infants are listed in accordance with their most positive response to the stranger's offer of toys, whether it was made to the first toy offered or a later one. The second column takes into account all infants who showed a particular negative or tentative response at least once during subepisode 3c. These data are presented solely to underline the frequency of mild negative and tentative responses that are necessarily obscured in identifying for each infant the most positive response. It may be noted that the total of the first column is only 87. In addition, and not included in the table, there were eighteen infants who merely watched the stranger and made no active response toward or away from her or from her toy, and one infant who was very upset and took no interest whatsoever in what the stranger was doing with her toy.

Thus outright rejection of the stranger's toy occurred but rarely. Mild snubs were observed more frequently, although in all but five infants they later gave way to a tentative or positive response. Twenty-four infants responded no more than tentatively to the stranger's offer, but as the second column indicates, tentative responses were not infrequently shown by infants who later responded more positively. Indeed, a few infants followed an early positive response with tentative or even negative responses. When making a tentative response a baby seemed to be torn between a desire to take the toy and reluctance to do so. Slightly more than half the sample responded positively to the stranger's offer, with or without initial reluctance, and 29 played with the stranger's toy at least briefly. Only seven responded to the extent of engaging in interactive play with the stranger; undoubtedly more would have done so had not subepisode 3c terminated after 1 minute.

Conflict Between Behavioral Systems

It is our belief that most of our sample of one-year-olds showed behavioral signs of conflict between behavioral systems simultaneously activated by the stranger—a fear-wariness system on the one hand and an affiliative system on the other hand. In general, the behaviors suggesting that the fear-wariness system has been activated are those expressive of distress and those involving

TABLE 8. Responses to the Stranger's Offer of a Toy

Type of Response	Most Positive Response Shown by an Infant	Number of Infants Showing Response at Least Once
Negative responses		
Actively rejects toy	2 ⎱ 7	5
Mildly snubs toy	5 ⎰	23
Tentative responses		
Intention movements toward toy	7 ⎱	12
Approach or reach toy only	7 ⎬ 24	17
Touch toy only	10 ⎰	10
Positive responses		
Picks up toy only	20 ⎱	
Picks up and plays briefly with toy	29 ⎬ 56	
Interactive play with stranger	7 ⎰	

avoidance of the stranger. These may also express the simultaneous activation of the attachment system in that they involve seeking closer proximity to or contact with the mother. Specifically, the following behaviors are judged to indicate fear or wariness: crying, locomotor withdrawal from the stranger, leaning away from the stranger, gaze aversion, retreat to the mother, reaching for the mother, and rejecting or snubbing of the toy offered by the stranger. In addition, we suggest that mildly negative facial expressions, such as "sober," "sobering," "serious," and "apprehensive," are likely to accompany some degree of wariness, although since intermediate facial expressions were not systematically described by our observers, these were used only when repeatedly mentioned for a given baby for the analysis reported below.

In general, the behaviors suggesting that affiliative behavior has been activated by the stranger are those expressing some degree of willingness to enter into interaction with her, whether across a distance or in closer proximity. Specifically, the following behaviors were judged to be affiliative: smiling or vocalizing to the stranger, approaching her, touching her, offering her a toy, and accepting the toy she offered, whether by merely picking it up, playing with it, or playing with the stranger. In addition, if repeatedly mentioned, mildly positive facial expression was judged to be affiliative, such as an "open" or "pleasant" expression.

Of particular interest are behaviors or sequences of behaviors combining both wary and affiliative elements. One of these is the coy response, exhibited by thirteen infants, in which there was both gaze aversion and smiling. Another response in this category is the approach to and then immediate retreat from the stranger, shown by ten infants. Akin to this response is the partial approach—an approach that is begun and abruptly inhibited—and the intention movement in which the tendency to approach is shown by bodily movement and orientation that may not go as far as locomotion toward the stranger. Finally, all the tentative responses to the toy the stranger offered imply a conflict—not only the intention movements but also the partial approach to or reach for the toy with termination of the movement before the toy can be grasped, or the tentative touching of the toy with subsequent withdrawal of the hand.

As a descriptive enterprise only, the infants were sorted into seven groups in accordance with the extent to which they showed behavioral signs of fear-wariness and of affiliative tendency toward the stranger. In this sorting we considered not only frequency and intensity of behavior but also the type of behavior (e.g., considering approach more strongly affiliative than a smile across a distance). The results of this sorting appear in Table 9.

Twelve infants (11%) showed only fearful or wary behavior with no affiliative behavior toward the stranger whatsoever, whereas only four showed affiliative behavior with no sign of wariness. The great majority (85%) gave some indication that both wariness and affiliative tendencies had been activated by the stranger. We do not wish to generalize the findings summarized in Table 9 about the balance of fear-wariness versus affiliation that a stranger may activate in one-year-olds: the sorting was admittedly configurational and lacking in any precise way of estimating strength of either tendency, and surely the laboratory situation that was utilized affected the extent to which both behavioral systems were activated. The main finding we wish to stress is that the majority of infants responded to the stranger with both affiliative and wary behavior.

DISCUSSION

As implied in the introduction, we propose to discuss our findings in the light of a hypothesized interplay among four major behavioral systems that seem especially likely to have been activated in the strange situation. The final analysis in the Results section has already launched this discussion. The general background of our hypothesis lies in attachment theory as formulated by Bowlby (1969, 1973) and Ainsworth (1967, 1972, 1973; Ainsworth & Bell, 1970) and is not repeated here, although aspects relevant to the major points of discussion are presented. Let us consider each of the four systems separately at first.

The Fear-Wariness System

The fear-wariness system consists primarily of behaviors that serve the person in escaping from or avoiding an alarming stimulus object or situation. It includes, however, signaling behaviors, such as crying or calling, that attract a protector to approach. It also includes behaviors that serve to maintain distance between the person and an alarming stimulus. It is closely linked to the attach-

TABLE 9. Sorting of Infants According to Degree of Fear-Wariness and
Affiliative Tendency Toward Stranger

Degree of Fear-Wariness versus Affiliative Tendency	N
Fearful or wary only, no affiliative behavior	12
Mostly fearful or wary, some affiliative behavior	13
More wary than affiliative behavior	10
Equal amounts of wary and affiliative behavior	39
More affiliative than wary behavior	10
Mostly affiliative, some wary behavior	18
Affiliative only, no wary behavior	4
Total	106

ment system, insofar as both systems tend to be activated by an alarming stimulus, and since escape or avoidance behaviors tend not only to be away from the alarming stimulus but also toward an attachment figure, and signaling behaviors also promote proximity to such a figure.

Rheingold and Eckerman (in press) argue that fear of strangers may not be normative during the second half of the first year because crying or approaching the mother is infrequent when the infant is confronted by a stranger. Distress and escape reactions, however, may be viewed as anchoring one end of a behavioral continuum. Less extreme, but on the same continuum, are the variety of responses mentioned earlier (gaze aversion, intention movements, etc.); such responses include elements of wary behavior.

Wary behavior, in distinction to overt distress and locomotor avoidance, operates to maintain distance between the infant and a stranger and to inhibit or work against other systems (affiliative and exploratory) that might decrease that distance. Rheingold and Eckerman (in press) omitted from their behavioral coding the behaviors that we would consider to be wary behaviors. Our findings confirm theirs that distress is a relatively infrequent reaction toward strangers in infants nearing the end of the first year, but nevertheless they offer ample evidence that the stranger activates the fear-wariness system in a majority of one-year-olds.

Whereas we think of "fear" as referring to the more intense portion of a behavioral continuum and "wariness" to the less intense portion, Bronson (1972) and Freedman (1965) used the term "wariness" to comprehend the entire range of behaviors from crying and explicit avoidance to mere gaze aversion. Bronson made his distinction between fear and wariness not in terms of behavioral intensity but on ontogenetic and etiological grounds. While acknowledging his distinctions as having substantial theoretical interest, we can see no behavioral basis for distinguishing between fearful and wary behavior as Bronson defines them; hence we treat them as belonging to the same behavioral system.

Schaffer, Greenwood, and Parry (1972) used the term "wariness" to refer to the behavior shown by infants of 8 months and older between the presentation of a novel object and reaching for it; these infants engaged in prolonged visual inspection of the object and inhibited other activity. Younger infants, in contrast, reached for the object as soon as it was presented. Prolonged visual inspection with inhibition of activity describes the initial response of most of our infants to the stranger's entrance at the beginning of episode 3. Furthermore, other behaviors that we have classed as wary have the same implication of inhibition of activity—partial approaches abruptly terminated, intention movements, and tentative responses to the stranger's offer of a toy that also involve inhibited approaching, reaching, or grasping. Thus although we did not include prolonged gazing as a behavioral indication of wariness in the analysis shown in Table 9, we believe a case could be made for doing so, even though some infants smiled in the course of prolonged gazing. Wariness in Schaffer's sense implies a period of alertness during which there is the potential for various subsequent responses, presumably depending on how the infant processes the information he obtains from his visual inspection. As a result of this inspection, the novel object or person may be perceived as alarming and the child may withdraw or signal distress; or it may be perceived as harmless but interesting and he may approach and explore it or interact with it; or he may continue in a state of wary alertness, continuing to inhibit interaction; or, indeed, it may be perceived as harmless but insufficiently interesting and he may turn back to other activities that were interrupted by the stimulus object in question. Some may argue that this period of alert inhibition of activity does not belong to the same behavioral system as overt distress and avoidance behavior, but to us it seems well justified to class it as "wary." Furthermore, the implications of caution in any definition of wariness link it to fear.

Gaze aversion implies avoidance of interaction. As Hutt and Ounsted (1970) suggested, "failure to make eye contact has important inhibitory effects upon social interaction." Gaze aversion reduces or cuts off the opportunity to interact, at least temporarily. Hutt and Ounsted also suggest that gaze fixation signifies a readiness for interaction. Did the prolonged looking at the stranger shown commonly by infants in our sample imply such readiness for interaction? Not necessarily. It was our impression that prolonged looking rarely implied prolonged eye-to-eye contact. Indeed, it is likely that in most instances gaze aversion was aimed at terminating prolonged looking when eye-to-eye contact occurred. The strangers in our study did not watch the baby steadily; on the contrary, they were careful to avoid eye-to-eye contact if they sensed that it was disturbing to the infant.

At first glance it might seem that moving away from the stranger might imply intense activation of the fear-wariness system, but we do not believe that this is necessarily so. Since the mother was readily available in our situation, moving away from the stranger almost invariably implied approaching the mother. Among those who retreated to the mother were included almost all those few babies who approached the stranger. Their approach to the stranger would suggest that they were the least fearful in the sample, even though they also moved away from the stranger. This example, as well as other instances of the intermingling or alternation of fearful or wary behavior with behaviors identified with other systems, supports our main thesis that response to a stranger must be viewed as a resultant of the activation and interaction of several behavioral systems.

The Exploratory System

Episode 2 of the strange situation was devised specifically to activate exploratory behavior; indeed, nearly all infants explored the toys, most of them quite actively. It seems reasonable that the toys, still present in episode 3, might continue to elicit exploratory behavior, competing with the stranger (and the mother) for the baby's interest. Ainsworth, Bell, and Stayton (1971) reported, however, that interest in the stranger tended strongly to override exploration of the toys in episode 3, even though a minority of infants maintained such behavior fairly actively. There remains the question of whether the exploratory system is implicated in the baby's interest in the stranger or whether only the fear-wariness and affiliative systems are involved.

It has been generally assumed (e.g., Hebb, 1946; Schaffer, 1966; Bowlby, 1973) that a strange person belongs to the general class of strange or unfamiliar stimulus configurations. It has also been generally accepted (e.g., Hebb, 1946) that an unfamiliar stimulus object may evoke either fear or exploratory behavior. Bowlby's (1973) account, as well as a number of earlier ones, proposes that the ready availability of an attachment figure may support exploration, whereas its absence strengthens the likelihood of fear behavior. Furthermore, Hebb and others have suggested that the degree of discrepancy between the unfamiliar object and familiar objects with which it shares some common elements determines the likelihood of fear rather than exploratory behavior. Nonetheless, neither existing theory nor empirical findings to date offer any clear basis for predicting whether a "discrepant" stimulus of this type will activate avoidance or approach and manipulation.

Another issue in the response to strangeness is whether a strange person is merely one more unfamiliar object, or whether there is a distinction to be made in the infant's response to strange persons and unfamiliar inanimate objects. Like Eckerman and Rheingold (1974), we found that few infants spontaneously approached the stranger, very few touched her, and none explored her person, whereas nearly all infants spontaneously approached the toys and manipulated them. Furthermore, in our strange situation the presence of the stranger overrode exploration of the toys; thus the amount of exploratory behavior sharply declined after she entered (Ainsworth & Bell, 1970). Clearly the stranger is not treated just like another unfamiliar object. Moreover, the stranger is bigger than a toy, and she is capable of moving about on her own initiative, hence is probably perceived by even a one-year-old as not under his direct control. It is features such as this, in addition to mere degree of unfamiliarity, that must enter in as determiners of whether the stranger will activate fear or wariness or approach and exploration.

Furthermore, it is by no means clear that the "positive" behavior likely to be activated by the stranger is exploratory behavior. Indeed, it is more plausible to interpret most of it as affiliative behavior. This does not imply that a baby never explores an unfamiliar person. In the familiar environment of the home, infants in our longitudinal study sometimes touched and manipulated the visitor's pen, notebook, clothing, or jewelry. But we rarely observed a baby exploring the face or body of an unfamiliar person, even the home visitor to whom he had become habituated.

It is reasonable to suppose that the exploratory system was to some extent activated by the stranger's offer of a toy, especially if the baby did in fact accept it and play with it. Nevertheless the wariness that many babies displayed when faced by this offer (as shown by their negative or tentative responses to it) suggests that the stranger's toy was somehow perceived as an extension of the stranger. Thus wariness often tended to inhibit exploratory tendencies in subepisode 3c, although in some babies affiliative and exploratory tendencies combined were strong enough to override wariness.

Is looking at the stranger a form of exploration? All infants looked at her when she entered. More looks were directed to her than to the mother when both were present, and (as Ainsworth & Bell, 1970, reported) more looks were directed to her than to objects in the still relatively unfamiliar physical environment. A majority of infants subjected the stranger to prolonged visual scrutiny. Bowlby (1969) regarded looking as an orienting behavior. Looking may be implicated in many different behavioral systems. In the absence of concomitant behaviors that may help identify the system or systems that have been activated, looking has ambiguous significance. Whether looking implicates the attachment, fear-wariness, affiliative, or exploratory system or some combination of these is impossible to ascertain from the mere fact of looking. During prolonged looking with concomitant inhibition of action, one might suppose that looking is playing an exploratory role; but if so, it is a cautious exploration while maintaining distance—exploration (or appraisal) in the service of wariness.

The Attachment System

Attachment behavior was activated in a substantial minority of the infants in our sample, nearly half of them achieving close proximity to the mother at some time during the stranger-present episode, some through distress signals, more through active approach. That proximity-seeking behavior was activated by alarm rather than merely by a desire to interact with the mother was suggested by the behavior of the babies after they achieved proximity; most of them turned to face the stranger. It was as though the fear-wariness system had been reduced in intensity of activation through proximity to the attachment figure, and the baby could then continue to engage in the wary exploration implicit in frequent or prolonged looking at the stranger.

We have already mentioned that nearly all infants who spontaneously approached the stranger immediately retreated to the mother after their adventurous excursion, two repeating the approach and withdrawal several times. One of us (I.B.) who played the role of unfamiliar playmate in a play situation (Main, 1973) observed that infants who came very close to her in the course of interaction with her might then rush back suddenly to the mother, as though alarmed that they had been so intimate with the stranger. And, of course, Morgan and Ricciuti (1969), Bronson (1972), and others have noted that infants responded more positively and less negatively to a stranger when held by the mother than when several feet away from her.

What of the larger proportion of the sample who did not seek proximity to the attachment figure? It could well be that for most of these one-year-olds, who were near the toys, the mother was close enough to prevent activation of the fear-wariness system at a high level of intensity, especially since they were free to move toward her if they wished. Nevertheless, signs of wariness or conflict between wary and affiliative tendencies directed toward the stranger were plentiful enough to indicate that the mother's presence did not wholly prevent the activation of the fear-wariness system. Furthermore, it is probable that some infants' experience with their mothers may have fostered distrust of her responsiveness; thus the attachment system, even though activated, does not result in proximity seeking because of expected rebuff (Ainsworth & Bell, 1970; Ainsworth, Bell, & Stayton, 1971). This possibility adds further complexity to the mélange of conflicting behavioral tendencies. We make no further discussion of individual differences because enough information is available for only a minority of subjects in the total sample to enable us to hazard explanations of the behavior of an individual infant.

The Affiliative System

The findings of this study show that the stranger activated in most infants some degree of affiliative response. When the stranger was at a distance and initiated no interaction, a majority of babies nevertheless smiled at her at least once. On the other hand, few infants spontaneously approached her, and even fewer touched her. Although two infants approached her with a toy, none actively and unequivocally invited her to play.

When the stranger herself took the initiative in inviting the baby to play, more than half were able to respond in some positive degree to her overtures, either accepting the toy she offered or showing by intention movements or other tentative responses that they were tempted to do so. Except for the two infants who remained in contact with the mother, the infants who had retreated to the mother when the stranger approached eventually responded to the stranger and let go of the mother. To be sure, the stranger invited them to approach through the intermediary of a toy; but since the toy clearly seemed to be an extension of the stranger, the eventual approach to the toy implied some degree of acceptance of the stranger.

Smiling as an expression of affiliative tendency deserves some comment. Attachment theory classifies smiling when it first emerges as a precursor attachment behavior that is proximity promoting in that it attracts conspecifics to approach and to remain close. It has been assumed that smiling becomes discriminating and directed more specifically toward familiar figures than toward unfamiliar ones. Both the present study and the longitudinal study reported by Stayton, Ainsworth, and Main (1973) suggest that smiling becomes differential to the mother in regard to its intensity, but there is no unequivocal evidence either in these studies or in the literature generally that smiling is differential to attachment figures in regard to frequency.[10] Although it is reasonable to conclude that smiling remains an attachment behavior as differentiation between familiar and unfamiliar figures proceeds, it seems equally reasonable to think that it also serves as an affiliative behavior in response to relatively unfamiliar conspecifics.

Smiling as an affiliative behavior—that is, directed at persons other than attachment figures—may still have the same "predictable outcome" that it did in the early months, namely, to attract people to come and to remain closer. Nevertheless, smiling may be used in contexts that imply that it is a propitiatory behavior, part of the fear-wariness system, much like the sexual presenting posture of nonhuman primates. In such a context it signals affiliative intent as a means of eliciting benign behavior. It is our hypothesis that at least some of the smiles of our one-year-olds were propitiatory rather than invitations to closer interaction. In support of this hypothesis we note that more babies smiled in subepisode 3a when the stranger's silent immobility made it difficult for the in-

---

[10]Investigators such as Ambrose (1961) and Gewirtz (1965) found a peak in the frequency of smiling to an unfamiliar experimenter somewhere between 3 and 5 months, earlier for family-reared than for institution-reared babies. The subsequent decline in smiling to an unfamiliar person is generally attributed to the infant's having learned to discriminate between persons and to smile more frequently to the mother than to others. There is no report in the literature, however, of direct comparisons of frequency of smiling to the mother and to unfamiliar persons. Furthermore, analyses of our longitudinal data yield no evidence of differential frequency of smiling to the mother versus a relatively unfamiliar visitor at any time during the first year, either in enter-room situations (Stayton, Ainsworth, & Main, 1973) or in face-to-face situations (Blehar, Lieberman, & Ainsworth, in preparation).

fant to guess what she might do next. Moreover, some babies smiled while in the middle of a prolonged look, which otherwise suggests Schaffer's wary scrutiny, and the coy smiles given by some babies seem to be resultant of conflicting affiliative and wary tendencies. Smiling, therefore, seems to have multiple functions and seems to be tied into at least three of the four behavioral systems with which we are concerned—the attachment, affiliative, and wary systems. Lest anyone think it far-fetched to hypothesize thus, approach provides a clearcut example of a behavior with multiple functions. Approach to an attachment figure is by definition an attachment behavior, since it increases proximity to that figure. Approach to an attachment figure may at the same time serve the fear-wariness system. Usually such an approach simultaneously increases distance from an alarming feature of the situation. Sometimes, however, it is necessary to go closer to the alarming object to reach the attachment figure, and in such instances there is conflict between two behaviors, which have both been activated by alarm. Approach is often an element in exploratory behavior, and it also may be an element in affiliative behavior.

Interplay Among Behavioral Systems

The strange situation was specifically designed to activate a variety of behavioral systems. A novel array of toys was expected to activate exploratory behavior. A sequence of stresses, including the entrance of the stranger in episode 3, was expected to activate both fear behavior and attachment behavior, at least in some children. And yet since the behavior of the stranger was intended to be minimally threatening and optimally friendly, it might be expected to activate affiliative behavior. Thus the situation was implicitly intended to facilitate both conflict and interplay among these four behavioral systems, and to judge by the present findings, it succeeded.

We have already provided some indication of what we mean by interplay among behavioral systems in the presentation and discussion of findings. To be more explicit, let us mention three main ways in which interplay can be viewed. First, a single behavior may serve two or more systems that are not in themselves conflicting. Thus moving away from the stranger to the mother is at the same time a fearful or wary behavior and an attachment behavior. Second, and perhaps more interesting from the viewpoint of our thesis, are the behaviors that seem to reflect a conflict between affiliative tendencies and wariness. There is the coy response with simultaneous gaze aversion and smiling that resembles the "flirting response" observed in many cultures by Eibl-Eibesfeldt (1970). Not only does it indicate a conflict between affiliative and wary behavior, it also constitutes a resultant of both tendencies. Other behaviors that reflect a similar conflict are intention movements, tentative responses to the stranger's toy, and the like.

Third, the interplay among systems may be manifested sequentially. The

162   Inge Bretherton and Mary D. Salter Ainsworth

most striking example of this is the approach to the stranger followed immediately by retreat to the mother, which a few children repeated, providing a classic illustration of an approach-avoidance conflict. With some babies affiliative behavior seemed to override wariness as long as the stranger was at a distance, only to be overridden by wary behavior and the attachment behavior with which it was often interlocked when the stranger approached. Even more common were the many ways in which wary behavior gave way to approach to the stranger as she enticed the baby with a toy.

Of course different situations would have a differential effect on the balance among these behavioral systems. That affiliative behavior was as conspicuous as it was in our situation, we attribute to three main conditions—the presence of the mother, the mobility of the infant, and the sensitive and contingent behavior of the stranger. Fearful and wary behavior may have been as frequent as it was because all strangers were totally unfamiliar and were confronted in an unfamiliar situation. Equally obviously, there were great individual differences among infants. To be able to trace the dynamics of interplay among different behavioral systems in much more detail than we have done would involve a large number of individual case studies, which optimally would include relevant information about individual development and history of experiences, instead of focusing on behavior in a very brief laboratory situation.

References

Ainsworth, M. D. S. *Infancy in Uganda: Infant care and the growth of love.* Baltimore: Johns Hopkins University Press, 1967.

Ainsworth, M. D. S. Attachment and dependency: A comparison. In J. L. Gewirtz (Ed.), *Attachment and dependency.* Washington, D.C.: Winston, 1972. (Distributed by Wiley, New York.) Pp. 97–137.

Ainsworth, M. D. S. The development of infant–mother attachment. In B. M. Caldwell & H. N. Ricciuti (Eds.), *Review of child development research.* Vol. 3. Chicago: University of Chicago Press, 1973.

Ainsworth, M. D. S., & Bell, S. M. Attachment, exploration, and separation: Illustrated by the behavior of one-year-olds in a strange situation. *Child Development,* 1970, **41,** 49–67.

Ainsworth, M. D. S., Bell, S. M., & Stayton, D. J. Individual differences in strange-situation behavior of one-year-olds. In H. R. Schaffer (Ed.), *The origins of human social relations.* London and New York: Academic Press, 1971. Pp. 17–52.

Ainsworth, M. D. S., Blehar, M. P., & Wall, S. N. Responses of one-year-olds to the mother and to a stranger in a strange situation. Monograph in preparation.

Ainsworth, M. D. S., & Wittig, B. A. Attachment and exploratory behavior of one-year-olds in a strange situation. In B. M. Foss (Ed.), *Determinants of infant behaviour.* Vol. 4. London: Methuen; New York: Wiley, 1969. Pp. 111–136.

Ambrose, J. A. The development of the smiling response in early infancy. In B. M. Foss (Ed.), *Determinants of infant behaviour*. London: Methuen; New York: Wiley, 1961. Pp. 103–105.

Bell, S. M. The development of the concept of the object as related to infant–mother attachment. *Child Development*, 1970, **41**, 291–311.

Blehar, M. P., Lieberman, A., & Ainsworth, M. D. S. Responses of young infants to mother and to a stranger in face-to-face situations. In preparation.

Bowlby, J. *Attachment and loss*. Vol. 1. *Attachment*. London: Hogarth; New York: Basic Books, 1969.

Bowlby, J. *Attachment and loss*. Vol. 2. *Separation: Anxiety and anger*. London: Hogarth; New York: Basic Books, 1973.

Bronson, G. W. Infants' reactions to unfamiliar persons and novel objects. *Monographs of the Society for Research in Child Development*, 1973, **37** (3, Whole No. 148).

Eckerman, C. O., & Rheingold, H. L. Infants' exploratory responses to toys and people. *Developmental Psychology*, 1974, **10**, 255-259.

Eibl-Eibesfeldt, I. *Ethology: The biology of behavior*. New York: Holt, Rinehart & Winston, 1970.

Freedman, D. G. The infant's fear of strangers and the flight response. *Journal of Child Psychology and Psychiatry*, 1961, **2**, 24

Gewirtz, J. L. The course of infant smiling in four child-rearing environments in Israel. In B. M. Foss (Ed.) *Determinants of infant behaviour*. Vol. 3. London: Methuen; New York: Wiley, 1965. Pp. 205-248.

Grant, E. C. Human facial expression. *Man*, 1969, **4**, 525-536.

Hebb, D. O. On the nature of fear. *Psychological Review*, 1946, **53**, 259–276.

Hutt, C., & Ounsted, C. Gaze aversion and its significance in childhood autism. In S. J. Hutt & C. Hutt (Eds.), *Behaviour studies in psychiatry*. Oxford: Pergamon Press, 1970.

Lewis, M., & Brooks, J. Self, other and fear: The reaction of infants to people. Chapter 8; this volume.

Maccoby, E. E., & Feldman, S. Mother-attachment and stranger reactions. *Monographs of the Society for Research in Child Development*, 1972, **37**, 146.

Main, M. Exploration, play, and level of cognitive functioning as related to child-mother attachment. Unpublished doctoral disseration, Johns Hopkins University, 1973.

Morgan, G. A., & Ricciuti, H. N. Infants' responses to strangers during the first year. In B. M. Foss(Ed.), *Determinants of infant behaviour*. Vol. 4. London: Methuen; New York: Wiley, 1969.

Rheingold, H. L., & Eckerman, C. O. Fear of the stranger: A critical examination. In H. W. Reese (Ed.), *Advances of child development and behavior*. New York: Academic Press, in press.

Scarr, S., & Salapatek, P. Patterns of fear development during infancy. *Merrill-Palmer Quarterly*, 1970, **16**, 53–90.

Schaffer, H. R. The onset of fear of strangers and the incongruity hypothesis. *Journal of Child Psychology and Psychiatry*, 1966, **7**, 95–106.

Schaffer, H. R., & Emerson, P. E. The development of social attachments in infancy. *Monographs of The Society for Research in Child Development*, 1964, **29**, (3, Whole No. 94).

Schaffer, H. R., Greenwood, A., & Parry, M. H. The onset of wariness. *Child Development*, 1972, **43**, 165–175.

Spitz, R. A. Anxiety in infancy: A study of its manifestations in the first year of life. *International Journal of Psycho-Analysis*, 1950, **31**, 138–143.

Stayton, D. J., Ainsworth, M. D. S., & Main, M. B. The development of separation behavior in the first year of life: Protest, following and greeting. *Developmental Psychology*, 1973, **8**, 213–225.

Tennes, K. H., & Lampl, E. E. Stranger and separation anxiety in infancy. *Journal of Nervous and Mental Diseases*, 1964, **139**, 247–254.

CHAPTER 7

Fear of Strangers and Specificity of Attachment in Monkeys [1]

LEONARD A. ROSENBLUM AND
STEPHANIE ALPERT

Primate Behavior Laboratory, Downstate Medical Center

OVERVIEW

During the last decade a significant body of data has been developed concerning early attachment formation in the human infant. Much of this work focused on the initial attachments of infants during the first year of life; hence a basic theme of this work has been its consideration not only of cultural and other experiential influences but of the likely importance of basic biological factors in regulating the unfolding patterns of behavior that are observed. As a result of an unusual degree of interdisciplinary stimulation, research on nonhuman primates has provided a considerable amount of parallel evidence on attachment formation in monkeys and apes, thus nurturing further a number of hypotheses regarding the biological anlagen of human attachments.

Regardless of the mechanisms through which various theorists hypothesize the development of attachments, there is general agreement that patterns of behavior subsumed under the attachment concept are directed toward *particular* individuals rather than toward a *class* of conspecifics. Furthermore, although the behaviors encompassed may change in character with age (Yarrow, 1972; Bowlby, 1969; Ainsworth, 1972), they are directed toward a specific individual over a sustained portion of the infant's life (Schaffer & Emerson, 1964) and are not situation-specific (Ainsworth, 1972; Schaffer & Emerson, 1964; Cairns, 1972). Similarly, it is widely accepted that new attachments may be formed at any time in the life cycle; thus the range of observed behaviors will derive from the changing sensory, motor, and cognitive capacity of the organism, as well as from the pattern of prior life experiences of both members of

[1] This research was supported by Grants MH 15965 and MH 22640 from the National Institute of Mental Health, U.S. Public Health Service. The authors wish to thank Barbara Turner for her assistance in carrying out these studies.

the dyad. Nonetheless, early in life at least, the core of the attachment concept is "... the tendency of the young to seek the proximity of certain other members of the species" (Schaffer & Emerson, 1964, p. 6). This essential characteristic of the concept is held by most current theorists even those postulating a stimulus–response reinforcement process of attachment formation (Gewirtz, 1972). In evaluating attachment behaviors, some theorists (Gewirtz, 1972; Cairns, 1972) consider only the degree to which the presence of a specific individual regulates or controls a defined set of responses in the infant, regarding the use of negative behavioral indices of attachment as theoretically suspect. However, most workers consider the corollary to proximity-seeking of the attachment figure to be affective and behavioral disruption on separation from the attachment figure (e.g., Bowlby, 1969; Schaffer & Emerson, 1964; Ainsworth, 1969, 1972; Yarrow, 1972) and to varying degrees, relative avoidance of and/ or behavioral disturbance in the presence of strangers (Ainsworth, 1969, 1972; Morgan & Ricciuti, 1969; Tennes & Lampl, 1964; Yarrow, 1972).

As a concomitant cognitive development for the attainment of what Ainsworth (1972) refers to as "clear-cut attachments," theorists suggest that the infant must first develop a capacity to sustain some representation of the mother in the absence of immediate perceptual cues. In this context, several authors point to the pertinent work of Piaget and his colleagues on the progressive stages of sensory-motor development (e.g. Schaffer & Emerson, 1964; Yarrow, 1972; Ainsworth, 1972), and they stress that infants do not begin to show evidence of searching for lost or hidden objects until about the eighth month of life (Piaget, 1937; Décarie, 1965; Bell, 1970). It has been suggested that it is not until the beginning of the acquisition of this capacity to respond to objects as having "independent existence in time and space" or "object-permanence" that clear-cut attachments can occur. And indeed, Ainsworth (1972) indicates that such a capacity "... may be seen as a necessary condition for attachment" (p. 104).

Mother-Infant Attachment

A consideration of studies of the development of infant attachment and related phenomena in nonhuman primates offers some interesting corollaries to the human material. As a result of the stimulation provided by Harlow's artificial mother-surrogate work (Harlow & Zimmerman, 1959) we now have available both systematic and more qualitative observation of mother–infant relations in perhaps two dozen species of primates, observed in both field and laboratory. Both the temporal and the behavioral parameters describing the dyadic relationship vary from species to species. In monkeys at least, there is usually a gradual decay in close contact, proximity, and orientation to the mother from virtually continous levels initially to almost complete absence within 6 months to 2 years, depending on the species (Rosenblum, 1971a; Rheingold, 1963; Poirier, 1972).

Harlow's classic work on artificial mothers suggested the saliency of "contact comfort" in facilitating attachment formation and the more minimal and transient contributing effects of movement, warmth, and feeding (Harlow, 1961). Except for the research of Sackett (1970) and his coworkers, however, we have gained little additional systematic information regarding the very earliest stages of the formation of the infant monkey's attachment to the mother. These investigators have demonstrated that young rhesus, at least, appear to have a strong, unlearned tendency to respond positively to the general class of adult-female-conspecifics. Despite the relative lack of information regarding the initial onset and selective focusing of attachment in nonhuman primate infants, a fairly large body of data has been developed regarding the long-term course of the relationship, the factors regulating its intensity and rate of decay, as well as some of its sequelae.

Most of the studies on attachment in nonhuman primates have utilized one or another of the basic measures of attachment described in the child literature. These measures include: contact-maintenance and proximity-seeking; sustained visual orientation; marked disruption of behavior in the absence of the mother, particularly when such separations are sudden and prolonged; and prominent greeting responses and return to normative developmental or somewhat regressive patterns on the return of the attachment figure. As also suggested in the human literature (Schaffer & Emerson, 1964; Cairns, 1966; Brody & Axelrod, 1971), there are indications in nonhuman primates that more intensive maternal interaction with infants enhances the degree of infant attachment (Rosenblum & Kaufman, 1967; Mitchell, Ruppenthal, Raymond, & Harlow, 1966; Rosenblum, 1971a,b), as well as its long-term duration as a prominent organizing factor in the expression of social behavior (Rosenblum, 1971b). Similarly, as suggested by various child development workers (e.g., Bowlby, 1969; Gewirtz & Gewirtz, 1965; Stevens, 1971; Yarrow, 1972), the character of the environment in which the dyad lives influences the course of attachment. This has been shown to be true both in terms of the environment's physical structure (Jensen, 1969; Jensen, Bobbitt, & Gordon, 1968) and its social organization, particularly with regard to the infant's opportunity to interact with other conspecifics (Rosenblum, 1968, 1971b, 1974; Hinde, 1969; Jay, 1963; Poirier, 1969; Kaplan & Schusterman, 1972a,b). Each of these factors has been identified as influencing the intensity, duration, and breadth of attachment behaviors observed in monkeys.

Thus the work on primates during the last 10 to 15 years supports the contentions that many of the phenomena observed in the development of early attachments in children represent in part the operation of basic biological systems and that the nonhuman primate is an appropriate model with which to study these systems. Quite obviously, however, many gaps remain in the growing structure of our pertinent comparative knowledge of development.

Despite the significance suggested for human infants to develop the capacity to discriminate and respond preferentially to the visual features of the mother or other primary caregivers, and to manifest subsequent wariness or fear of strangers, we still lack systematic information of parallel developments in non-human primates. Bearing in mind that the infant rhesus is capable of simple discrimination learning by 10 to 20 days (Zimmerman & Torrey, 1965), Harlow and Harlow (1965) have suggested that in rhesus "There is every reason to believe that the infant learns attachments to a specific mother (*the* mother) long before our postulated reflex stage has passed (n.b. 15–20 days) . . ." (p. 291).

Bowlby (1969), reporting that Hinde endorses the Harlow position, suggested that "within a few days of birth, a rhesus baby orients its own mother in preference to other monkeys" (p. 195). Bowlby also cited other anecdotal observations pointing to very early discrimination of and preferential response to specific individuals by a baboon and a patas monkey. All these informal observations, however, failed to distinguish between differential responsiveness to a specific *individual* and the infant's tendency to respond to a specific class of eliciting *behaviors* exhibited by an appropriate member of his species. Just as a human infant early in development responds with visual orientation or a smile to a soft voice or to a smiling face, if only the mother presents the appropriate set of cues to the infant, it would be a mistake to interpret the infant's response to the mother as a preferential response to her as a specific individual. Sackett (1970) has made the same point in considering various interpretations of "preferential" responding of young rhesus to conspecific females in his selection-circus. Similarly, as an example of such pseudodiscrimination, free-responding squirrel monkey infants at 2 weeks of age appeared to "discriminate" their calling, agitated mother rather than the mother of another infant of similar age (Rosenblum, 1968).

Furthermore, there are indications in the literature that monkey infants may neither discriminate the mother nor respond preferentially to her until considerably later than the age suggested by Harlow and Hinde. Jensen and Bobbitt (1965), studying pigtails *(Macaca nemestrina),* demonstrated that it takes the monkey *mother* about 2.5 weeks to completely discriminate her own infant from a same age infant; when *infants* were tested until 30 days of age, Jensen ". . . saw no consistent differences in the attraction of the own and peer infant to the separated mother" (p. 308). Takeda (1967) noted in a hand-reared Japanese macaque *(M. fuscata)* that "attaching behaviors" to other than the caretaker did not decline until some time after 80 days of life and that the infant could readily be left with a stranger before that time. Even more dramatically, Jensen and Tolman (1962) showed that two pigtail infants, each raised in isolation with its mother, when exposed to a stranger at 5 and 7 months of age, respectively, attempted " . . . to achieve the closeness customarily experienced with their own mothers" (p. 134). It was not until several trials of exposure that infants "learned" to avoid the stranger. It is noteworthy that in the same article Jensen and

Tolman quoted Harlow's observation that "monkeys raised with artificial cloth mothers do not show a specific attachment to one but will accept any artificial cloth mother offering similarly comforting properties . . ." (p. 134).

There is some possibility of course that in the Jensen and Tolman study the isolation rearing retarded the appearance of appropriately discriminative responding. However, the recent hypotheses of Hoffman, Rainer, and Eiserer (1972) on imprinting processes and Cairns' (1972) recent speculations might well have suggested an enhancement of the discrimination and fear of the stranger under circumstances of isolate rearing. Cairns, for example, said:

"Maternal animals in several species isolate themselves and their offspring from others following parturition. Such isolation promotes, among other things, the establishment of individual recognition and mutually supported response patterns . . . such an outcome seems consistent with the proposal that mutual discrimination develops most readily in the course of insulated and exclusive interactions [p. 58]."

Fear of Strangers

With regard to the development of avoidance or fear of strangers, the information on nonhuman primate infants is exceedingly sketchy. Even the general maturation of fearful behavior has not been fully assessed. Harlow and Zimmerman (1959) indicated that for surrogate-reared rhesus, initial fear responses to stimuli placed in the home cage appear at about 22 days of age in most subjects; however, they also observed that ". . . most fear stimuli evoke many positive exploratory responses early in life and do not consistently evoke flight responses until the monkey is 40–50 days of age" (p. 424). Sackett (1970) in his studies on response to various types of visual stimuli also concluded that "until about day 80 none of the stimuli produced fear, withdrawal or disturbance. From day 80 to day 120 the frequency of these behaviors rose markedly whenever threat pictures were presented even though these pictures had not produced fear before this time" (p. 125).

In an earlier study, Bernstein and Mason (1962) noted the initial appearance of fear grimaces and screeches in one-month-old rhesus infants in response to complex stimuli. These authors also indicated, however, that actual withdrawal from approaching, complex, novel objects appeared some time after 3 months of age.

Despite this rather sparse and fragmentary information, after reviewing the existing data, both Candland (1971) and Bronson (1968) concluded that fearful responses to external stimuli may first emerge at about 3 to 4 weeks of age in macaques, developing further in intensity and specificity thereafter. Even less is known about fear of strange social stimuli. As indicated previously, some authors have suggested very early and selective attachments in monkeys. However, under appropriate conditions young monkey infants readily accept transfer to others and may be handled, carried, and even nursed by a number of others without manifesting any apparent fearfulness. This has been shown by the field studies of langurs (Jay, 1963), vervets (Gartlan, 1969), and squirrel monkeys (Dumond, 1968), and by the laboratory studies of alternating mothers in rhesus (Mitchell et al., 1967) and "aunting" and foster-mothering in rhesus (Harlow, Harlow, & Hansen, 1963), bonnets, and squirrel monkeys (Rosenblum, 1971). Furthermore, as already noted, Takeda (1967) reported that in a human-reared Japanese macaque, fear of strange humans did not appear until after 100 days; it will also be recalled that 5- to 7-month-old pigtail macaques reared alone with their mothers showed no fear of strangers on initial exposure (Jensen & Tolman, 1962). Thus, although visual discrimination of mother may begin fairly early in life, actual proximity-avoidance and/or fear of strangers may not emerge until several months of age.

Object Permanence

Finally, it is also important to consider the information available regarding one additional aspect of the development of specific attachments and response to strangers in nonhuman primates. As indicated earlier, various observers of the development of human attachments have suggested the critical significance of the infant's development of what is generally referred to as "object permanence" (i.e., the demonstration of a capacity to respond to objects, in the absence of immediate sensory input from them and independent of their location). A number of workers have speculated on the development and function of the object permanence concept, although a variety of terms with partial or complete overlap of characteristics have been employed. Fraiberg (1969) concluded from her review of this literature that "nearly all writers consulted, link the achievement of libidinal object constancy with some form of mental representation of the mother" (p. 21). It is clear from her paper that complete attainment of the object concept at about 18 months of age, as operationally defined in Piagetian terms as stage VI of sensory-motor development, coincides with the analytic concept of "evocative-memory" and fits with Freud's notion of "the capacity to bring before the mind once more something that has once been perceived, by reproducing it as a representation without the external object having still to be there" (1925, p. 237).

Of course "mental representations" in animals have a long and tortured history in comparative psychology. It is not our intention to speculate on what is "going on in the animal's mind" but rather to treat such presumed cognitive functions as a set of intervening variables between the stimulation of an animal with an exposed and then hidden object and a series of operationally defined behavioral responses to those objects. It is assumed that such capacities are dependent on a matrix of prior maturational and experiential events. Viewed in this framework, the primate literature does offer some fragments of pertinent information. Classically, the delayed response procedure, particularly that involving the "direct method" (Fletcher, 1965) in which S is shown an object (usually food) that is then covered in his view, closely parallels the procedures and capacities considered in stage IV of Piaget's materials.

Putting aside for the moment the behavioral mechanisms through which a monkey subject may mediate such delayed responding (perhaps not very different from those of the 8-month-old child), we note that adult monkeys can handle delays of several minutes under appropriate circumstances. Chimpanzees can apparently delay response even after returning to the home cage for the night, making their response the following morning (Yerkes, 1943). However, infant rhesus, 60 days of age, cannot respond reliably following only a 5-second delay, even after 900 training trials; 90-day-old infants do only slightly better after prolonged training (and hence aging). On the other hand, 120- and 150-day-old infants achieved 90% correct scores after a 5-second delay within 600 trials (Harlow, Harlow, Rueping, & Mason, 1960). Even these older infants, however, had some difficulty with delays as long as 40 seconds. Zimmerman and Torrey (1965) concluded that "the infant monkey is not capable of performing efficiently at longer delays until eight or nine months of age, while five months appears to be a minimal age for attaining a high performance level on the shorter delays" (p. 436).

In a recent study, purporting directly to test object permanence in the squirrel monkey, Vaughter, Smotherman, and Ordy (1972) found that a 6-month-old infant did not respond to an object (banana) covered before his eyes even after 100 training trials (although partially covered objects were readily retrieved). A 9-month-old, although initially poor at the same task, gradually responded (within the 30 seconds allowed) at 80 to 90% correct within 100 trials. A 12-month-old and an adult were proficient at this task almost immediately. However, when the object underwent a single observed displacement (i.e., first set under one object, then placed beneath another), performance of even the older S s was more variable, and the 9-month-old took an additional 100 trials before achieving reliable performance. Vaughter et al. suggest that these abilities may appear earlier in monkeys raised in more enriched environments. Décarie (1965) has proposed the same type of difference exists in home- and institution-reared human infants. (This point has also been suggested by Gruber, Girgus & Banuazizi, 1970, on the development of object permanence in cats; it should also be noted that delayed response is poorer in deprivation-reared chimpanzees; Davenport & Rogers, 1968.) In general it seems reasonable to suggest that infant monkeys may not be significantly beyond the equivalent of stage IV responsiveness nor develop the functional equivalent of more complete object permanence in the Piagetian sense until some time after 4 to 6 months of life. Nonetheless, although perhaps presumptive on the basis of this limited evidence, it is pertinent to include here the conclusion of Vaughter et al. that "the object concept develops in the squirrel monkey and that its development generally follows along the sequence described by Piaget" (p. 37).

In this general consideration of the development of object permanence in non-human as well as human primates, it must also be noted that spatial factors are often extremely influential in directing an S's response during learning, particularly early in life. Harlow (1959) reports extreme emotionality in attempts to reverse training in a very readily acquired spatial discrimination task in 15- and 45-day-old rhesus. The senior author had similar experiences in attempting to teach an observational learning task using the mother-surrogate as reward in 30- to 50-day-old rhesus infants. Infants were overwhelmingly reluctant to turn toward the new alley in a maze (in which they had repeatedly seen the mother), once having had several initial trials in which she was found in the opposite alley. Perhaps most instructive in this regard are some early observations by Yerkes (1943) on his chimpanzees. In one study he used different colored boxes, one placed in each corner of a large room. While the subject watched, its breakfast was placed into one box and the lid closed. The animal was removed briefly and the location of the boxes changed. Upon their return Ss would invariably choose the box, irrespective of its color, that happened to be in the corner where the food had been placed, and they persisted in these spatially fixed attempts even after several trials, growing more disturbed each time. Yerkes commented, "I recall instances in which a subject, having opened the box which was in the position where it had seen the food placed, searched thoroughly within and without the box as if unwilling to trust its senses, and then throwing itself on the empty box, cried piteously" (p. 104). Thus for these chimpanzee subjects (age not indicated), although *the object was searched for*, the animals could not carry that search beyond the general spatial locus at which the object had last passed from their perceptual field.

Certainly a variety of other primate and comparative studies (Kohler, 1925; Kluver, 1933) have provided data of pertinence to the functional attributes of object-permanence attainment. In our own laboratory, we have been able to show in pilot work that two, 2-year-old bonnet macaques could successfully respond to double displacements of a desired food object with a minimum of prior training. These subjects have also shown some evidence of responding appropriately to a hidden displacement after the second observed one, by continuing to search and finally opening the experimenter's closed hand, which contained the desired raisin. Nonetheless, we have almost no knowledge of the development of these abilities in primates, nor have prior attempts been undertaken to relate the appearance of such abilities to particular antecedent events nor to correlate their development with attachment processes.

MOTHER PREFERENCE AND FEAR OF STRANGER

The research described below was initiated in light of the pivotal significance for primate development inherent in the establishment of selective responsiveness to the mother and related or opposed reactions to others. The studies are an attempt to provide for the first time systematic data on the emergence of these critical developmental phenomena in monkeys. First, however, we must present a broad developmental chronology within which the various age points to be discussed can be placed. All our subjects belong to the *Macaque* genus, the most widely dispersed primate taxa. As far as is known, gestation in macaques lasts approximately 5.5 months. Single infants are by far the most frequent outcome of pregnancies. Under both wild and appropriate laboratory conditions, mature females will produce an infant at yearly intervals. This implies that the mother returns to active sexual activity when her infant is approximately 4 to 5 months of age and conceives her next offspring while her still suckling infant is about 6 months old. In general, active weaning of the infant occurs between the fourth and tenth months of life, although even the birth of the next offspring does not abruptly terminate the ongoing infant–mother relationship. There is evidence, however, that the long-term duration of the close bond between the infant and the mother probably terminates more rapidly in males than in females, and in the infants of some species, such as the bonnet, more rapidly than in other species, such as pigtails. Both these species have been studied extensively in our laboratory (Rosenblum, 1971a) and are the subjects of the current research. Although precise ages for the attainment of puberty under wild conditions have not been extensively studied, in appropriate laboratory environments females are sexually mature at 2.5 to 3 years and males about a year later; in general, these figures are likely to be somewhat earlier than those which may be expected in the natural environment.

Our own detailed studies of mother–infant relations and infant development in monkeys have focused on two macaque species, the bonnet *(Macaca radiata)* and the pigtail *(M. nemestrina)* (Rosenblum & Kaufman, 1967; Rosenblum, 1971a,b). The developmental pace and early behavior of infants of these two species have much in common. Infants are born with strong reflex systems that facilitate early survival, and infants spend the first several weeks of life in close, virtually exclusive contact with the mother (see Figure 1). Following initial excursions from the mother beginning at about 2 weeks of age, there is a gradual decline in levels of close mother–infant contact (see Figure 2). This decline is quite parallel for the infants of these two species under comparable laboratory conditions.

Since both pigtails and bonnets are group living under wild conditions, our laboratory subjects are also born and reared within conspecific social groups. As any human observer of an unfamiliar grouping of animals or humans can

FIGURE 1. A young pigtail infant in close ventral-ventral contact with its mother.

attest, it is initially difficult to discern the distinctive individual characteristics of the group members. This occurs, even though individuals vary, because conspecifics possess so many similar morphological features (see Figure 3). With repeated exposure, however, distinctive features become apparent. As alluded to in our discussion of the literature, despite any innate sensitivity to selected monkey features that may assist the monkey infant in making such distinctions, consistent discrimination of an individual member of a group may be a difficult task for the infant monkey.

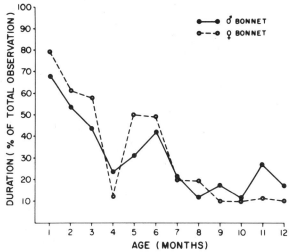

FIGURE 2. The decrease in ventral–ventral contact between male and female bonnet infants and their mothers during the first year of life. These data are derived from systematic observations of eight male and eight female infants reared in complex social groups.

FIGURE 3. A portion of a bonnet social group, showing a mother, clutching her newborn infant, huddled in contact with two other adult females. Note the relative similarity of facial and general physical features.

Method

The data presented below represent a series of tests on a total of 25 macaque infants: 11 female and 7 male bonnet macaques and 7 female pigtail macaques. A number of additional males and females of both species are being tested further, and although their data have not been formally analyzed, the results of their testing are essentially in keeping with the material presented below. All infants were conceived and born in the Primate Behavior Laboratory of the Downstate Medical Center. All were reared in conspecific group settings containing a number of mothers and other infants; all such groups lived in relatively large and complex pens of approximately 600 cubic feet (see Rosenblum & Youngstein, 1974, for details). To assess responsiveness to mothers and strangers across the widest possible age range, all infants available in the laboratory during the last 2 years have been tested; some were tested only once, others as many as eight times. Thus various infants have begun testing at different ages with repeated tests, never less than 3 to 4 weeks apart. Careful assessment of the data has indicated that neither age at the onset of testing nor the number of repetitions of tests has any systematic influence on the age-related data obtained. Figures and data presented below are the results of testing five to seven male and female bonnet infants within each successive age block beginning at 3 weeks of age. One exception to this is the 19- to 26-week period, for which only two male and two female bonnet subjects are represented. Very recent data obtained on several more male and female subjects during this age range essentially substantiate the initial data. The pigtail data represent scores on at least five subjects at each age range. Unfortunately, until very recently too few pigtail males had been born in the laboratory to allow systematic evaluation of their performance on these tests.

All testing was carried out in a chamber 8 feet long, 18 inches wide, and 2 feet high (see Figure 4). The interior of the chamber was painted flat black, and the floor was covered with shaggy carpeting to facilitate locomotion in young infants. The chamber had hinged Plexiglas lids covered with fine mesh screening to prevent the infants from seeing out of the test chamber. The center 2-foot area of the chamber was enclosed by two guillotine Plexiglas doors that could be raised and lowered remotely by the observer. The infant was placed in this start area through a small door on the side wall of the chamber. Observation of the interior of the chamber with minimal distraction for the infant was made possible by a large mirror hung at about a 45° angle, 3 feet above the chamber itself. Of critical significance to the operation of the test procedure were the two end walls of the chamber, each containing a large one-way-vision glass window. No illumination was provided within the chamber itself, whereas each stimulus chamber (an open-mesh transport cage) was brightly illuminated by means of a 20-W fluorescent fixture. Thus because of the one-way glass and the differential lighting, the infant was easily able to see the mother, the strang-

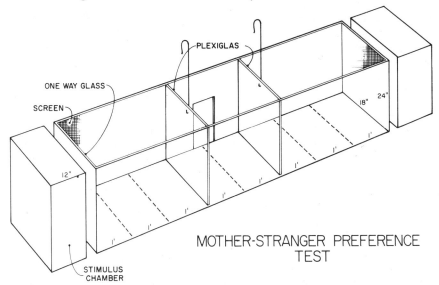

FIGURE 4. The mother–stranger preference test apparatus. The apparatus had hinged Plexiglas lids covered with fine mesh screening. The floor contained shaggy carpeting to facilitate locomotion. Observations were made through a mirror hung at about a 45° angle, 3 feet above the apparatus (not illustrated).

er, or an empty stimulus compartment, but stimulus animals could not see the infant within the test chamber. Thus differential response to the infant by the stimulus animals was effectively eliminated. Except for the use of the one-way-vision screens, which ensured that the infant was responding primarily to the visual appearance of the mother or stranger rather than to specific behaviors directed toward it by either animal, this test apparatus was essentially similar to those utilized by Sackett (1970) and subsequently by Kaplan and Schusterman (1972). Although olfactory stimuli were not specifically controlled for, it seemed unlikely that they could be utilized for discrimination. Vocalizations, although perhaps a potential problem, were very intermittent in appearance and seemed to be difficult to localize because of the construction of the pen; when they did occur, such sounds failed to result in any systematic alteration in infant responsiveness (i.e., some infants showed no response, some moved toward and others away from the source of sounds on different occasions).

To begin testing, a mother–infant dyad was captured and the infant removed from the mother while the latter was restrained in a squeeze-chamber. The mother was then transferred to the stimulus chamber. Adult females, from conspecific groups other than the one in which the test infant lived, often with infants of their own removed for testing the same day, served as "strangers." The infant was placed in the center 2-foot start area to begin testing and restrained there by the two clear Plexiglas doors. Thirty seconds after the placement of the appropriate stimuli at the ends of the chamber, the Plexiglas doors were raised and the trial begun. Each test day the infant was given seven, 180-second trials. Several minutes elapsed between each trial, and during this time the infant was restrained once again in the center start area. Each set of trials was begun with an adaptation trial in which each of the two stimulus chambers was empty. Then on each test day infants received two trials for each of three conditions: (1) mother versus empty chamber, (2) stranger versus empty chamber, (3) mother versus stranger. All conditions were balanced for side on each test day and otherwise balanced for sequence, except that the mother–stranger trials always concluded a set of trials on a given day.

When the Plexiglas doors were raised to begin a trial, the observer, using a clock-counter device, recorded each entry into each 1-foot segment of the test chamber, and the total duration of time that the infant spent in it. A number of emotional and exploratory behaviors were also recorded separately. However, the primary measures utilized were the frequency and duration measures scored when the infant was in either of the two, 1-foot segments closest to the stimulus compartments, *the choice area*. In addition, the frequency and duration scores for visual orientation of the infant when occupying these primary choice areas were used. Orientation was scored whenever the infant's nose was clearly pointed to one or the other end of the apparatus in a plane approximately parallel to the floor. The trials in which mother and stranger were presented simultaneously were run to provide a sensitive measure of discrimination of and preference for the mother as opposed to the stranger. These preferences were measured in terms of the average percentage of the trial spent in either choice area.

RESULTS AND DISCUSSION

Bonnet Macaques

The responses of male and female bonnet infants in these trials give the first indication of the relatively undifferentiated response of very young infants and the gradual emergence of clear preferences for the mother (see Figure 5). By the last portion of the 3- to 10-week age block, female infants had begun to show some preference for mother, averaging 52.7% of the trial at the mother's end of the chamber and only choosing the stranger during 24.8% of the trial. This difference, however, did not achieve statistical significance for the total age block. Male infants, on the other hand, showed virtually no distinction in response to mothers and strangers during this initial age period, spending 31% of the trial near the mother and 34.4% near the stranger. Both male and female infants showed marked increases in preference for the mother in the 11- to 18-week age range. Females in particular displayed a dramatic rise, choosing the mother during 79.6% of the trial and the stranger only 11.7% of the trial. Males had a less dramatic increase in preference, responding to the mother for slightly more than half the trial and to the stranger for less than a quarter of the trial. Nonetheless, infants of both sexes showed significant preference for the mother on these trials during the first half of the 11- to 18-week age range (t tests; $p < .02$). Females continued to respond to mothers between 75 and 85% of each trial and to the stranger for 11% or less throughout subsequent testing. Males, on the other hand, as reflected in Figure 5, did not achieve such high levels of preferential response to mother until the 27- to 34-week age range. Females thus showed significantly greater preference for mother on these mother–stranger trials during the 11- to 26-week age period when compared with male infants (Mann Whitney U; $p < .02$).

Figure 6 reveals that from the outset females also stayed considerably longer with the mother when they chose her as opposed to when they chose the stranger. For males, on the other hand, the bout-lengths of excursions to the mother's as opposed to the stranger's end of the chamber hovered around a ratio of 1:1, until about the twenty-seventh week of life, when it rose dramatically to values comparable to those of females. Female infants, even in the 3- to 10-week age range, showed bout-lengths 4 to 6 times greater when the mother was chosen than when the stranger was chosen. Thus the relative difference in bout-lengths of mother and stranger choices reflects further the earlier development of preferential responsiveness to mother as compared to strangers in female as opposed to male bonnet infants reared under similar conditions.

Furthermore, on examining the behavior of both male and female infants during the mother–stranger test trials, one may also detect a more subtle change in response to strangers as the infants develop. The amount of time spent looking at the stranger during the time that a choice of mother had been made (i.e., while the infant was standing or sitting within 2 feet of the mother's stimulus compartment) undergoes an interesting change with age (see Figure 7). During weeks 11 to 26 of life there was a sudden increase in time spent looking at the stranger at the opposite end of the apparatus. Whereas before and after this age period, infants directed nearly three-quarters of their scored orientations toward the mother, during this period infants spent about the same amount of time looking toward the stranger and looking toward the mother, next to whom they were sitting. As we see below, such heightened visual orientation toward the stranger during this age period, particularly in females, reflects an important shift in the nature of response to strangers at this age. There is some suggestion with regard to female infants, at least, that this behavior contains elements of a growing wariness and distinct hesitancy to physically move toward strange conspecific females.

The growth of preferential response to mother in the mother–stranger trials does not, however, indicate that conspecific females, when presented by themselves in the highly arousing circumstances of this test environment, have become aversive stimuli for these young infants. As indicated in other chapters

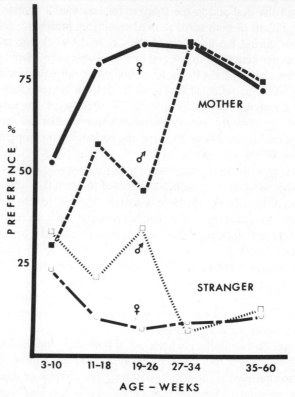

FIGURE 5.   The percentage of each trial spent choosing either the mother or the stranger by male and female bonnet infants on mother–stranger tests.

in this volume regarding response to strangers by human infants, a considerable amount of positive responsiveness to strangers may be evidenced by infants of all ages. This readiness to respond positively to strangers may continue to appear even during age periods normally designated as those in which the most pronounced fear or avoidance of strangers is shown.

Our own data indicate that on the stranger-empty trials, throughout the age range tested, male and female infants each averaged more than 60% of the trials at the stranger end of the test chamber. Female infants, unlike the males who responded quite steadily at this level to strangers at all ages, showed a slight decline in responsiveness to strangers in the empty trials during the last half-year of testing. We could evaluate further the relative preference for choice of mother as opposed to stranger by tabulating the ratio of mother choice to stranger choice on the two types of empty trials (see Figure 8). Female infants, in contrast to their male counterparts, exhibited a gradual but pronounced increase in this measure of relative preference for the mother as they grew older. Male

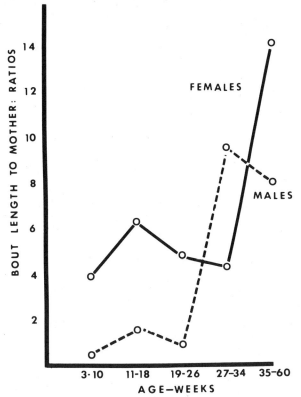

FIGURE 6. Ratio of bout-length of mother choice to stranger choice in the mother-stranger trials. Ratio is the average bout-length to mother divided by the average bout-length to stranger. "Bout-length" is the average duration in the choice area divided by the average frequency in the choice area.

infants, however, showed only slightly greater relative preference for the mother; at no point was movement toward her more than 20% greater than movement toward the stranger. Thus a comparison of responses to stranger on empty trials and to mother on similar trials provided a second index of relative preference for approaching the mother as opposed to stranger on trials that did not allow for simultaneous comparison of the two stimuli.

One of the primary purposes of this study was to determine whether we could discern in these infants any evidence for wariness or fear of strangers, as opposed to simply greater positive responsiveness toward mother. The 8-foot-long chamber utilized for this testing allowed considerable opportunity for an infant not merely to manifest very obvious approach responses but, on the empty trials, to move a considerable distance away from either stimulus animal. If we consider that the amount of time spent at the empty end of the chamber when

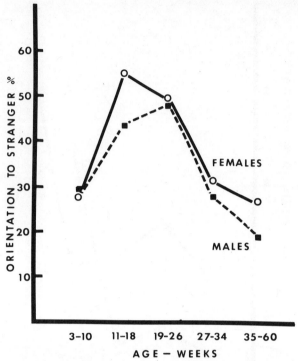

FIGURE 7.   Percentage of total visual orientations directed toward the stranger, while male and female bonnet infants were seated next to the mother on mother-stranger trials.

mother was present reflects a basic level of infant activity and exploratory interest in the apparatus, it seems reasonable to suggest that the ratio of time spent at the empty end when stranger was present (as opposed to when mother was present) should reflect the relative avoidance of the stranger by infants at any given age.

As indicated in Figure 9, these ratio scores show an important sex difference and a striking change with age in females. As a reflection of the nonselective behavior of the youngest infants, both males and females initially made almost identical movements to the empty end when mother or stranger was present. Male infants thereafter showed only slightly greater tendencies to move to the empty end when stranger was present as compared with trials in which the mother was available. Female infants, on the other hand, throughout weeks 11 to 34 of life, showed a very marked relative avoidance of the strange female. Indeed, during this age range, females spent more than 10 times as much of the period at the empty end of the chamber when stranger was present as compared with trials in which mother was available (20.3 vs. 1.9%). This relative

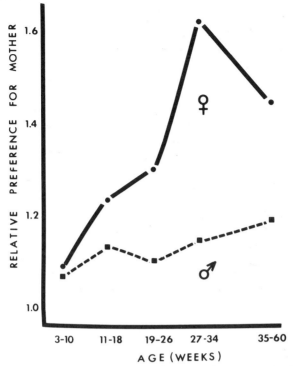

FIGURE 8. Relative preference for response to mother as opposed to stranger by male and female bonnet infants as reflected in the ratio of choice scores for mother to choice scores for stranger on empty trials.

avoidance of strangers by female infants virtually disappeared in the last quarter of the first year of life.

A further reflection of this female avoidance of strangers is suggested in Figure 10, which indicates the durations of average excursions (bout-lengths) to the empty end of the chamber when either mother or stranger was present alone. After about the nineteenth week of life, females, on the average, spent nearly half a minute on each excursion to the empty end of the chamber when stranger was present, but only 4 to 8 seconds on such excursions in the presence of the mother. Male infants, however, failed to make such prolonged excursions to the empty end of the chamber in the stranger's presence until the end of the first year of life. Conceivably, in light of the relatively delayed emergence of strong preferential response to mother that occurs in male infants as compared with females, the whole process of differentiation, preference, and avoidance may indeed be delayed for as long as 6 months in male infants as compared with their female counterparts when all have been reared in complex social group conditions.

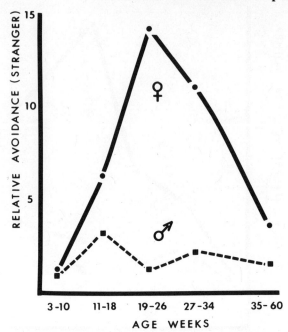

FIGURE 9.   Relative avoidance of strangers by male and female bonnet infants reflected in ratio of time spent at empty end of chamber when stranger was present as opposed to time spent at empty end when mother was present.

It is evident from the material presented thus far that even when a well controlled and circumscribed test condition is utilized, different measures may be more sensitive to elucidating differential response to mother and stranger at different ages. Figure 11 portrays some of the measures of approach and orientation obtained from the several test conditions across all ages in group-reared bonnet females. To enable ready comparisons, each score is expressed in ratios of mother and stranger scores. Although the general pattern of preference for mother and wariness of strangers in females is suggested by the relative heightening of the first four bars and by the subsequent increase in the scores for behaviors 5 to 7, it is clear that at any given age the measures do not all equally reflect the patterns of response to mother and strangers, nor do any of the measures follow precisely parallel developmental courses. Thus, for example, boutlength measures (item 2, 4, 6) may precede or follow more overt measures of movement in indicating relative preference or wariness. It seems clear, therefore, that at the nonhuman primate level, as well as for children, a number of measures must be obtained across a wide range if we are to systematically assess the age of onset and actual termination of various forms of responsiveness both to attachment figures and to strangers.

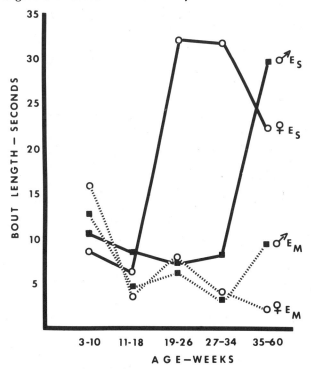

FIGURE 10. Bout-lengths of time spent at empty end of chamber by bonnet male and female infants in the presence of either the stranger or the mother. (Em = mother-empty trials; Es = stranger-empty trials).

Pigtail Macaques

Before turning to a consideration of the responses of pigtail female infants in our test situation, we must briefly summarize some salient features of social organization and maternal behavior that have served in our past studies to distinguish pigtail and bonnet macaques. Results of a series of studies have indicated that bonnet adults, both before and after the birth of infants, spend considerable parts of the day and evening in close contact and proximity with one another. When infants are born, a great deal of positive interaction between other members of the group and the newborn infant is allowed by the bonnet mother. As a concomitant of this allowance of interaction with her young infant, the bonnet mother engages in relatively low levels of maternal restraint and protection of the infant. As a result of these social and maternal patterns, bonnet infants, often within the first hours of life, are observed to have relatively high levels of passive and active social interaction with both adult and peer conspecifics.

In pigtail groups on the other hand, even though observed under the same

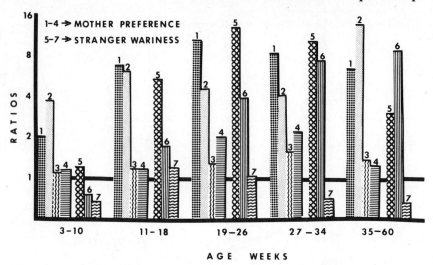

FIGURE 11. The development of various measures of preference for mother and wariness of stranger in group-reared bonnet females: 1 = mother preference score on mother-stranger trials; 2 = bout-lengths for mother choices versus stranger choices on empty trials; 3 = ratio of mother to stranger choices on empty trials; 4 = bout-lengths for mother choices versus stranger on empty trials; 5 = relative avoidance of stranger on empty trials (ratio of empty scores on mother-empty trials to empty scores on stranger-empty trials); 6 = bout-lengths of excursions to the empty end when mother is present compared with bout-lengths to the empty end when stranger is present; 7 = visual orientation toward the stranger while sitting near the mother in mother–stranger trials.

physical circumstances and structurally identical social groups, both the social pattern and the maternal behaviors are markedly different from those observed in bonnets. Pigtail adults are rarely found in close proximity or physical contact with one another except while engaging in sexual, grooming, or aggressive activity. In our experience, aggressive activity is considerably higher even in stabilized pigtail groups than is commonly observed in bonnets. Moreover, the appearance of young infants, if anything, often exaggerates the group spacing pattern, with mothers actively preventing exploration or interaction with their newborns, either through flight or overt, protective maternal aggression. As a corollary of these behaviors, the pigtail mother, when compared with the bonnet mother of infants of similar age, engages in appreciably more restraint and related protective behaviors of her young infant. One outgrowth of these pigtail patterns is the characteristic tendency of the pigtail infant to engage in significantly less interaction and close proximity and contact with other members of his group than do bonnets. Finally, several of our studies have demonstrated that pigtail infants manifest intense and enduring attachment to their mothers, as indicated in severe depressive reactions to maternal loss and long-term orientation

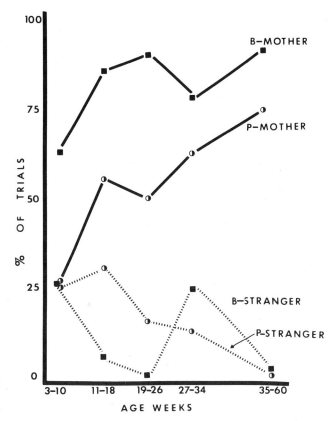

FIGURE 12. A comparison of trials in which at least a 10% preference for either mother or stranger was shown by bonnet (B) and pigtail (P) female infants on mother-stranger trials.

to the mother and siblings when compared with our laboratory-reared bonnets (Rosenblum, 1971a,b; Rosenblum & Kaufman, 1967).

Although it could have been anticipated that the relatively restricted rearing and social experience of pigtails might result in earlier, more dramatic preferential response to the mother, as well as great timidity and withdrawal in the presence of strangers, our current findings suggest precisely the opposite. Figure 12 presents the data for mother–stranger trials for pigtail female infants, as well as those for bonnet females, in terms of the percentage of trials within which at least a 10% greater duration of response, either to mother or to stranger, was displayed. Even utilizing this relatively conservative index of preferential response, it can be seen that pigtail females, although generally paralleling the development of preferential response to mother as seen in bonnet females, proceeded at a markedly slower pace. Even by 6 months of age, pigtail females showed a preference for mother on only slightly more than half the test trials. Bonnet females, on the other hand, showed an unquestionable preference for mother some 3 months earlier. Thus it would appear that differentiation of and preference for the mother takes several months longer to appear in pigtail females than in their bonnet counterparts.

An examination of the trials in which the mother and stranger were each compared with an empty stimulus chamber provided an even more striking distinction between group-reared bonnet and pigtail female infants. As Figure 13 reveals, using the same measure of relative avoidance of stranger discussed earlier, pigtail females throughout the period of testing failed to manifest any overt indication of stranger avoidance. Bonnet females, however, did display marked avoidance of stranger during the 11- to 34-week age range. Pigtail females in this regard seem to be strikingly similar to the previously discussed bonnet males, within whom there was also no indication of strong wariness of strangers.

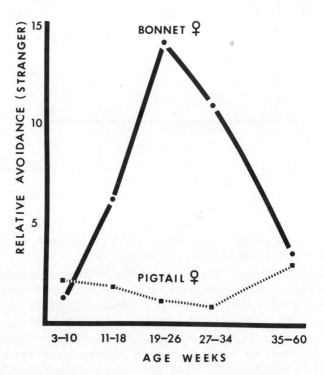

FIGURE 13.   Relative avoidance of stranger by bonnet and pigtail female infants on empty trials (see Figure 9).

Isolate Bonnet Dyads

Before considering these data further, it is pertinent to mention briefly some of our recent findings regarding the test performance of bonnet females reared with their respective mothers in social isolation. Two such isolate-dyad bonnet female infants have been studied. All measures indicate that their performance closely parallels that obtained on group-reared pigtail females and stand in marked contrast to the data discussed previously on group-reared bonnet females. The isolate-dyad bonnets, including the oldest, now tested at 39 weeks of age, have never manifested any measurable index of stranger wariness. Similarly, although the testing is incomplete, these infants show a strikingly slow development of preferential response to mother, even in the mother-stranger tests.

Summary

It is of course difficult at this stage of our research to make more than the barest speculations regarding any possible integrations of these data. We are nonetheless struck with the following facts. Even the earliest phases of the development of infant attachment may show very marked sex differences in nonhuman primates. Whether such differences are entirely genetic or the result of very early and perhaps extremely subtle differences in maternal responsiveness to male and female infants remains to be determined. Nonetheless, the subsequent differences in the lifelong relations of males and females to their mothers, which have been reported in numerous species under wild conditions and appear to play a critical role in the nature of the species' social adaptations to their environment, have their origins in the very first days or at most weeks of life. Next, assuming that our data on isolate dyads prove to be reliable, there is evidence that the pace of the infant's differentiation and preferential response to mother, as well as the appearance of subsequent wariness to strangers, can indeed be influenced significantly by the nature of the infant's early social experience. Furthermore, it seems likely that some species, as a result of characteristic social patterns and concomitant forms of maternal behavior, can produce a marked degree of interactive isolation of young infants. This in turn suggests that the speed of acquisition and intensity of preferential response to mother, as well as variations in approach and avoidance tendencies toward conspecific strangers, may in and of themselves have significant adaptive value for different species. It is of course possible that species differences of the type described here are primarily attributable to genetic rather than ontogenetic factors. Although this possibility would not alter the adaptive significance of different forms of attachment behavior and its selectivity, a more precise determination of the contribution of genetic and ontogenetic factors and their interaction will play an important role in our ultimate appreciation of the processes governing the development and significance of social attachments and fears in the human child.

References

Ainsworth, M. D. S. Object relations, dependency, and attachment: A theoretical review of the infant–mother relationship. *Child Development*, 1969, **40**, 969–1025.

Ainsworth, M. D. S. Attachment and dependency: A comparison. In J. Gewirtz (Ed.), *Attachment and dependency*. Washington, D.C.: Winston, 1972. Pp. 97–138.

Bell, S. M. The development of the concept of the object and its relationship to infant–mother attachment. *Child Development*, 1970, **41**, 291–312.

Bernstein, I. S., & Mason, W. A. The effects of age and stimulus conditions on the emotional responses of rhesus monkeys: Responses to complex stimuli. *Journal of Genetic Psychology*, 1962, **101**, 279–298.

Bowlby, J. *Attachment and loss*. Vol. 1. *Attachment*. London: Hogarth; New York: Basic Books, 1969.

Brody, S., & Axelrod, S. Maternal stimulation and social responsiveness of infants. In R. Schaffer (Ed.), *The origins of human social relations*. New York: Academic Press, 1971. Pp. 195-215.

Bronson, G. W. The development of fear in man and other animals. *Child Development*, 1968, **39**, 409–431.

Cairns, R. B. Attachment behavior of mammals. *Psychological Review*, 1966, **73**, 409–426.

Cairns, R. B. Attachment and dependency: A psychobiological and social learning synthesis. In J. L. Gewirtz (Ed.), *Attachment and dependency*. Washington, D.C.: Winston, 1972. Pp. 29–80.

Candland, D. K. The ontogeny of emotional behavior. In H. Moltz (Ed.), *The ontogeny of vertebrate behavior*. New York: Academic Press, 1971. Pp. 95-170.

Davenport, R. K., & Rogers, C. M. Intellectual performance of differentially reared chimpanzees. I. Delayed response. *American Journal of Mental Deficiency*, 1968, **72**, 674–680.

Décarie, T. G. *Intelligence and affectivity in early childhood*. New York: International University Press, 1965.

Dumond, F. V. The squirrel monkey in a seminatural environment. In L. A. Rosenblum & R. W. Cooper (Eds.), *The squirrel monkey*. New York: Academic Press, 1968. Pp. 87–145.

Fletcher, H. J. The delayed response problem. In A. M. Schrier, H. F. Harlow, & F. Stollnitz (Eds.), *Behavior of nonhuman primates*. New York: Academic Press, 1965. Pp. 129–166.

Fraiberg, S. Libidinal object constancy and mental representation. *Psychoanalytic Study of the Child*, 1969, **24**, 1–47.

Freud, S. Negation (1925). In *Collected Works,* Standard Edition. Vol. 19. London: Hogarth, 1961. Pp. 235–239. Cited in Fraiberg (1969).

Gartlan, J. S. Sexual and maternal behavior of the vervet monkey, *Cercopithecus aethiops. Journal of Reproduction and Fertility,* 1969, Suppl. 6, 137–150.

Gewirtz, J. Attachment, dependency and a distinction in terms of stimulus control. In J. Gewirtz (Ed.), *Attachment and dependency.* Washington, D.C.: Winston, 1972. Pp. 139–178.

Gewirtz, J. L. & Gewirtz, H. B. Stimulus conditions, infant behaviors, and social learning in four Israeli child-rearing environments. In B. M. Foss, (Ed.), *Determinants of infant behaviour.* London: Methuen; New York: Barnes & Noble, 1969. Pp. 161-179.

Gruber, H. E., Girgus, J. S., & Banuazizi, A. The development of object permanence with the cat. *Developmental Psychology,* 1971, **4,** 9–15.

Harlow, H. F. The development of affectional patterns in infant monkeys. In B. M. Foss (Ed.), *Determinants of Infant Behavior.* Vol. 1. London: Methuen; New York: Wiley, 1961.

Harlow, H. F., Harlow, M. K., & Hansen, E. W. The maternal affectional system of rhesus monkeys. In H. L. Rheingold (Ed.), *Maternal behavior in mammals.* New York: Wiley, 1963.

Harlow, H. F., Harlow, M. K., Rueping, R. R., & Mason, W. A. Performance of infant rhesus monkeys on discrimination learning, delayed response, and discrimination learning set. *Journal of Comparative and Physiological Psychology,* 1960, **53,** 113–121.

Harlow, H. F., & Zimmerman, R. R. Affectional responses in the infant monkey. *Science,* 1959, **130,** 421–432.

Hinde, R. A. Influence of social companions and of temporary separation on mother–infant relations in rhesus monkeys. In B. M. Foss (Ed.), *Determinants of infant behaviour.* Vol. 4. London: Methuen; New York: Barnes & Noble, 1969.

Hoffman, H. S., Ratner, A. M., & Eiserer, L. A. Role of visual imprinting in the emergence of specific filial attachments in ducklings. *Journal of Comparative and Physiological Psychology,* 1972, **8,** 399-409.

Jay, P. Mother–infant relations in langurs. In H. L. Rheingold (Ed.), *Maternal behavior in mammals.* New York: Wiley, 1963. Pp. 282–304.

Jensen, G. Environmental influences on sexual differentiations: Primate studies. *Symposium on Environmental Influences on Genetic Expression,* Bethesda, Md.

Jensen, G. D., & Bobbitt, R. A. On observational methodology and preliminary studies of mother–infant interaction in monkeys. In B. M. Foss (Ed.), *Determinants of infant behaviour.* Vol. 3. London: Methuen; New York: Wiley, 1965.

Jensen, G. D., Bobbitt, R. A., & Gordon, B. N. Effects of environment on the relationship between mother and infant pigtailed monkeys *(Macaca nemestrina). Journal of Comparative and Physiological Psychology,* 1968, **66,** 259–263.

Jensen, G. D., & Tolman, C. W. Mother–infant relationship in the monkey, *Macaca nemestrina.* The effect of brief separation and mother–infant specificity. *Journal of Comparative and Physiological Psychology,* 1962, **55,** 131.

Kaplan, J. Differences in the mother–infant relations of squirrel monkeys housed in social and restricted environments. *Developmental Psychobiology*, 1972, **5**, 43–52.

Kaplan, J., & Schusterman, R. J. Social preferences of mother and infant squirrel monkeys following different rearing experiences. *Developmental Psychobiology*, 1972, **5**, 53–59.

Kluver, H. *Behavior mechanisms in monkeys.* Chicago: University of Chicago Press, 1933.

Kohler, W. *The mentality of apes.* London: Routledge & Kegan Paul, 1925.

Mitchell, G. D., Harlow, H. F., Griffen, G. A., & Moller, G. W. Repeated maternal separation in the monkey. *Psychonomic Science*, 1967, **8**, 197–198.

Mitchell, G. D., Ruppenthal, G. C., Raymond, E. J., & Harlow, H. F. Long-term effects of multiparous and primiparous monkey mother rearing. *Child Development*, 1966, **37**, 781–791.

Morgan, G. A., & Ricciuti, H. N. Infants' responses to strangers during the first year. In B. M. Foss (Ed.), *Determinants of infant behaviour*. Vol. 4. London: Methuen; New York: Barnes & Noble, 1969.

Piaget, J. *The construction of reality in the child.* New York: Basic Books, 1954. (Originally published: 1937.)

Poirier, F. E. The Nilgiri langur *(Presbytis johnii)* Mother-infant dyad. *Primates*, 1969, **9**, 45–68.

Poirier, F. E. *Primate socialization.* New York: Random House, 1972. Pp. 3–28.

Rheingold, H. L. The effect of a strange environment on the behavior of infants. In B. M. Foss (Ed.), *Determinants of infant behaviour*. Vol. 4. London: Methuen; New York: Barnes & Noble, 1969.

Rosenblum, L. A. Mother–infant relations and early behavioral development in the squirrel monkey. In L. A. Rosenblum & R. W. Cooper (Eds.), *The squirrel monkey*. New York: Academic Press, 1968. Pp. 207–233.

Rosenblum, L. A. The ontogeny of mother–infant relations in macaques. In H. Moltz (Ed.), *Ontogeny of vertebrate behaviour*. New York: Academic Press, 1971a. Pp. 315–367.

Rosenblum, L. A. Infant attachment in monkeys. In R. Schaffer (Ed.), *The origins of human social relations*. New York: Academic Press, 1971b. Pp. 85–113.

Rosenblum, L. A. Sex differences in mother–infant attachment in monkeys. In R. L. Vande, R. M. Richart, & R. C. Friedman (Eds.), *The psychology of sex differences*. New York: Wiley, in press.

Rosenblum, L. A., & Kaufman, I. C. Laboratory observations of early mother–infant relations in pigtail and bonnet macaques. In S. A. Altmann (Ed.), *Social communication among primates*. Chicago: University of Chicago Press, 1967. Pp. 33–41.

Rosenblum, L. A., & Youngstein, K. P. Developmental changes in compensatory dyadic response in mother and infant monkeys. In M. Lewis & L. A. Rosenblum (Eds.), *The effect of the infant on its caregiver*. New York: Wiley, 1974. Pp. 141–161.

Sackett, G. P. Unlearned responses, differential rearing experiences, and the development of social attachments by rhesus monkeys. In L. A. Rosenblum (Ed.), *Primate behavior: Developments in field and laboratory research*. Vol. 1. New York: Academic Press, 1970. Pp. 112–140.

Schaffer, H. R., & Emerson, P. E. The development of social attachments in infancy. *Monographs of the Society for Research in Child Development*, 1964, **29** (3, Serial No. 94).

Takeda, R. Development of vocal communications in man-raised Japanese monkeys. II. *Primates*, 1967, **7**, 73–116.

Tennes, K. H., & Lampl, E. E. Stranger and separation anxiety in infancy. *Journal of Nervous and Mental Disease*, 1964, **139**, 247–254.

Vaughter, R. M., Smotherman, W., & Ordy, J. M. Development of object permanence in the infant squirrel monkey. *Developmental Psychology*, 1972, **7**, 34–38.

Yarrow, L. J. Attachment and dependency: A developmental perspective. In J. Gewirtz (Ed.), *Attachment and dependency*. Washington, D.C.: Winston, 1972. Pp. 81–96.

Yerkes, R. M. *Chimpanzees: A laboratory colony*. New Haven, Conn.: Yale University Press; London: Oxford University Press, 1943.

Zimmerman, R. R., & Torrey, C. C. Ontogeny of learning. In A. M. Schrier, H. F. Harlow & F. Stollnitz (Eds.), *Behavior of nonhuman primates*. New York: Academic Press, 1965. Pp. 405–477.

CHAPTER 8

Self, Other, and Fear: Infants' Reactions to People [1]

MICHAEL LEWIS AND JEANNE BROOKS

Educational Testing Service

The infant's reactions to other humans has both an affective and a cognitive component, since social perception involves both domains. Fear of the strange is a phenomenon that can be employed to observe both attachment to a familiar person and differentiation among strangers. Although attachment usually is defined by a positive approach to the mother, as measured by proximal and distal behaviors (Coates, Anderson, & Hartup, 1972; Lewis & Ban, 1971; Lewis, Weinraub, & Ban, 1973), or by separation from the mother as measured by distress (Ainsworth & Bell, 1970; Goldberg & Lewis, 1969; Schaffer & Emerson, 1964), attachment can also be explored by examining the infant's responses to other persons when the mother is or is not present.

Fear of the strange is also related to cognitive development. For example, Hebb (1946, 1949), Piaget (1952), and Schaffer (1966) have argued for a relationship between fear and novelty and have considered it indicative of motivational constructs. Also, increased cognitive capacity may influence the development of fear; for example, object permanence, at least in primitive form, might be necessary for social differentiation to occur (Scarr & Salapatek, 1970; Schaffer, 1966). General cognitive capacity might also be related to earlier recognition and differentiation.

Although the strange can include objects and events as well as people, most of the work on fear of the strange has involved people. We mention in passing that loud noises—in fact, intensity in general—have the possibility of frightening the infant (see Scarr & Salapatek, 1970). It is not our intention to deal with this dimension of stimulus events. We restrict our discussion further to include only the infant's social world, leaving out the study of nonsocial stimuli.

Fear of strangers or stranger anxiety has been studied, most of the work

[1] This research was supported by the National Institute of Child Health and Human Development, under Research Grant 1 PO1 HD01762 and by the National Institute of Mental Health, under Research Grant MH-24849-01. We wish to thank Marsha Weinraub and Gina Rhea who helped formulate the problem and collect the data.

growing out of the ethological-attachment literature (Ainsworth & Bell, 1970; Schaffer & Emerson, 1964). Fear of strangers usually appears in the second half of the first year and extends, for some, long into the second year. In the ethological-imprinting position, fear of strangers is seen as a way of binding the infant to his caregivers; like Rheingold and Eckerman (1971), however, we recognize that not all infants exhibit fear of strangers. Some infants show only signs of wariness or differential smiling toward unfamiliar people, while others show no negative affect at all. However, since we are not interested in fear per se but in differential fear, behaviors such as wariness, crying, sobering, and shyness exhibited to a stranger but not to a familiar person are all relevant measures.

For all the current research on fear in infancy, there has been relatively little effort directed to the social dimensions that elicit fear or wariness. Thus far, age of onset, number of infants exhibiting fear, and specific fears of inanimate objects have received the most attention. We are interested in the infant's response to strangers and to familiar persons, and in the social dimensions that are relevant to such differentiations. Only one study (Morgan & Ricciuti, 1969) touches on social dimensions. A male and a female stranger approached infants who were seated by the mother or on her lap. Fear responses were greater for the older infants, for the infants seated in a "Tenda" by the mother, and for the male stranger condition. Even though we do not know why the infants exhibited more fear in the presence of the male, it seems that amount of negative response was related to the nature of the social event. More concretely, our current study comes from an observation of an 8-month-old female. We observed that an approach by an adult stranger produced extreme fear. The infant screamed, cried, and tried desperately to escape. How different when a stranger 3 or 4 years old approached her: smiling, cooing, and reaching behavior was then exhibited. Why should this be? The others were equally strange. Would this hold for children who were generally fearful? What does it mean for the cognitive functioning of the infant, let alone its significance for any theory of attachment? As a first step, this casual observation had to be repeated and extended. To further study such differential reactions, we observed infants' responses to five different social events: a strange adult male and female of the same physical size, a strange female child 4 years of age, the infant's mother, and the infant itself. We expected to find that infants would not only differentiate between strange and familiar but would respond differently to the strangers as a function of various social dimensions.

EXPERIMENTAL PROCEDURE

Twenty-four subjects (14 girls and 10 boys), 7 to 19 months old, were seen. Only infants who were firstborn or who had siblings over 5 years of age were included: 20 were firstborn. Infants with siblings under 5 years of age were excluded to minimize familiarity with small children. Since the analyses indicated no difference between first and later borns, all subjects were pooled.

When the infant was brought to the laboratory by his mother, he was greeted by and interacted with one experimenter to reduce exposure to strangers not involved in the experiment. Each infant was seated in a Tenda at one end of a 10 × 14 foot carpeted room that contained a few pieces of furniture and pictures. The mother sat next to the child, and each of the strangers, one at a time, knocked on the door. The mother greeted the stranger as the door opened and remained silent during the remainder of the episode. The stranger slowly walked toward the infant. On reaching the infant the stranger bent down and touched the infant's hand. Throughout the episode the stranger smiled but did not vocalize. Movements were deliberately slow to avoid eliciting startle responses. After touching the infant, the stranger turned, slowly walked to the door, and left the room. The three strangers were a male adult and a female adult, both of the same physical size, and a 4-year-old female child. The order of appearance was balanced for the three stranger conditions.

The self-or-mother condition followed the stranger conditions. In the mother condition the parent went to the door without leaving the room and walked toward the infant in the same manner as the strangers. For the infant–self condition, it was necessary for the infant to see itself. The mother moved the Tenda directly in front of a mirror placed at the opposite end of the room. She slowly moved the Tenda toward the mirror so that the infant was able to see his reflection *without* observing his mother. When the Tenda was next to the mirror, the mother moved away. We did not have the mirror approach the infant to avoid the effect of novelty (mirrors do not walk). There was approximately a 2-minute interval between conditions. If the infant exhibited fear, the mother comforted him without removing him from the Tenda.

The mother was then interviewed for background and information about her child's fear of strangers. The questionnaire was similar to that of Schaffer and Emerson (1964).

BEHAVIORAL SCALES

Three behavior scales—facial expression, vocalization, and motor activity—were used to rate the infant's reactions to the stranger conditions (see Table 1). A score of 3 indicated a neutral response; 1 was the most negative and 5 the most positive response possible. The checklist is similar to the one developed by Morgan and Ricciuti (1969).

The infants' responses were measured at four distances for each stranger condition. The distances are defined below.

Distance 1 (far)   : — stranger entered room.
Distance 2 (middle): — stranger was in the middle of the room, approximately 7 feet from the subject.

TABLE 1. Behavioral Scales

Facial Expression		Vocalization	
+2	Smile broad	+2	Laugh or giggle
+1	Slight smile	+1	Coo, babble
0	Neutral expression	0	Neutral vocalization
0	Sobering	0	No vocalization
−1	Slight frown	−1	Fuss, whimper
−2	Marked and pronounced puckering	−2	Cry, scream

	Motor Activity to M and to E
+2	Reaches out to E, tries to approach, cling
+2	Touches E's hand or body when nearby
+1	Makes gross body movement − hand waving toward E
0	Looks at E
0	Inattention − sleeping, squirming
0	Explores surroundings (to room)
0	Attention directed away from stranger (to M)
−1	Waves arms and legs while looking at E with negative expression
−1	Avoids E's glance
−1	Pulls hand away from E
−2	Attempts to escape from E (withdraw)
−2	Reaches for mother, tries to approach, touches

Distance 3 (close) : — stranger was 3 feet from the infant.

Distance 4 (touch): — stranger touched the infant's hand.

Lines on the floor indicated the distance from the infant. In the following analysis the terms far, middle, close, and touch indicate the distances. When distances 1 and 2 are summed, they are termed distal. Proximal indicates that distances 3 and 4 have been summed.

Observer reliability was measured by the proportion of agreements (PA) between two observers for the first eight subjects. The mean PA for the three scales was .90 (range .75–1.00). Reliability was highest for vocalization and lowest for motor activity.

A second visit was scheduled in the laboratory to obtain data on the infant's perceptual cognitive development. Each infant was seated in a junior chair or on his mother's lap in front of a screen. Various slides were presented at eye level by rear-screen projection 2 feet from the infant. Two visual episodes were presented. An episode consisted of six presentations of one stimulus, each 30 seconds in duration with a 15-second intertrial interval. The seventh trial was a novel stimulus. Visual stimulus A was 20 straight colored lines (first six trials) and 3 straight colored lines (seventh trial). Visual stimulus B was 20 straight lines (first six trials) and 20 curved lines (seventh trial). Half the infants received stimuli A first, half received stimuli B first.

Fixation for each trial was recorded on an event recorder by an observer who could not be seen by the infant. Habituation, or the speed with which the redundant information is processed, was obtained. Response recovery, or the effect of the novel stimulus presented on the seventh trial, was also calculated. A complete description of the procedure can be found in Lewis et al. (1969).

FEAR OF STRANGERS

The mean data for the facial expression scale and the motor activity scale appear in Figure 1. The similarities between the two scales are striking. Since the responses are almost identical, the facial and motor scales are combined (see Figure 2). The vocalization scale is not included in the analysis or further discussion because there was almost no vocalizing, fretting, or crying.

Differences in Social Events

The data are rather clear. Affective social differentiation increases with the approach of the social agent. Thus few positive or negative responses are exhibited to a social event in a distal position. As the person approaches, differential affect is observed. The male and female strangers elicit the only negative response, whereas the child stranger elicits a positive response. The most positive responses occur when the mother and self are in proximity. In an analysis of variance with the social events and distance as the principal effects, the social event (or stimulus) effect, the distance effect, and the stimulus $\times$ distance interaction were all significant $(F = 11.25, p < .001; F = 16.10, p < .001; F = 18.04, p < .001$, respectively).

To test the differences among stranger conditions at distance 4 (touch), Wilcoxon matched-pairs signed-rank tests were performed for each comparison. All the pair differences for both scales are significant except those between male and female between mother and self. Even though the difference between the male and female adult strangers is not significant, the responses to the male are consistently lower than those to the female. This is similar to the Morgan and Ricciuti study. The infants seem to be making three general distinctions: strange adult (male and female), strange child, and familiar persons (mother and self).

The Effect of Distance

To examine the stranger and distance interaction effect, an analysis of change across distance was performed for each stimulus condition. Distances 1 and 2 were summed, as were distances 3 and 4, and the proximal and distal affect scores were compared for each stimulus condition. In terms of numbers of infants exhibiting the expected changes, fourteen and ten subjects showed an increase in fear to the male and female strangers, respectively, whereas only two subjects responded negatively to child, mother, and self. Conversely, more positive responses are related to proximity in the child, mother, and self conditions (16, 15, and 10 subjects, respectively) than to the male and female strangers $(\chi^2 = 33.5, df = 4, p < .001)$. Motor activity responses are similar to the facial

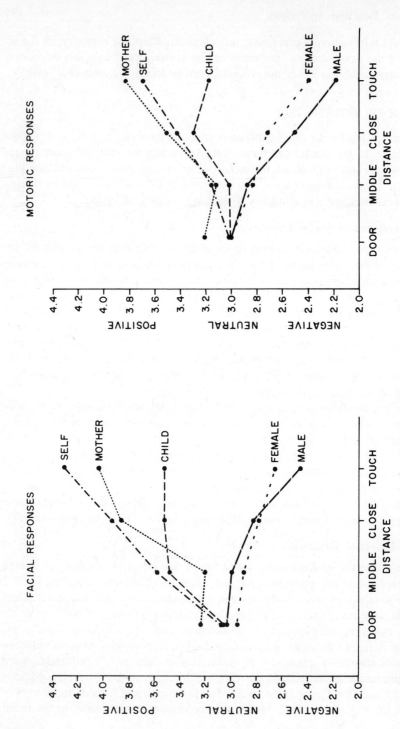

FIGURE 1. Mean data for the facial expression and the motor activity scale.

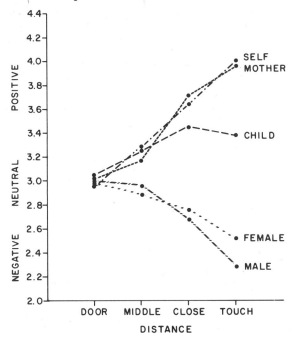

FIGURE 2.   Mean data for the facial and motor scales combined.

expression measures $(\chi^2 = 39.85, df = 4, p < .001)$.

It has been reported that social differentiation does not occur unless the person is approaching and is quite close to the infant (Bronson, 1972; Morgan & Ricciuti, 1969; Schaffer, 1966; Shaffran & Décarie, 1973). When adult strangers approached, infants first stared, then looked at their mothers, but did not exhibit negative affect until the stranger was close. The absence of fear and the prolonged staring may be due to the novelty of the stranger, since novelty may result in increased attention. When the stranger is in close proximity, however, he is not only novel but frightening (since something strange and close can hurt). Schaffer (1966) reports that 13% of his infants refused to observe the stranger approaching and continued to watch the mother, avoiding the impinging event. Bronson (1972) found prolonged staring in his 3- to 4-month-old infants, but he observed the avoidance pattern in infants older than 6 months. He hypothesizes that the younger infants are attempting to process information but have difficulty doing so because the familiar referent has not been firmly encoded. By 6 months, the infant recognizes that the stranger is unfamiliar, and he is also able to avoid or resist the stranger. The rule for infants over 6 months might be: stay and attend as long as the event does not get close; if it approaches, withdraw.

Several alternative explanations for the delay in wariness have to do with information processing. Bronson (1972) suggested that time spent in the presence of the stranger might be relevant. The longer the stranger is in the infant's presence, the more likely he is to exhibit fear. Thus time in room and distance are confounded. If the stranger does not approach, would fear still occur? Morgan and Ricciuti (1969) controlled for the effect of time and distance and found that time was not a relevant dimension.

Hunt (1963) and Schaffer (1966) have suggested that a rapidly approaching stranger cannot be assimilated because there is a limit on *rate* of information processing. The inability to assimilate the approaching stranger results in avoidance or distress. However, we have found that a rapid rate of approach may result in positive *or* negative affect, depending on who is approaching; thus rate of approach cannot be used to account for negative affect.

Bronson (1972) also suggested that the latency to cry is longer than the latency to smile. However, positive affect in the mother and self conditions was not observed earlier than fear responses for the strangers.

It is interesting to note that positive affect toward the infant's mother was not faster than the negative affect toward the strangers. Since the mother is known and easily recognizable at these ages, one might have anticipated earlier positive responses. A possible explanation is that the infants anticipated that the mothers would behave in a certain way (expectations due to normal nonexperimental interactions) and the mothers failed to do so. Thus lack of earlier positive behavior may be an indication of anxiety due to the unusual conditions.

Age Differences

Differentiation of responses to the various social events is related to age as well as distance. When the sample is divided by median age, twelve subjects are between 7 and 11.5 months of age and twelve subjects are 12 to 19 months old. We realize that the small sample size and the arbitrary division of the infants into two age groups limits generalization; however, interesting age differences emerge. Figure 3 presents the mean data on the facial and motor responses for the two age groups.

Although the patterns for the two age levels are most similar, older infants exhibit a greater range of responses than the younger ones. The older infants are more positive to self, mother, and child and more negative toward the adult strangers. The age difference for the adult strangers is significant when Mann Whitney U tests are performed (female stranger, $U = 36.5$, $p < .025$; male stranger, $U = 42$, $p < .05$). Differences for child, mother, and self were not significant, although there is a trend indicating that the older infants exhibit more positive affect $(p < .10)$. Maturation of motor skills may contribute to the differences between age groups, since the older subjects exhibit both more negative and more positive responses. It is important to note that these age differences appear only when the social event is in close proximity. The greater

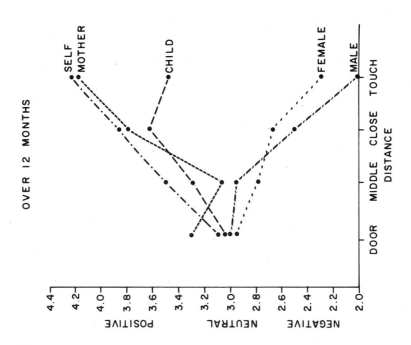

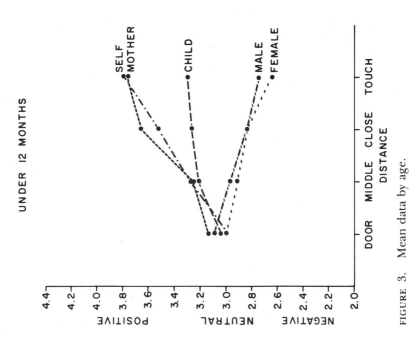

FIGURE 3. Mean data by age.

203

age and presumably greater cognitive development of the infants older than 1 year did not result in *prompter* affective responses. Approach may determine the timing, whereas age affects the intensity of the response.

Similar age differences in the *intensity* of fear responses have been found by Schaffer (1966), Morgan and Ricciuti (1969), and Scarr and Salapatek (1970). Findings on the age of onset, however, are conflicting. In the experiments of Morgan and Ricciuti, infants 4½ to 10½ months old did not exhibit negative responses to the adult strangers, and the younger infants were, in fact, positive toward the strangers. When sobering was considered to be an index of fear, the 4½–and 6½–month-old infants still exhibited positive affect. However, Bronson (1972) reports that infants as young as 4 months respond negatively to strangers. The discrepancies concerning age of onset are difficult to interpret.

Sex Differences

The sex of the infant as well as the sex of the stranger may be related to the production of fear. It has been repeatedly demonstrated that infants are more negative to male than to female adult strangers (Benjamin, 1961; Morgan & Ricciuti, 1969; and Shaffran & Décarie, 1973). Our infants were slightly more fearful of the male stranger, and the difference between the male and female strangers was not significant. Significant differences may have been absent because our social objects did not vocalize during the approach. Vocalization may serve as an additional cue for distinguishing between social events. Lieberman (1967) has shown that infants differentiate male and female voices; thus the perceptual capacties exist to utilize these cues. In addition, the male and female strangers in the present study were approximately the same height, but they were not in the Morgan and Ricciuti (1969) study. Therefore, the failure to differentiate between male and female strangers may be due to the fact that size and vocalization cues were not available.

The sex of the infant may also be related to the affective response to persons (Lewis & Weinraub, 1973). We have found that year-old boys look more at their fathers than their mothers during a free play situation, whereas the reverse was true for girls. However, the negative and positive responses of the boy and girl infants in this experiment were similar. Figure 4 presents the mean data on the facial expression scale for boys and girls. Girls tended to be more fearful of the male stranger than did the boys, although this was not significant.

Reports on sex differences in infants' responses to strangers show limited consistency. Schaffer (1966) and Robson, Pederson, and Moss (1969) found that the onset of wariness is earlier in girls. Girls also exhibit more intense fear than boys (Tennes & Lampl, 1964) and are more variable in their response (Bronson, 1972; Shaffran & Décarie, 1973). Shaffran and Décarie (1973) and Morgan and Ricciuti (1969) learned that boys are

Infants' Reactions to People

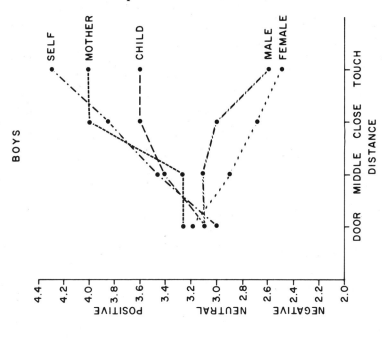

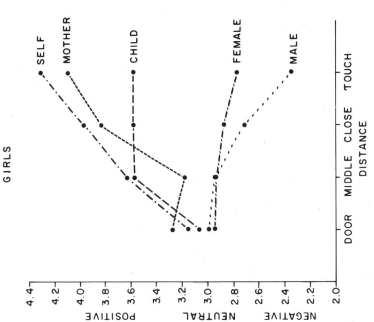

FIGURE 4. Mean data on facial expression scales by sex.

205

more positive to a female stranger, and Bronson (1971) reported that 16-month-old girls were more interested in a female adult stranger than were boys. Maccoby and Feldman (1972) found that girls 2, 2½, and 3 years old were more likely to interact with a female stranger than were boys, although these differences were not significant.

It seems clear from this review that the sex difference data with regard to strangers and fear are not at all conclusive. The data on eye regard as a function of sex of the observer and of the observed indicate that infants are capable of showing differential behavior toward the two sexes. Moreover, this behavior is often a function of the sex of the infant itself (Lewis & Weinraub, 1973). These differences are pursued in a later section of this chapter.

Attention and Differentiation of Social Events

The cognitive ability to differentiate between familiar and unfamiliar seems necessary for the onset of wariness or fear. To recognize that a person is unfamiliar requires a certain level of perceptual development and cognitive capacity. Therefore, one might expect the onset or intensity of fear responses to be related to cognitive development. However, such a relationship has not been found. Scarr and Salapatek (1970) and Bronson (1972) did not find fear of a female stranger and object permanence to be related, Goulet (in press) observed no relationship between fear and causality, and Scarr and Salapatek (1970) reported that motor development and fear reactions are not related. Perhaps only the development of object permanence and causality is necessary before any differentiation can occur, and therefore differentiation requires so low a level of cognitive skill that all infants exhibiting fear are capable of it. Shaffran and Décarie (1973) have suggested that no relationship exists because the fear response is so unstable in the first year of life.

Perhaps the ability to differentiate between familiar and unfamiliar social events is related to the attentional capacities of infants. Thus is there any relationship between infants' responses to slight stimulus changes and their responses to social events?

To study this problem, the infants were seen one week after experiencing the social events in a perceptual cognitive task in which a series of redundant stimuli was followed by a novel stimulus. Measures of response decrement and response recovery were obtained. Habituation, the rate at which a redundant stimulus is processed, is computed by the formula 1st trial-6th trial/1st trial. Response recovery compares looking times for the novel stimulus and the redundant stimulus: 7th trial-6th trial/6th trial. These scores were averaged over the two series. Rapid response recoveries are considered to be measures of general perceptual cognitive ability (Lewis, 1969, 1971).

The first issue was the relationship between the intensity of response (either negative or positive) to the social events and the infant's attentional behavior

TABLE 2. Pearson Product Moment Correlations Between Attention Measures

	Facial and Motor Scale	
	Recovery	Decrement
Social event (N)		
Male stranger (21)	−.23	−.19
Female stranger (21)	−.46	−.27
Child stranger (21)	−.09	−.07
Mother (17)	.20	−.28
Self (20)	.04	.18
Social differentiation		
Male-female	.31	.08
Male-child	.12	.10
Male-mother	.38	.07
Male-self	.21	.22
Female-child	.33	.14
Female-mother	.29	.12
Female-self	.33	.24
Child-mother	.11	.22
Child-self	−.16	.15
Mother-self	.03	.01

(Table 2). A negative correlation indicates that greater response decrement is related to greater negative affect. The same is true for response recovery. It was predicted that a positive relationship should exist between these variables for mother and self and a negative one for the strangers. The data indicate that there is no relation between the amount of affect expressed and the attentional data. Interestingly, in three out of four cases the mother and self correlations are positive, and in six out of six the stranger correlations are negatively related to attention. Although not significant, the affect–attention response to strangers is somewhat different from that of mother and self.

Although intensity of affect response does not appear to be related to attentional capacities, differentiation of affect may be. Differentiation scores for each possible combination of social events, taken two at a time, were obtained; the absolute affect differences between each pair were then correlated with the attention scores (Table 2). The data disclose no relation between any of the differentiation scores to the social events and the attentional scores.

The attentional data then seem to agree with the results obtained with other measures of perceptual-cognitive capacities. This finding is not unreasonable in that it would be hard to imagine infants by 9 months of age having difficulty in perceptually differentiating these kinds of social event. The differential affective responses to these events can hardly be due to discrimination capacities; rather, the nature of the stimulus and its meaning to the infant must be the controlling elements.

Within-Subject Consistency

The infant's response consistency across the five social events was determined and is found in the Pearson Product Moment correlation matrix of Table 3. The magnitude of the correlations is not terribly large, but two clusters of social events are observable: the three strangers—child, male, and female—are positively correlated, whereas the mother and self events are positively correlated with themselves and negatively correlated with the strangers. Among the strangers, the most positive correlations are between the two adults, then between the two females (adult and child), and last between the adult male and the female child. Interestingly, a similar pattern emerges when we look at the negative relationships between mother and strangers. The most negative is between mother and male, then mother and child, and last mother and female. Finally, the least negative relationship involving the self event is the self-child correlation. Recognizing the level of these correlations, we can only speculate that this may represent some ordering of the infant's representation of similarity. If so, adult strangers of either sex are perceived as most similar to each other and different from mother and self, whereas self is least different from mother and child.

The infant's responses to mother and self events are negatively related to their responses to the strangers; thus infants who responded most positively to their mothers and themselves were the ones who responded most negatively to the strangers. The difference between the correlation of male to female strangers (which was positive) and male to mother and male to self (which was negative) was significant $(t_{(16)} = 2.17, p < .05; t_{(19)} = 4.44, p < .001)$, as was the difference between female–child strangers and female–self correlations $(t_{(19)} = 4.32, p < .001)$. This lends support for the clustering of two categories of social events, familiar and unfamiliar.

Morgan (1973) reported a similar correlation $(r = .66)$ between infant's response to male and female strangers. Likewise Shaffran and Décarie (1973) noted a moderate relationship in responding to three adult strangers. The consistency of an infant's response to a stranger should be influenced by the nature of the stranger as well as by the situational context. Such context variables might include the presence or absence of the mother, the familiarity of the surroundings, and the expectations due to past experience or anticipations due to plans or strategies.

Only one study has reported consistency for repeated approaches by one stranger. Robson, Pederson and Moss (1969) found a correlation of .65 for two approaches within one hour. However, Sroufe et al. (Chapter 3) demonstrated that the infant's response to strangers is not consistent, varying from wariness to smiling. Shaffran and Décarie (1973) also report that only one-sixth of their subjects consistently responded negatively. Interestingly, their positive responses were consistent. These results support the view that the context of experience may play an important role in determining the infant's affect, either

TABLE 3. Intercorrelations of Infant's Responses to the Five Social Conditions

	Female	Child	Mother	Self
Male	+.71*	+.10	−.33	−.36**
Female		+.14	−.11	−.57*
Child			−.20	−.13
Mother				+.12

*$p < .01$ two-tailed.
**$p < .10$.

by alternating the nature of the stimulus by making it more familiar or by changing some expectations. Thus a masked face presented after another masked face has two effects, at least of making the mask more familiar, and creating an expectation that masks may appear.

Situation differences tend to be more important for consistency of response than stranger differences. Morgan (1973) found that correlations for same stranger–different situation were lower than for different stranger–same situation. In addition, his data suggest that the more stressful situations were more likely to be related than the less stressful ones. When the infant was in the mother's lap, for example, the consistency between responses to two strangers was only .35; the correlation was .66 when the baby was in an infant seat.

THEORETICAL PERSPECTIVES

The major finding of our study is that infants respond differently to five social events; specifically, infants respond positively to self, mother, and child stranger, and negatively to the male and female adult strangers. It is especially interesting that infants not only differentiate between familiar and unfamiliar, but between strangers. How are we to account for the negative affect directed toward the adult strangers and the positive affect directed toward child stranger and to mother and self? We would expect fear of the stranger; thus the negative expression toward the adult strangers comes as no surprise. However, if strangeness alone elicits fear or negative affect, why no fear (in fact, a positive affect) toward the child stranger?

Both ethological and cognitive theorists have attempted to account for fear of the strange, and we next examine the ability of these two theories to account for the experimental data. A third concept, that of the self as referent which may help explain fear of the strange, is also presented.

Ethological Explanation

The ethological approach generally explains universal human behaviors, such as attachment to a caregiver in terms of biological adaptation and evolutionary mechanisms. For example, ethologists such as Bowlby (1969, 1973) have attempted to explain fear and attachment in terms of their salience for species survival. Fear of the strange is considered to be a homolog of flight in other primates and mammals (Bowlby, 1969; Freedman, 1961). Such fear is adaptive insofar as it protects the infant from threatening and harmful situations and strengthens the attachment bond to the mother. Therefore, strangeness per se accounts for fear. Obviously, this observation does not explain the experimental data. Morgan (1973) and Shaffran and Décarie (1973) both reported that both positive and negative responses may be directed toward the same stranger, since infants are quite variable with respect to fear of strangers. Also, infants do not act consistently toward different strangers; for example, they are more negative to males than females, and they are positive, not negative, to a child stranger.

Fear may also be maladaptive. Organisms need novelty to expand existing schema and to increase competency. But novel events are more likely to be perceived as harmful and therefore may elicit fear and flight. How, then, is the organism able to resolve the conflict between the cognitive demand for exploration and the demand for survival? We will present one possible solution. Exploration may be less harmful or threatening if the novel event is not in close proximity or is not approaching. That is, attend but do not flee as long as the strange does not approach; withdraw if the strange is in close proximity. In this model, both exploration and fear are acknowledged to be important, but they do not interfere with each other. This model requires the use of little or no cognitive processes.

As stated earlier, ethological theory cannot explain the infant's positive response to the child stranger. However, we might postulate that young organisms should be more frightened of large than small strange events, since large things are more likely and more able to cause harm. Therefore, infants may be less frightened of strange events that are the same size or smaller than themselves. One might argue, then, that size is the crucial factor that explains the positive response to the child.

However, another dimension fits in the ethological framework and can be used to differentiate the child from the adult strangers. Facial configuration changes over age, and the infant may respond to these differences. Hess (1970), for example, proposed that the facial configuration of young organisms may be an innate releasing mechanism (IRM) for parental behavior. Perhaps facial configuration also acts as an IRM for infants. Still open to investigation is the question of whether size or facial configuration or both are the salient factors determining the infant's response. The experimental varying of size is rather difficult—we have obtained the services of a small adult to see whether her approach elicits the response pattern characteristic of a child or of an adult.[2]

We have also approached this problem directly from another point of view. By presenting the picture of a child's or an adult's face and by filling the slide with the head, we have eliminated size as a variable. It is then possible to study the infant's response to different people without size as a variable. Unfortunately, when slides are used, no negative affect is elicited. This phenomenon has been demonstrated repeatedly (Kagan, Henker, Hen-Tov, Levine, & Lewis, 1966; Lewis, 1969), even when distortions of slides are presented. This result suggests that infants are capable of treating slides as quite different from "real-life people." Whether this is only a function of the fact that slides do not approach and people do, needs to be explored. However, even though little or no negative affect is elicited by slides, it is still possible to determine whether infants can discriminate and show any preference for children's faces over those of adults.

Fifty-three infants 9 to 18 months old were shown a series of pictures that included faces of 5-year-olds and of adults (Lewis & Brooks, in press). The fixation data are presented in Figure 5. Both male and female infants across ages looked more at the adults than at the 5-year-olds. This difference was significant for the total sample $(t_{(51)} = 2.44, p < .02)$. However, only the female infants showed significant differentiation $(t_{(23)} = 3.70, p < .01)$.

As expected, the affect data showed no negative responses. Thus, infants as young as the first year of life are capable of discriminating adults from children on the basis of facial cues. Although size may be a more salient feature, it is not necessary for differentiation between children and adults. Exactly what facial cues the infants utilize needs to be investigated.

The ethological view does not adequately explain the data on fear of the strange. The variability in responses and the positive affect exhibited to a child

[2]We have just completed the data collection and are in the process of analyzing the results of a study comparing infants' reactions to children, adults, and a small adult. Six different persons including a male and female child, a male and female adult, and a small female adult the same height as the children, approached 40 infants. The procedure was identical to the one reported here. The results indicate that the infants seemed to respond as if there were three classes of strangers—children, adults, and small adults. The infants were most likely to respond with what is traditionally termed fear (e.g., crying, frowning, and gaze averting) to the strange adults. However, they were less likely to exhibit those behaviors in the presence of the small adult and did not exhibit them in the presence of the children. This suggests that size of the approaching person is an important determinant of the amount of negative affect.

In addition, the infants responded differently to the children and the small adult in terms of other behaviors. Infants smiled and reached toward the children but not toward the small adult. The most characteristic response to the latter was prolonged and concentrated staring with little movement or affect exhibited. This seems to indicate that the size-face discrepancy present in the small adult is perceived by the infant although it does not produce distress.

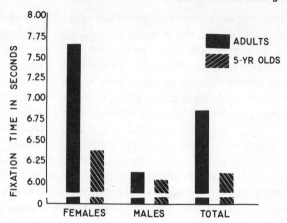

FIGURE 5.   Mean fixation time for pictures of adults versus 5-year-old facial stimuli by sex of the observer.

stranger suggest that fear is not exhibited to all that is strange or novel. This approach is too simplistic, since it fails to consider the cognitive capacities as well as the past experience of the infant.

Incongruity Hypothesis

Cognitive theorists have taken a different approach to the question of fear. The cognitive ability to distinguish between familiar and unfamiliar persons and objects is considered to be a necessary precondition for the occurrence of fear. Therefore, discrepancies between external events and internal representations or schema are central to the incongruity hypothesis. Incongruity presupposes differentiation, since the schema of familiar referents must exist in the infant's mind and also must be utilized for recognition of the strange to occur.

Berlyne (1960) suggested that the unfamiliar or the novel event may evoke fear *or* pleasure, contingent on the conditions. Pleasure is evoked when the stimulus is novel or curious "to the right degree" (Berlyne, 1970). Learning in general takes place through conflict or disequilibrium; if the organism lacks information about a stimulus event, uncertainty is generated. To reduce the uncertainty, the organism actively explores the event. Although Berlyne's concept of conflict reduction may explain general exploration, it does not explain the infant's negative responses to adult strangers. Also, one wonders what characteristics of the child stranger categorized it as an event with "the right degree" of conflict arousal.

Berlyne's theorizing leads us to the incongruity hypothesis. Hebb (1946, 1949) was the first to relate incongruity to affect. Fear is evoked by events that are highly discrepant from previous experience. For example, the head of a monkey shown to other monkeys produces extreme fear because of its incongruity (Hebb, 1946). A number of assumptions about incongruity are implicit in this statement. First, incongruity between an internal representation or schema and the external stimulus event must be perceived. Therefore, a representation or schema must be present in the organism for discrepancy to occur. Fear cannot develop without a central patterning that defines the familiar or comparison figure (Schaffer, 1966). Second, the schema of the familiar that serves as a comparison figure for the impinging social event is usually considered to be the mother. Schaffer (1966) states that fear is not observed in infants before the development of an attachment to a specific human, usually the caregiver. The attachment figure becomes the comparison figure. Therefore, a specific attachment figure, amount of exposure, and general cognitive capacity (object permanence in some rudimentary form must be present) may be related to the concept of incongruity and the appearance of fear.

Third, the incongruity hypothesis states that some discrepancy is required for fear of the strange (Hunt, 1961; Kagan, 1970). A curvilinear relationship between affectual response and novelty of the stimulus is specified, such that an optimum amount of incongruity is necessary for approach. If the social event is too similar to the schema, boredom will occur and the organism will not attend to the event. If the social event is too dissimilar, no information can be processed, observation may not take place, and avoidance and distress occur.

One problem immediately confronting the incongruity hypothesis is determining why highly discrepant events can produce both little attention and fear. It must be argued that the lack of attention is produced by fear; that is, fear causes the infant not to attend. Several difficulties are associated with this approach. First, how does the child know a stimulus is novel if he does not attend? Clearly we must talk in terms of degree of attention, not whether attention occurs. Second, observation of infants interacting with events that seem to be causing fear shows that the infants *do* attend. In the present experiment they continued to look at the approaching stimulus. In Schaffer's study (1966) only 13% of the infants avoided the stranger. From at least one standpoint, it does not make much sense in terms of survival to take one's eyes away from an event that is eliciting fear.

The incongruity hypothesis is also a post hoc explanation of the data. It is difficult to determine on an ad hoc basis the similarity or congruity of a series of events. This is why prediction of a specific fear response is nearly impossible. Moreover, the infant may have different categories for comparing internal schema and external events; thus depending on what schema is used as the referent, different orders of similarity may be generated. For example, I may order my mother, my nephew, and a strange adult female differently. If familial relationships is the comparison, mother and nephew would be judged to be similar, whereas if sex is the comparison, mother and strange adult female would be judged to be similar. Therefore, the comparison figure and the infant's strategy must be taken into account. If the judgment of congruity in our experiment is made with the mother as the referent, the strange female is least incongruent, the strange male more so, and the strange child, most. Thus the child stranger should elicit the most negative response instead of a positive one. Two explanations are possible: (1) incongruity may not be the sole determinant of fear; and/or (2) the mother may not be the only referent for the infant in his interaction with social events. If another comparison figure is used, a different order would occur. If the self is the referent, the child stranger would be least, not most, discrepant.

Another inadequacy of the incongruity hypothesis is pointed up by the failure of the familiar to consistently elicit boredom or withdrawal. The approach of the mother elicits very high positive affect. In the study of infants' responses to pictures of faces, discussed earlier, the picture of mother was looked at longest and was responded to most positively (Lewis & Brooks, in press). Affect preferences based on familiarity may be salient to the infant. There can be no question that infants enjoy and show positive affect to familiar events, the mother being the best example.

Other problems occur when the incongruity hypothesis is evoked. How does incongruity theory explain why approach often is necessary to elicit both positive and negative responses? The capacity of infants to develop specific aversions to individuals (Bronson, 1972) may be better explained by previous experience than by discrepancy. An infant may be fearful of a babysitter because in its past experience the sitter's arrival has meant that the parent is leaving. This conditioned fear has nothing to do with incongruity but rather with the infant's past experience. In general, the infant may be able to evoke internal representations of past experiences that were painful or frightening and associate them with current events. Interestingly, since the current event has an internal representation, we would have to consider it to be familiar rather than novel. Thus in this case a familiar event elicits fear.

In a paper on the acquisition and violation of expectancy, Lewis and Goldberg (1969) have suggested that the chief function of violation of expectation—or, in this case, discrepancy—is to alert the organism. This is a general arousal. In the Lewis and Goldberg (1969) study arousal was measured by observing the surprise expression on the 3- to 4-year-old child's face. Thirteen out of fourteen cases of surprise occurred in response to a violation of expectation. The specific affective behavior (in the experiment reported, it was smiling) occurred after. Thus it would appear that the chief function of violation of expectancy or discrepancy is to arouse the organism. What determines the specific affective behaviors depends on the context of the violation and the nature of the other cognitions the infant utilizes at that point.

Thus, for example, a mother's putting on a mask may lead to a violation of expectancy for the infant. This would lead to arousal. Whether the infant laughs or cries is then dependent on the contextual situation and the infant's specific cognitions. For example, the infant may cry if the mask is put on when the mother is about to read him a bedtime story but laugh when it is put on during playtime. In both cases the infant recognizes the discrepancy that arouses him, but in the former it produces fear because he understands it not to be related to bedtime, and in the latter it produces happiness because he understands it to be related to play. Thus the discrepancy of mask has only the arousing effect; other cognitions determine its affective value. One particular cognition, which we wish to pursue, is that of the infant's cognition of itself.

The Concept of Self

The following comments are related to the possibility that the infant utilizes referents other than its mother in its social interactions. The referent to be explored is that of the self, and the following discussion is intended to initiate the consideration of this construct.

We wish to explore two aspects of the self: the first and most common is the categorical self (I am female, or I am intelligent, or I am big or small, or I am capable); the second, and by far the more primitive, is the existential statement "I am." The basic notion of self—probably as differentiated from other (either as object or person, the mother being the most likely other person)—must develop first. There is no reason not to assume that it develops from birth and that even in the early months some notion of self exists. We would argue that this nonevaluative, existential self is developed from the consistency, regularity, and contingency of the infant's action and outcome in the world. Self is differentiated by reafferent (or information) feedback; for example, each time a certain set of muscles operates (eyes close), it becomes black (subject cannot see). That is, the immediacy, simultaneity, and regularity of action and outcome produce differentiation and self. The action of touching the hot stove and the immediacy of the pain tells me that it is my hand that is on the stove. This self is further reinforced if, when I remove my hand, the pain ceases. The infant's world is full of such relationships, and they vary from its own action on objects to its relationship with a caregiver. In these social interactions, the highly directed energy of the caregiver (touch, smile, look, etc.) is contingent on and specific to infant action (smile, coo, etc.).

The relationship of self to the mirror is, likewise, related. Looking in the mirror is pleasurable because of the consistency, regularity, and contingency of the viewer's action and the viewed outcome. In no other situation is there such consistent action–outcome pairing. In other words, the mirror experience contains the elements that generally make up the fabric of the infant's growing concept of self. It is difficult to know when the infant is aware that the image is himself. Awareness is a difficult concept to study in nonverbal organisms, but it is clear that by the time one-word utterances such as "self" or "mine" emerge, the infant has the concept of self. It is reasonable to assume that the concept existed prior to the utterance. In fact, if we consider the research on the development of object permanence (e.g., Charlesworth, 1968), we find that for the most part object permanence has been established by 8 months of life, in many cases even earlier. If infants have the cognition available to preserve memory of objects no longer present, how can we deny them the ability to have self-permanence? Indeed, is it reasonable to talk of object-permanence capacity without self-permanence capacity? Given that this first self–other distinction is made very early, the various categorical dimensions of self may also proceed to unfold. The unfolding of the categories—whether sequential, hierarchical, or otherwise—and the dimensions of the various categories, are uncertain.

Self-Recognition as a Measure of Self

Self-recognition is only one part of the self construct, but it is easy to define and to observe. The kinesthetic feedback produced by our actions is continuous, and such action–outcome contingencies must theoretically form the basis for self-recognition. However, observing self-recognition experimentally may be more difficult than defining it theoretically. For example, facial recognition should be universal in our society because everyone is repeatedly exposed to mirrors and pictures. The only adults who would have difficulty recognizing their faces visually would be psychotic patients and patients suffering from certain dysfunctions of the central nervous system (Cornielson & Arsenian, 1960; Frenkel, 1964). Therefore, there is usually a high degree of correspondence between the general concept of self and facial recognition, although we recognize that these two constructs are not synonymous. Even though we realize that self-recognition and the construct of self are not synonymous, the demonstration of the former may give us insights on the development of the latter. In addition, visual self-recognition is only one aspect of self-recognition—one that in fact may be the hardest and last formed. For example, proprioceptive or auditory recognition may occur much earlier. Thus visual self-recognition may not be demonstrable in infants who do in fact already have some self-recognition and concept of self.

The development of self-recognition has been studied in primates and in human infants. The most comprehensive work has been done by Gallup (1970), who has observed chimpanzees and rhesus monkeys in front of mirrors. First Gallup distinguishes between self-directed and other-directed behaviors: "self . . . is the referent through the reflection, where in cases of social behavior the reflection is the referent" (1970, p. 86). Chimpanzees with as little as 10 hours of mirror play are able to groom visually inaccessible parts of their bodies with the use of the mirror. To experimentally demonstrate his belief that primates engage in self-recognition, Gallup devised a situation for experimentally testing self- versus mirror-directed responses. Red dye was painted on chimpanzees' and rhesus monkeys' ears while the animals were anesthetized. A control group, also anesthetized, received no red dye. When the primates awoke, their mirror behavior was observed to see whether they would reach for the dye by touching the ''mirror ear'' or whether they would reach for their ''own ear.'' The experimental chimpanzees reached for their ''own ears'' while looking in the mirror. Neither the control nor the rhesus monkeys showed the reaching for their own ear. In this experiment chimpanzees did not reach for the chimp-in-the-mirror-with-a-strange-color but instead reached for their own ear. That is, they recognized the image in the mirror as *their own,* and reached for the strange dye on themselves, instead of reaching toward the reflection. By this demonstration Gallup argues that there is an evolutionary history, since primates lower than chimpanzees do not have the capability to recognize themselves visually, even after repeated exposures to a mirror. Since chimpanzees are able to recognize themselves after limited experience with a mirror, it would not be unreasonable to expect human infants also to demonstrate this ability. Infants are not only cognitively sophisticated, but they spend much time engaging in mirror play. Mothers often report that their infants enjoy mirror play and sometimes use a mirror to soothe a fussy infant. Therefore, we believe that a study of infants' responses to mirrors will indicate that visual self-recognition is present from an early age.

In fact, when the various studies are examined, a consistent pattern of the development of self-recognition appears. From 3 to 12 months of age, infants approach the image socially; they smile at, vocalize to, and pat the mirror (Amsterdam, 1972; Dixon, 1957; Gesell & Thompson, 1938). In the second 6 months, friendly approach is coupled with repetitive activity and deliberate movements (Amsterdam, 1972; Dixon, 1957). By 12 months, the infants begin to withdraw from the image and actively attempt to avoid it. Self-directed behaviors are observed around 18 months.

To experimentally distinguish between self- and mirror-directed behaviors and to discover the developmental timetable for self-recognition, we adapted Gallup's situation to human infants. We observed 23 infants with rouge on their noses in front of a mirror. (The rouge was applied by the mothers under the guise of wiping the infants' faces.) After the application, the infants were brought to a floor-length mirror. All the 22-month-olds $(N = 8)$, one-third of the 19-month-olds $(N = 9)$, and none of the 16-month-old subjects $(N = 6)$ touched their noses. Amsterdam (1972) has reported that marked directed behaviors first occur at 18 months and are common by 20 months. Thus the development of self-recognition as measured by self-directed behavior is consistent across two studies and indicates that facial self-recognition exists in many infants by 18 months. Unfortunately, there is yet no information on the relation between recognition and prior experience, social interactions, and cognitive ability.

If more mirror experience had been provided, perhaps the infants would have shown self-directed behavior even earlier. Gallup found that mirror experience was necessary for the chimpanzees to show self-directed behavior. However, human society differs from that of other primates in that the mirror has been a very common human artifact. Even though all infants in our study had had prior experience with mirrors, *extensive* experience may not be necessary. The proprioceptive feedback system and the cognitive system (especially that of permanence) only need to be integrated to produce recognitory behavior. In other words, it may be that only a few trials with the appropriate feedback are needed in order to elicit visual recognition.

Another method that we have used to determine whether infants can recognize themselves is to show them slides of pictures of themselves and of infants of both sexes who are the same age as the subjects. Fifty-three infants age 9 to 18 months were seen. Each infant received two trials of a picture of itself and a male and female infant the same age. The pictures were of the head, and the trials were 15 seconds long. Figure 6 presents the fixation data, which indicate that infants looked longest at the same-sex and least at opposite-sex infants. When the fixation times between self and other infants (independent of sex) were observed, no significant difference could be found. However, when sex of the same-age infant was included, self was differentially regarded. The analysis of self to same-sex infant indicated no difference, whereas the comparisons between self and opposite-sex infant did (sign test $z = 1.68$, $p < .05$). This effect was most significant for girls (sign test $p < .02$).

These results lend some support to the supposition that infants below 18 months of age are capable of differentiating themselves from other infants their own age. These data together with the mirror data bolster our hypothesis that by 18 months an infant is capable of recognizing himself. A concept of self exists prior to the ability to use labels such as ''self'' and ''mine'' correctly. As stated earlier, the development of self-recognition may be intimately related to the notion of permanence as well as to the kinesthetic feedback system. That the self is distinct from other environmental events is a necessary condition for the later development of self identity (Guardo & Bohan, 1971). The origins of self permanence may occur quite early, since the parallel system of object permanence develops in the first year of life. The development of the self as subject may also be related to social differentiation. The mother–other distinction occurs between 3 and 9 months; the self–other differentiation should be evolving at the same time. The infant certainly has as much experience with itself as with its mother.

Self and the Explanation of Fear of Strangers

Is our understanding of the phenomenon of fear helped by evoking the concept of self? We would argue that it is. For example, Hebb (1949) found that monkeys exhibited great fear when a monkey's head was placed in their cage. Consider that the animals were fearful because they saw a monkey without a body

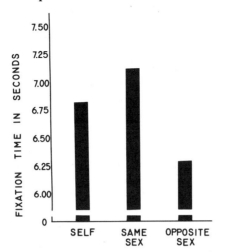

FIGURE 6.   Mean fixation time for facial pictures of self, opposite-sex, and same sex infants of the same age.

and they were aware that they, too, were monkeys. Maybe they too could lose their heads to a mad professor. Would not humans placed in a similar situation show fear for their lives or safety? Hebb argues for an incongruity hypothesis but he, like others following him, has not always separated incongruity from content.

The notion of self may also explain the positive response to the child stranger and the negative responses to the adult strangers in our study. The referent for the social comparison may not always be the infant's mother. There could be multiple referents, one of them being the mother, another being the self. Perhaps the positive response to the child stranger is produced because the infants find the child to be like themselves; that is, they use themselves as referent, find the child to be like them, and are therefore not afraid. In this case the categorical dimension of self may have to do with size. I am small vis-à-vis other social events, and the child is also small, and therefore it is like me. Although we have no direct data to support the notion of multiple referents, the interrelationship among the social events is suggestive evidence. Infants who were very fearful of the male were also fearful of the female stranger, but there was no significant relationship between self and mother. Thus although there is a division into strange and familiar, the two familiar events are hardly similar.

In addition, gender identity, which is part of the self concept, may explain why female infants are more frightened than male infants of male adult strangers. The male infant recognizes that the male stranger is like himself and is therefore not as fearful.

The concept of self has for us two aspects—the earlier differentiation of self from other, and the later categorical self. The earlier differentiation should take place at the same time the child is differentiating its mother and acquiring object permanence. We see no difficulty in this differentiation.

The categorical self is somewhat different. First, the categorical self is subject to many changes. Ontogenetically it should change as a function of the child's other cognitive capacities as well as with changing social relationships. The categorical self, then, undergoes a lifelong process of change. Some categories, like gender, remain fixed; others change either by being added to or by being altered entirely. Historically and socially this categorical self should be expected to change. Thus the category of self in feudal society should be somewhat different from that in an industrial society. In the former, self is defined by social units larger than itself such as the family (in fact, that one was named "the son of" denotes self-references as relationships to others). Socially, the categorical self is also affected; for example, the redefinition of a woman (or man) in our society as a function of the feminist movement will change the categories people use (Miss versus Mrs. becomes irrelevant as Ms. is used).

If this conceptualization is at all valid, it becomes necessary to consider what categories may be available to the infant and how these change. One category that has received some attention is gender.

Gender as a Category of Self

Gender is an important category of self that is established early and remains invariant over life. Sex may be a salient cue for differentiating others and recognizing oneself. Even though the ability to label gender (self and others) correctly is considered a preschool task (Kohlberg, 1966), the origins of gender invariance and differentiation may be found in infancy.

One problem associated with looking at gender identity or for that matter at any categories of self in infancy is the lack of the organism's verbal facility either to respond to a task or to understand the requirements. Thus our studies must be limited to observation of the infant's differential behavior. One behavior of particular interest is the infant's visual regard. We shall make use of this to see whether it is possible to talk about gender identity in the very young. Special use is made of the interaction between the sex of the infant and the sex of the object, since we believe that any interaction should reflect the two characteristics necessary to argue for gender identification. These are gender differentiation, or the ability to discriminate between the two sexes, and own gender recognition. A sex of subject–sex of object interaction makes these points.

At two ages we have found this interaction. First, when one-year-old infants were observed with both parents (one at a time) in a playroom situation, male infants looked more at their fathers and female infants looked more at their mothers (Ban & Lewis, 1971). This was a significant interaction. At 2 years

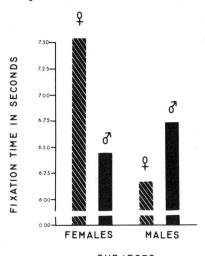

FIGURE 7.   Mean fixation time for facial pictures of infants by sex of stimulus and sex of the observer.

of age there was more visual regard to the same-sexed parent during play. In still another study, briefly mentioned earlier, we observed the fixation data of a group of 54 male and female infants from 9 to 18 months of age. Here too, a significant interaction was found. Figure 7 shows that male infants looked at male infants more than females, the reverse being true for females. This interaction was tested by a second-order difference score $(t_{(49)} = 2.08, p < .05)$.

Recall also Figure 6, which indicated that pictures of the self were most easily differentiated when compared with infants the same age of the opposite sex.

An infant's gender may also affect his negative responses to other persons. We found, as have others (Benjamin, 1961; Morgan & Ricciuti, 1969; Shaffran & Décarie, 1973), that infants exhibit more negative affect toward male than toward female strangers. In our sample, this effect was more pronounced for the female infant.

Finally, in a study of peer group interaction, eight sets of four one-year-old infants and their mothers were observed at play in a laboratory playroom. Preliminary analysis indicates that the infants tend to look more at the same-sex infants (Brooks, Michalson, & Lewis, 1974). Preferences for same-sex playmates have also been observed in dyads and groups of preschoolers (Abel & Sahinkaya, 1962; Langlois, Gottfried, & Seay, 1973).

All these gender data lend support to our thesis; however, some of the strongest data come from the study of hermaphrodites. Money and his colleagues have found that by 2 years of age infants having undergone gender change are most reluctant to give up their original gender identity (Money,

Hampson, & Hampson, 1957). We have little theory to support such early sex
of subject–sex of object interaction. Differential behavior as a function of the
sex of the object does not explain why the behavior of the infant varies as a
function of its sex. We have hypothesized that early in life the child develops
such a category (i.e., gender) and utilizes it in his interactions with others. All
things being equal, we would predict that children will model and attempt to
behave like the same-sex objects. We are currently involved in a series of experiments to elucidate this matter.

Peer Relationships

The most interesting finding of our study is that the infants responded positively, not negatively, to the child stranger. Only three other studies have compared infants' responses to adults and children; results similar to those reported
here were found. Using our methodology, Greenberg, Hillman, and Grice
(1973) learned that infants react more negatively to the approach of an adult
than to that of a child stranger. When Lenssen (1973) placed two infants and
their mothers in a playroom, the infants ignored their mothers and directed significantly more behavior toward the strange infant, as compared with the strange
adult. Infants also preferred to interact with strange infants rather than strange
female adults when four infants and their mothers were observed together. In
a study just completed we observed the infants' interaction with peers, adult females, and their mothers at the same time. Eight sets of 12- and 18-month-old
infants were seen in a laboratory playroom. Each set consisted of four dyads
of a mother and her infant; half the children were male and half female. Looking, touching, and proximity-seeking behaviors, among others, were obtained.
The data indicate that infants spent more time in interaction with peers than
with adult females, either mother or stranger. Looking behavior directed toward
peers is more than twice that directed toward mother or strange adult female
(Brooks, Michalson, & Lewis, 1974). Infants seem to enjoy, not fear, interaction with other infants and children. Perhaps the infant realizes that the child is
like himself and, therefore not threatening. Thus the use of a categorical self as
a referent for social comparisons may have implications for peer relationships.
Exactly what categories the infant uses to relate to peers is not clear. Size,
which has been suggested, might be critical in the comparison. The positive response of the infants to the child and infant strangers is consistent with other
primate evidence, all suggesting that infant peer interactions may have a special
quality. According to anecdotal evidence, infants often seem to follow and learn
faster from an older sibling than from their parents. For example, later-born infants exhibit less fear of strangers than firstborn children (Schaffer, 1966; Collard, 1968). This may be because a later-born infant has other infants to observe
and play with from the beginning of its life. Peers have been known to serve

quite well as adult substitutes in early attachment relationships (Freud & Dann, 1951; Chamove, 1966). In fact, Harlow was surprised at the lack of social emotional deviance in his mother-deprived, peer-attached monkeys. "Early experience with multiple peers produces ties among group members which maximize play and affiliative behavior and minimize aggression within the group or towards outsiders" (Harlow & Harlow, 1969, pp. 27–28). Moreover, the data make clear that if infant–peer relationships can be sustained (as, e.g., in laboratory colonies) infant–peer relationships satisfy many of the socioemotional requirements we view as important for the growth of the infant (Harlow, Harlow, & Suomi, 1971).

Finally, an interesting implication of peer relationships has to do with animals for whom imprinting is a major source of social bonding. Among birds, for example, can the young be as easily or more easily imprinted on a peer than on an adult member? On whom is a duckling imprinted as its family swims single file on the pond? The mother, or the young duckling in front of it? If the ducklings maintain their order, only the first is behind the mother. If they vary their order, then each duckling spends more time behind a peer than behind mother. Peer attachments, even in infancy, have great importance for a general theory of socioemotional development. Certainly it must modify our views on infants' fear.

Summary

A wide variety of theoretical perspectives has been presented to explain the child's dealing with the strange, the familiar, and the novel. We have suggested that it is not unreasonable to evoke a concept involving the cognitive capacity of the infant. This cognitive capacity rests on our belief that the infant by 2 years of age has already acquired a conceptualization of itself that we call self. Moreover, the self, which is subject to change and modification, is utilized by the young organism in its dealings with its social world. We recognize that some of the discussion is speculative; however, we consider it important to postulate alternative cognitive models of the child's interaction with its world. Neither the ethological nor incongruity hypothesis satisfactorily explains the existing data, and we hope by this exercise to stimulate alternative views.

We wish to summarize by listing our three major points:

1. Violation of expectation or discrepancy is not the only factor in fear-producing events. Conditioning to past events cannot be omitted as a major determinant.

2. Violation of expectation or discrepancy does not lead to fear itself. Rather, violation of expectancy leads to general arousal (see Lewis & Goldberg, 1969). The specific affective behaviors that follow this general arousal are totally de-

pendent on at least the set of cognitions and contextual cues the infant utilizes at the moment of arousal.

3. Within the infant's dealings with its social world, it is necessary to evoke the specific cognition of self to understand the infant's affective expression toward other people.

The infancy literature of the past decade makes it quite clear that we do not have to await the infant's language acquisition to talk about complex and sophisticated cognitive skills, employed in an executive fashion and dependent on context, plans, and strategies. It is important to keep in mind that one of the first words of the infant is "mine," used as it *pulls an object toward itself.*

References

Abel, H., & Sahinkaya, R. Emergence of sex and race friendship preferences. *Child Development,* 1962, **33,** 939–943.

Ainsworth, M. D. S., & Bell, S. M. Attachment, exploration, and separation: Illustrated by the behavior of one-year-olds in a strange situation. *Child Development,* 1970, **41,** 49–67.

Amsterdam, B. Mirror self image reactions before age two. *Developmental Psychobiology,* 1972, **5**(4), 297–305.

Ban, P., & Lewis, M. Mothers and fathers, girls and boys: Attachment behavior in the one-year-old. Paper presented at the Eastern Psychological Association meetings, New York, April 1971.

Benjamin, J. D. Some developmental observations relating to the theory of anxiety. *Journal of the American Psychoanalytic Association,* 1961, **9,** 652–668.

Berlyne, D. E. Children's reasoning and thinking. In P. Mussen (Ed.), *Carmichael's manual of child psychology.* Vol. 1. New York: Wiley, 1970. Pp. 939–982.

Berlyne, D. E. *Conflict, arousal and curiosity.* New York: McGraw-Hill, 1960.

Bowlby, J. *Attachment and loss.* Vol. 1. *Attachment.* London: Hogarth; New York: Basic Books, 1969.

Bowlby, J. *Attachment and loss.* Vol. 2. *Separation.* London: Hogarth; New York: Basic Books, 1973.

Bronson, G. W. Infants' reactions to unfamiliar persons and novel objects. *Monographs of the Society for Research in Child Development,* 1972, **37**(148).

Bronson, W. C. Exploratory behavior of 15-month-old infants in a novel situation. Paper presented at the Society for Research in Child Development meetings, Minneapolis, April 1971.

Brooks, J., Michalson, L., & Lewis, M. Peer and adult attachment behavior in the one-year-old infant. Unpublished paper, 1974.

Chamove, A. S. The effects of varying infant peer experience on social behavior in the rhesus monkey. Unpublished MA thesis, University of Wisconsin, 1966.

Charlesworth, W. R. Cognition in infancy: Where do we stand in the mid-sixties? *Merrill-Palmer Quarterly*, 1968, **14**, 25–46.

Coates, B., Anderson, E. P., & Hartup, W. W. Interrelations in the attachment behavior of human infants. *Developmental Psychology*, 1972, **6**(2), 218–230.

Collard, R. Social and play responses of first born and later born infants in an unfamiliar situation. *Child Development*, 1968, **39**, 324–334.

Cornielson, F. S., & Arsenian, I. A study of the responses of psychotic patients to photographic self image experience. *Psychiatric Quarterly*, 1960, **34**, 1–8.

Dixon, J. C. Development of self recognition. *Journal of Genetic Psychology*, 1957, **91**, 251–256.

Freedman, D. G. The infant's fear of strangers and the flight response. *Journal of Child Psychology and Psychiatry*, 1961, **2**, 242–248.

Frenkel, R. E. Psychotherapeutic reconstruction of the traumatic amnesic period by the mirror image projective technique. *Journal of Existentialism*, 1964, **17**, 77–96.

Freud, A., & Dann, S. An experiment in group upbringing. In *The psychoanalytic study of the child*. Vol. 6. New York: International University Press, 1951.

Gallup, G. G. Chimpanzees: Self recognition. *Science*, 1970, **167**, 86–87.

Gesell, A., & Thompson, H. *The psychology of early growth*. New York: Macmillan, 1938.

Goldberg, S., & Lewis, M. Play behavior in the year-old infant: Early sex differences. *Child Development*, 1969, **40**, 21–31.

Goulet, J. Notion de causalité et réactions à la personne étrangère chez le jeune enfant. In T. Gouin-Décarie (Ed.), *La réaction à la personne étrangère*. Montreal: Presses de l'Université de Montréal, in press.

Greenberg, D. J., Hillman, D., & Grice, D. Infant and stranger variables related to stranger anxiety in the first year of life. *Developmental Psychology*, 1973, **9**, 207–212.

Guardo, C. J., & Bohan, J. B. Development of a sense of self identity in children. *Child Development*, 1971, **42**, 1909–1921.

Harlow, H. F., & Harlow, M. K. Effects of various mother–infant relationships on rhesus monkey behaviors. In B. M. Foss (Ed.), *Determinants of infant behavior*. Vol. 4. London: Methuen; New York: Wiley, 1969.

Harlow, H. F., Harlow, M. K., & Suomi, S. J. From thought to therapy: Lessons from a primate laboratory. *American Scientist*, 1971, **59**, 538–549.

Hebb, D. O. On the nature of fear. *Psychological Review*, 1946, **53**, 259–276.

Hebb, D. O. *The organization of behavior*. New York: Wiley, 1949.

Hess, E. H. Ethology and developmental psychology. In P. Mussen (Ed.), *Carmichael's manual of child psychology*. Vol. 1. New York: Wiley, 1970. Pp. 1–38.

Hunt, J. McV. *Intelligence and experience*. New York: Ronald Press, 1961.

Hunt, J. McV. Piaget's observations as a source of hypotheses concerning motivation. *Merrill-Palmer Quarterly*, 1963, **9**, 263–275.

Kagan, J. The determinants of attention in the infant. *American Scientist*, 1970, **58**, 298–306.

Kagan, J., Henker, B., Hen-Tov, A., Levine, J., & Lewis, M. Infants' differential reactions to familiar and distorted faces. *Child Development,* 1966, **37,** 519–532.

Kohlberg, L. A cognitive-developmental analysis of children's sex-role concepts and attitudes. In E. E. Maccoby (Ed.), *The development of sex differences.* Stanford, Calif.: Stanford University Press, 1966. Pp. 82–173.

Langlois, J. H., Gottfried, N. W., & Seay, B. The influence of sex of peer on the social behavior of preschool children. *Developmental Psychology,* 1973, **8,** 93–98.

Lenssen, B. G. Infants' reactions to peer strangers. Unpublished manuscript, 1973.

Lewis, M. Infants' responses to facial stimuli during the first year of life. *Developmental Psychology,* 1969, **1,** 75–86.

Lewis, M. Individual differences in the measurement of cognitive development. In J. Hellmuth (Ed.), *Exceptional infant.* Vol. 2. New York: Brunner/Mazel, 1971. Pp. 172–211.

Lewis, M., & Ban, P. Stability of attachment behavior: A transformational analysis. Paper presented at the Society for Research in Child Development meetings, Symposium on *Attachment: Studies in Stability and Change,* Minneapolis, April 1971.

Lewis, M., & Brooks, J. Social perception in the infant. In L. Cohen & P. Salapatek (Eds.), *Perception in infancy.* New York: Academic Press, in press.

Lewis, M., & Goldberg, S. The acquisition and violation of expectancy: An experimental paradigm. *Journal of Experimental Child Psychology,* 1969, **7**(1), 70–80.

Lewis, M., Goldberg, S., & Campbell, H. A developmental study of learning within the first three years of life: Response decrement to a redundant signal. *Monographs of the Society for Research in Child Development,* 1969, **34**(9, Serial No. 133).

Lewis, M., & Weinraub, M. Sex of parent × sex of child: Socioemotional development. Paper presented at the International Institute for the Study of Human Reproduction Conference on Sex Differences in Behavior, Tuxedo, N. Y., October 1973. To appear in R. M. Richart, R. C. Friedman, & R. L. VandeWiele (Eds.), *Sex differences in behavior,* in press.

Lewis, M., Weinraub, M., & Ban, P. Mothers and fathers, girls and boys: Attachment behavior in the first two years of life. Paper presented at the Society for Research in Child Development meetings, Philadelphia, March 1973.

Lieberman, P. *Intonation, perception, and language.* Cambridge, Mass.: M.I.T. Press, 1967.

Maccoby, E. E., & Feldman, S. S. Mother-attachment and stranger-reactions in the third year of life. *Monographs of the Society for Research in Child Development,* 1972, **37**(1, Serial No. 146).

Money, J., Hampson, J. G., & Hampson, J. L. Imprinting and the establishment of gender role. American Medical Association, *Archives of Neurology and Psychology,* 1957, **77,** 333–336.

Morgan, G. A. Determinants of infants' reactions to strangers. Paper presented at the Society for Research in Child Development meetings, Philadelphia, March–April, 1973.

Morgan, G. A., & Ricciuti, H. N. Infants' responses to strangers during the first year.

In B. M. Foss (Ed.), *Determinants of infant behavior*. Vol. 4. London: Methuen; New York: Wiley, 1969.

Piaget, J. *The origins of intelligence in children*. New York: International University Press, 1952.

Rheingold, H. L., & Eckerman, C. O. Fear of the stranger: A cultural examination. Paper presented at the Society for Research in Child Development meetings, Minneapolis, April 1971.

Robson, K. S., Pederson, F. A., & Moss, H. A. Developmental observations of diadic gazing in relation to the fear of strangers and social approach behavior. *Child Development*, 1969, **40**, 619–627.

Scarr, S., & Salapatek, P. Patterns of fear development during infancy. *Merrill-Palmer Quarterly*, 1970, **16**, 53–90.

Schaffer, H. R. The onset of fear of strangers and the incongruity hypothesis. *Journal of Child Psychology and Psychiatry*, 1966, **7**, 95–106.

Schaffer, H. R., & Emerson, P. E. The development of social attachments in infancy. *Monographs of the Society for Research in Child Development*, 1964, **29**(3, Serial No. 94).

Shaffran, R., & Décarie, T. G. Short-term stability of infants' responses to strangers. Paper presented at the Society for Research in Child Development meetings, Philadelphia, March–April, 1973.

Sroufe, L. A., Matas, L., & Waters, E. Determinants of emotional expression in infancy. Chapter 3, this volume.

Tennes, K. H., & Lampl, E. E. Stranger and separation anxiety in infancy. *Journal of Nervous and Mental Diseases*, 1964, **139**, 247–254.

Piaget, J. The Origins of Intelligence in Children. New York: International Universities Press, 1952.

Kagan, J. Change and Continuity in Infancy. New York: Wiley, 1971.

CHAPTER 9

Discrepancy, Temperament, and Infant Distress[1]

JEROME KAGAN
Harvard University

Sciences are nurtured by a dynamic, cyclic interaction between constructs and empirical reality. An interesting phenomenon is noted and given a preliminary name. Further inquiry leads to an inference regarding possible antecedents, and a hypothetical causal mechanism is generated and also named. The potential power of the mechanism is tested in the harsh empirical arena, and the new data generated often lead to changes in the names of both the phenomena and the mechanisms. This process is repeated indefinitely, with names changing for both events and causal processes. Consider, as an example, Newton's original paper on light and color in which an aether is postulated to understand the physical world.

"Perhaps the whole frame of nature may be nothing but various contextures of some aethereal spirits, or vapours, condensed as it were by precipitation, much after the manner that vapours are condensed into water or exhalations into grosser substances, though not so easily condensible; and after condensation wrought into various forms; at first by the immediate hand of the Creator, and ever since by the power of nature; which, by virtue of the command, increase and multiply, become a complete imitator of the copy set her by the protoplast. Thus perhaps may all things be originated from aether [Gillespie, 1960, p. 129]."

Three centuries later we know that the "aether" is not a useful construct, and physicists continue to search for the origins of matter, suppressing the uneasiness generated by the possibility that the physical world is a "labyrinth with an empty center" (Holton, 1973).

This necessary dialogue between naming and new information is less frequent in psychology. The research on human emotions, for example, has continued to use the labels philosophers invented more than 35 centuries ago—fear, joy,

[1]This research was supported by research grant HD-4299 from the National Institute of Child Health and Human Development, and grants from the Office of Child Development and the Spencer Foundation.

happiness, anger. The habit is so fixed that the names have become reified. We begin our work by assuming that fear, anger, and sadness are definite, palpable, and true entities, and we conceive of our task as discovering the events that produce them and devising methods of measuring them. However, putting the name aside temporarily and behaving as if there were none may be useful for psychology, whose lexicon has become encrusted with ancient, unexamined, and by implication misleading categories. Let us return afresh to the natural phenomena and see what new concepts we might generate. I am not opposed to the invention of hypothetical constructs—I have been too easily seduced into that exciting adventure—but it is often constructive to focus initially on the functional relations that exist in nature, deciding later what names to apply to them. Implementation of that suggestion to the phenomena that have been labeled fear may be useful.

REACTIONS TO UNEXPECTED EVENTS

There is a significant sequence during the first year of life in which the introduction of a visual or auditory stimulus in a particular context produces, within 1 to 5 seconds, lawful changes in the child's behavior and, by inference, his state. The change of primary concern is characterized by an alerting to the event and a temporary inhibition of ongoing activity. Following the initial alerting reactions, one of three behavioral sequences usually follows. On the one hand, the child returns to what he was doing and within 10 to 15 seconds appears to be as he was before the introduction of the event, without a display of "emotional" responses. A second possibility is that the child smiles, laughs, vocalizes, or shows excited motor activity. A third possibility is that the muscles of the child's face become tense, his eyes widen—a combination often called wariness—and he may turn away from the event and perhaps cry.

This description implies an original state (to be named) that is replaced by one of several different states, each of which also requires a label. I am assuming we agree that the initial event that may be followed by crying or smiling need not be a conditioned stimulus that was bonded through reinforcement to smiling or crying (although it might be). Typically the initiating event is either a sudden unexpected change in the physical aspects of the child's environment (movement, loudness, light intensity) or an event that is discrepant from the child's prior schema for that class of event (a face with distorted features or a dog that locomotes by slithering on the ground).

It is suggested that the term *event* is not synonymous with the more common term *stimulus*. It seems clear—Sroufe's chapter in this volume being a recent example—that a stimulus does not exist independent of a particular context and the individual's expectations. This principle is as valid for baboons as it is for man. Hence the word event (or discrepant event) is intended to refer to the unique gestalt described by the relations among all stimulus elements in a context, as well as the relation of those elements to the context. Introduction of a strange woman (a stimulus element) into a child's bedroom is an event different from the introduction of the same stranger into the doctor's office or the psychologist's laboratory. Since an adult's evoked potential to a light or tone depends on the context and his expectations, it is not reasonable to assume that the presentation of a stranger will have a fixed effect across contexts. Rather, it seems useful to argue that stimulus element and context are complementary components of the psychologically meaningful event. Hence the statement "A child's behavioral reactions to a stranger will depend on the context" is equivalent to saying "A child's behavioral reactions will differ in response to different events." The data described in this volume support this view, for infants display more inhibition than smiling if a strange woman walks directly toward them and touches them, but there is more smiling if the stranger approaches more indirectly and tentatively initiates play.

It is interesting to note that this position is in accord with Bohr's resolution of the problems created by Heisenberg's uncertainty principle (Bohr, 1934). In classical physics it was understood that the measurement of a molar physical phenomenon did not in any way interfere with the phenomenon. However, in quantum mechanics, which deals with "micro" events, that proposition is not true. In Newtonian physics the assumption of a sharp separation between the subject (or the investigator) and the object being investigated was not generally challenged. Quantum mechanic physics after 1900 acknowledged that the coupling between subject and object could only be cut in an arbitrary way. Bohr suggested that a phenomenon is a description of that which is to be observed as well as the apparatus used to obtain the observation. Bohr made the entire context of inquiry part of the event. We are suggesting, in a similar vein, that the context is not separate from the stimulus. A "stimulus in a context" is the psychological event we must study.

"As soon as the scientist sets up the observation tools on his workbench, the system he has chosen to put under observation and his measuring instruments for doing the job form one inseparable whole. Therefore the results depend heavily on the apparatus [Holton, 1973, p. 119]."

If we substitute context for apparatus in that sentence, the principle seems to be directly relevant for the study of human behavior.

SEQUELAE OF ALERTING

Since it is useful to name phenomena, we suggest the term "alerting" to designate the initially brief state, lasting 1 to 5 seconds, following the introduction of an event that is either a discrepancy or an unexpected change in physical parameters; others may prefer to call it the orientation reaction. It is characterized typically by inhibition of motor activity, decreased heart rate, and changes in motor tonicity. This state is neither fear, joy, nor excitement. It is a special state with alternative sequelae depending on the cognitive processes that follow.

The major factor that determines the sequelae of "alerting" is ease of assimilation of the event. If the event is primarily a change in physical qualities, rather than a change in psychological information, the child typically adapts quickly and his behavior returns to its original form. If the event violates an a priori expectation or is discrepant from a habituated standard, the child's postalerting behavior will depend on whether he can assimilate the event. If he can, either his behavior will return to baseline without any noticeable change in overt reaction, or he will show signs of nondistressful excitement (smiling, vocalizing, or increased motor activity). If he cannot assimilate the event he will either turn away and redirect his activity or display prolonged focusing of attention on the event, accompanied by inhibition of activity, and, on occasion, changes in facial expression and crying. How can we account for these differences? Let us consider first the assimilation arm of the process. Why do some children, following assimilation, simply return to baseline, whereas others vocalize, smile, or do both? We think at least two factors are important—effort invested in the assimilation, and a temperamental attribute.

If the event is assimilated easily and no effort is required, the child is likely to return to his prior posture without displaying signs of excitement. If the event is not assimilated easily, the child is likely to show prolonged attentiveness and, if successful, to issue signs of excitement, such as vocalization or smiling, but not necessarily both.

Relation of Discrepancy to Attention

This hypothesis engages the lively controversy concerning the relation between degree of discrepancy between event and schema and the behavior following alerting. We have argued that the child will show prolonged attention and signs of excitement to moderately discrepant events—events that share some dimensions with the child's previously acquired schema. Very familiar and very novel events, which share few or no dimensions with the schema, will generate shorter epochs of prolonged attention and less excitement.

The rival hypothesis maintains that the relation is not curvilinear but linear and that the more different the event is from the child's schema, the greater the attentiveness (and, by inference, the greater the attempt at assimilation).

During recent years we have attempted to show that the linear hypothesis is less able to explain the empirical data than the curvilinear principle. These data have been summarized in several places (Kagan, 1971, 1972; Super, Kagan, Morrison, & Haith, 1970; McCall & Kagan, 1967). The most recent demonstration, which is not yet published, is perhaps the clearest affirmation of the curvilinear form of the function.

One hundred forty infants of both sexes, 7½ months of age, were assigned to one of five discrepancy groups: no change, minimal change, two different levels of moderate change, and a novel or major change. The five stimuli, which were approximately equal in volume and were formed from papier-mâché, were: a sphere, a pear-shaped form, a club-shaped form, a cylinder, and an irregular, tooth-shaped object. The first four objects were all red with half-inch black stripes. The tooth-shaped object was green with no stripes. For the 80 infants tested in series 1, the sphere was the standard to which they were habituated; the discrepant object, presented following habituation, was either the pear-shaped form (minimal discrepancy), the club or cylinder (moderate discrepancy), or the tooth (novel or major discrepancy). For the 60 infants seen in series 2, the cylinder was the standard to which they were habituated, and the discrepant object was either the club (minimal discrepancy), the pear or sphere (moderate discrepancy), or the tooth (novelty). The control subjects who received no change continued to see the sphere in series 1 or the cylinder in series 2. Adult judgments of the stimuli revealed that the adults regarded the pear, the club, and the cylinder as progressively more elongated from the sphere. These judgments were in approximately equal intervals, with values of 0 for the sphere; 3, 6, and 10 for the pear, club, and cylinder, respectively; and a score of 20 assigned to the irregular-shaped tooth.

Each baby was seated on his mother's lap facing an 18-in. square window in front of a two-compartment box resembling a two-channel tachistoscope. A bright yellow padded lever extended from beneath the window. A lever press lighted one compartment and provided a 2.5-second view of the three-dimensional object. All objects revolved on a turntable at 16 revolutions per minute to maximize the attention-eliciting properties of the stimuli. The standard stimulus was changed to the discrepant stimulus by closing a switch in the control room which lighted the second chamber. Ambient illumination in the room was kept low and constant throughout testing. An observer, watching the subject through a 1×4 in. window behind one of the chambers, recorded fixation, vocalization, and fretting on a button box linked to a polygraph. Interobserver reliabilities for each of these variables were over .90. The infant's instrumental responses were automatically recorded on the polygraph.

Every 20 seconds the accumulated number of instrumental responses while looking at the stimulus (reinforced responses) was tallied on line from the automatic stimulus marking channel of a Grass polygraph. These calculations were immediately graphed and used to determine when each S had displayed criterial habituation and was ready for introduction of the discrepant stimulus. The following criteria for habituation were used:

1. Reinforced responding increased over base level.
2. Reinforced responding following peak responding in two consecutive periods decreased below 50% of the mean of the previous two 20-second periods.
3. The standard stimulus was available to each S for at least 3 minutes.

When these criteria were reached, the discrepant stimulus was illuminated. (Control infants continued to see the same stimulus.) The Ss must have had the discrepant stimulus available for viewing for at least 3 minutes to be included in the analysis. Discrepancy groups, series, and sex were the independent variables, with change in behavior between the last 2 minutes of the standard and the first 2 minutes of the discrepancy as the dependent variable treated in a repeated measures analysis of variance.

Table 1 shows the mean value for changes in behavior (initial 2 minutes of discrepant object less the last 2 minutes of the standard) for reinforced responses, total fixation time, nonfretful vocalization, and fretting for infants in both series. Sex and series differences were not significant.

Reinforced responses increased the most to the moderately discrepant object and decreased most to the novel and minimally discrepant objects. A trend analysis suggested a quadratic trend $(F = 2.30, df = 1/135; p = .16)$. The absence of a large drop in responding for the no-change controls was due to the increased restlessness produced by boredom and irritability. One result of this boredom was increased activity and smacking at the lever. Both fixation time and vocalization were greatest to the moderate discrepancies, and the quadratic component was significant for both variables. Fretting and crying were least likely to the moderate discrepancies and increased most to the no-change and minimal-change groups, suggesting boredom and restlessness.

Figure 1 illustrates the curvilinear function for reinforced responses and fixation time in clearer form as a result of pooling the no-change and minimal-discrepancy groups as well as the two moderate-discrepancy groups.

The moderate-discrepancy groups showed significantly greater recovery of instrumental responding than the minimal-discrepant groups $(t = 1.97, df = 110, p < .05)$ and a tendency toward greater recovery than the novel group $(t = 1.54, df = 82, p = .13)$. Similarly, there was greater recovery of fixation time to the moderate than to the minimal discrepancies $(t = 2.29, df = 110, p < .05)$.

Although smiling was infrequent in all groups, the moderately discrepant events produced the most smiling and the least crying.

It appears that events moderately discrepant from those for which the child possesses a schema are most likely to lead to prolonged attention, excitement, and even smiling—although the last response is least frequent. Moderately discrepant events are not likely to cause wariness or crying. Thus we assume that moderately discrepant events are usually assimilable. As for the causes of vocalization and occasional smiling, it is tempting (but I am not sure how helpful) to suggest that the effort at assimilation of a moderately discrepant event generates a tension that is resolved by the assimilation. That resolution produces the smiling, motoricity, and vocal discharge as epiphenomena. This phrasing is reminiscent of Freud's interpretation of laughter and is, of course, at the heart

TABLE 1. Change in Behavior Following Presentations of Discrepant Object

	Degree of Discrepancy						Trend Analysis		
	No Change	Minimal	Moderate 1	Moderate 2	Novel	Source	df	F	p
Reinforced responses (per minute)	-.069	-2.77	-0.73	+1.22	-1.97	Linear	1	<1	n.s.
						quadratic	1	2.30	.16
						residual	2	3.01	<.05
						error	135	—	—
Fixation time (seconds)	-5.46	-6.05	-3.09	+3.18	-2.99	Linear	1	2.13	.15
						quadratic	1	4.22	<.05
						residual	2	<1	n.s.
						error	135	—	—
Vocalizations (seconds)	-0.02	+0.81	+1.13	+3.44	-0.77	Linear	1	<1	n.s.
						quadratic	1	8.69	<.01
						residual	2	<1	n.s.
						error	135	—	—
Fretting (seconds)	+9.38	+4.09	+2.39	+1.27	+3.09	Linear	1	4.04	<.05
						quadratic	1	7.43	<.01
						residual	2	<1	n.s.
						error	135	—	—
n	28	28	28	28	28				

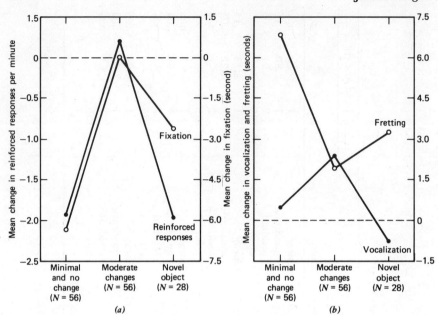

FIGURE 1. Change scores for instrumental responses, fixation, vocalization, and fretting for first 2 minutes of transformation minus last 2 minutes of the standard.

of the Miller-Dollard drive reduction explanation of reinforcement that was popular 20 years ago. Despite the notion's intuitive appeal, psychologists have been unable to find a way to measure this tension or its resolution. Unfortunately, it is not uniformly reflected in heart-rate change. We have not found any systematic relation—after 8 years of work—between heart-rate deceleration or acceleration, on the one hand, and the occurrence of smiling or vocal excitement, on the other. It is reasonable to assume that changes deep in the reticular activating system—or other loci in the brain—are the seat of the elusive tension; at the moment, however, we do not seem to be close to detecting the site of those subtle physiological events. Hence little is added, from an explanatory point of view, by speaking of tension enhancement and tension resolution. Although that language is phenomenologically satisfying and has the ring of correctness, such intuitions are often misleading.

THE ROLE OF TEMPERAMENT

A second factor that influences likelihood of smiling to a discrepant event is the child's temperament. To my knowledge, few investigators have found a visual or auditory event—tickling is excepted—that produced smiling in a laboratory context in 75% or more of infants tested. Typically, 20 to 50% of a group of infants smile to a moderately discrepant event, suggesting that some babies are not easily disposed to smile; some seem to have higher thresholds for this reaction. We assume the latter are potentially capable of a smile, but it takes greater or more (pick any magnitude adjective you like) effort to evoke a smile from some infants. This condition implies the operation of a constitutional variable related to the ability to establish and resolve whatever state changes accompany effort at assimilation. Freedman and Keller (1963) have reported that monozygotic twins are more similar in their tendency to smile than dizygotic twins, and Reppucci (1968), in our own laboratory, found substantial heritability ratios for smiling to masks in 4-month-old white infant twins, but low heritability for fixation time and vocalization. In a recent longitudinal study (Kagan, 1971) 4-month-old infants who smiled frequently at human masks were generally slower in tempo of play and larger in size than nonsmilers, although equally distributed from working and middle-class homes. Specifically, there was a group of children who smiled at 4 months to the human masks and at 27 months following successful solution of a perceptual problem. These "smilers," when contrasted with children who were low smilers at both 4 and 27 months, showed longer epochs of sustained attentiveness in play, as well as more inhibition in a conflict situation at 27 months of age. Moreover, endomorphic 2-year-old girls were high smiling infants; tall, heavy infant boys showed the most smiling to the perceptual problem.

This evidence, together with anecdotal reports from mothers of two or more children that one of their babies was more disposed to smile than the other, tempts us to posit a constitutional factor that predisposes an infant to smile. One consequence of that assumption is caution against interpreting absence of smiling as indicative of a failure to assimilate a discrepant event. We must find other indices of that dynamic process for low smiling children. It may be that the infants who return to baseline with no change in affective behavior, as well as those who smile, have assimilated the discrepant event in a similar fashion. The difference in affective behavior is due primarily to the temperamental disposition to smile.

THE BASES FOR DISTRESS

Let us now turn to the other set of alternative reactions following alerting; namely, continued inhibition, wariness, avoidance, redirection of activity, and crying. If the child cannot assimilate a discrepant event following initial effort, he is in a special state different from the one created by the initial appearance of the event. Some may wish to call this state "fear." But note that neither facial wariness nor crying necessarily occurs in this state, although we agree with others that changes in facial expression, patterns of motoric posture, and perhaps cardiac acceleration often accompany this state. Perhaps it should be given a more neutral name, like "uncertainty." The behaviors that follow the state of uncertainty will depend on the situation (availability of familiar figures or toys) and on the child's temperament. Is there a familiar toy available or an involving response that a child can initiate? If so, he is likely to initiate that response, and the resulting activity will inhibit crying, and, we believe, resolve or at least reduce the uncertainty. The child may suck his finger, bury his head in his mother's lap, hit an available object, or turn his face from the event. In a relevant study, Rheingold and Eckerman (1970) found that if a baby could crawl through an open door to locomote to his mother, whom he could not see, he did so and did not cry when he found himself alone in a strange room without visual access to anyone familiar. If he could not locomote to her, the child would cry.

We agree with Bronson (1971) that, as with smiling, some infants have a temperamental disposition to cry when uncertain; others have a higher threshold and require unusual levels of uncertainty before crying. Bronson (1971) found that young infants who showed early onset of signs of fear were more likely to show intense crying to a strange person at 12 months of age. We have found that 4-month-old babies who became restless and irritable after several presentations of an interesting stimulus were most likely to be fretful at 8 and 13 months and most likely to cry at 8 months when their mothers left them alone in a laboratory study of separation protest (Kagan, 1971). Nine boys and twelve girls in this study cried so intensely during the initial presentation of facial masks at 4 months of age that we had to stop the session. We brought these children back on a second day, but again they cried during the opening trials and the sessions had to be terminated. Each of these 21 highly irritable children was matched with a child of the same sex and social class who never fretted or cried to the masks, and we compared the pairs of children at 8, 13, and 27 months. Although there were no differences at 8 months, the extremely irritable 4-month-old girls behaved as if they were cognitively precocious to their nonirritable controls at later ages. They looked longer at discrepant events, vocalized more following termination of auditory events and showed less stereotyped play at 13 months, and were more talkative at 27 months. These differences did not emerge for boys.

Thomas, Chess, and Birch (1970) have also suggested that a temperamental disposition to irritability appears early in life, persists, and is at the core of one of their "personality types." Even rhesus monkeys raised in a laboratory display marked individual variability in their reaction to removal of the mother. Some infant monkeys respond with an inhibition of motor activity and little crying; others respond primarily with crying (Hinde & Spencer-Booth, 1971). Figure 2 summarizes the preceding discussion and labels the various states by number rather than by name, to emphasize the need for new labels.

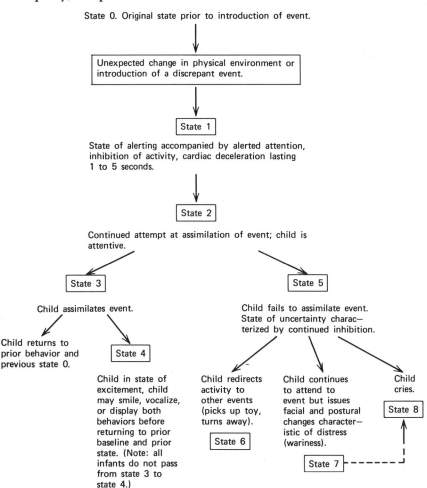

State 0. Original state prior to introduction of event.

Unexpected change in physical environment or introduction of a discrepant event.

State 1

State of alerting accompanied by alerted attention, inhibition of activity, cardiac deceleration lasting 1 to 5 seconds.

State 2

Continued attempt at assimilation of event; child is attentive.

State 3

Child assimilates event.

Child returns to prior behavior and previous state 0.

State 4

Child in state of excitement, child may smile, vocalize, or display both behaviors before returning to prior baseline and prior state. (Note: all infants do not pass from state 3 to state 4.)

State 5

Child fails to assimilate event. State of uncertainty charac—terized by continued inhibition.

Child redirects activity to other events (picks up toy, turns away).

State 6

Child continues to attend to event but issues facial and postural changes character—istic of distress (wariness).

State 7

Child cries.

State 8

FIGURE 2.   Hypothetical sequence to an alerting event.

The potential advantage of assigning numbers to the various fluid and dynamic states that flow one into the other is to underscore the ambiguity surrounding the term fear. Some investigators would call state 5 "fear" and view wariness and crying as operational signs of that state. But if temperamental and situational factors seriously influence the likelihood that crying will follow state 5— and we suggest that there is a poor relation between state 5 and the act of crying— then, as with smiling, although the occurrence of crying may be a sound basis for inferring state 5, absence of crying is not a reasonable datum on which to infer the absence of state 5. Others, who prefer to equate the reaction of crying with fear, view state 7 or 8 as the state of fear. At the moment, any of these practices is defensible, for the data are sufficiently ambiguous and the theory sufficiently fragile to permit any of a number of arbitrary classifications. The point we wish to make is that distressed facial expression and/or crying do not always occur when a child cannot assimilate a discrepant event he has spent a half-minute studying.

ACTIVATION OF HYPOTHESES

A second major theme in this chapter concerns a change in cognitive functioning that seems to occur during the second half of the first year. During the opening 6 to 8 weeks of life, the child alerts primarily to unexpected changes in physical aspects of his environment and, on occasion, cries following that alerting. After approximately 6 to 8 weeks, the child alerts with increasing frequency to events that are not merely changes in physical parameters but are transformations of his own earlier experiences—psychologically discrepant events. Some time after 7 or 8 months in Western children, a new mechanism emerges, and it seems to take the form of a cognitive competence. We have called that competence "activation of hypotheses" (Kagan, 1972), but the name is less important than a clear description of the process. Now the infant begins to actively retrieve cognitive structures—hypotheses—in the service of interpreting discrepant events, where a hypothesis is a representation of a relation between schemata. The infant not only detects and processes the discrepancy—as he did when younger—but he also attempts to transform it to his schemata for that class of events, and he activates hypotheses to serve that advanced cognitive function. Schaffer, in this volume, also notes the change at 8 months but uses slightly different language. Schaffer suggests that after 8 months the infant can consider several events simultaneously; he has progressed from sequential to simultaneous comparisons. Prior to 8 months the infant asks, "Have I or have I not seen this stimulus before?" Later he asks, "How does this stimulus compare with my other experiences?" It is not a coincidence that postulation of this new competence coincides with the time when the infant displays object permanence and separation fear—phenomena that require the child to activate an idea of an absent object or person.

The sources of support for the postulation of a new competence somewhere around 8 months come, first, from age changes in attention to the same set of events. Regardless of whether the event is a facial mask, a geometric design, or a dynamic sequence in which a rod turns on a bank of three light bulbs, there is a U-shaped relation between age and attention across the period 3 through 36 months, with the trough typically occurring between 8 and 13 months of age. Similarly, there is a U-shaped relation between age and search behavior to auditory stimuli across the period 3 through 20 months, with the trough again occurring around 8 months of age. Moreover, the probability of a cardiac acceleration to a particular discrepant event increases markedly toward the end of the first year; whereas cardiac deceleration is the modal reaction to the same event during the earlier months. Since studies of adults and young children indicate that cardiac acceleration accompanies mental work, whereas deceleration accompanies attention, the increased probability of acceleration toward the end of the first year implies that the infants are performing active mental work, or at least more active processing than occurred during the first 6 months of life.

The relevance of this new competence for this discussion is that the one-year-old is likely to treat the absence of a stimulus element in a context as a discrepant event. This phenomenon is rare in the very young infant. For the 4-month-old, a new event is usually created by introducing a material stimulus element into the situation. For the child of one year, who is capable of activating hypotheses, the removal of an element— such as his mother leaving the room—is perceived as a new event. This idea is supported by the observation that crying and sustained inhibition of play to maternal separation (signs of failure to assimilate) do not appear to any appreciable degree until 8 or 9 months of age, and increase in frequency and duration through 2 to 2½ years of age, after which they decline. This age function has the same form in middle-class Cambridge children, infants from an institution in Athens, and poor ladino infants from Antigua, Guatemala.

An Interpretation of Separation Anxiety

We now consider, in some detail, the work on "separation fear" and suggest that it fits the paradigm of an unassimilated discrepant event producing uncertainty (state 5 in Figure 2) and, occasionally, crying. That is, we treat the reaction to separation as we would the reaction to any discrepant event that cannot be assimilated.

In an early study, mothers were instructed to leave their 11-month-old infants either from a normally used exit in the home or from one that they rarely used (e.g., a closet or cellar door). The infants were more likely to be alerted and to cry when the mother left from the unfamiliar than from the familiar exit (Littenberg, Tulkin, & Kagan, 1971). Thus the generation of a change in affective behavior seemed to be produced not by the mother's leaving *qua* leaving, but by seeing her walk through a door she rarely took. The discrepancy that was difficult to assimilate was the event "leaving through an unfamiliar exit." More recently, in collaboration with Philip Zelazo, Milton Kotelchuck, Gail Ross, and Elizabeth Spelke, we have completed a series of studies similar in design and outcome. The scene was a laboratory playroom, and the actors were the mother, the father, the child, and an unfamiliar woman.

In the first study, (Kotelchuck, 1972), six cross-sectional samples were observed at 6, 9, 12, 15, 18, and 21 months of age. The total sample consisted of 144 infants, 12 boys and 12 girls at each of the six ages. All the infants were firstborn and had college-educated parents. The infant sat in the middle of a large playroom surrounded by many interesting toys and facing his mother and father who were seated at one end of the room. The parents were instructed to respond naturally but briefly if their child approached them. Every 3 minutes one of the adults entered or departed from the room. One of two nonbalanced orders was used to determine which adult—the mother, the father, or the stranger—would remain in the room with the child. The subjects who received order 1 experienced the following thirteen events: mother and father, father, father and stranger, stranger, stranger and mother, mother, mother and father, mother, mother and stranger, stranger, stranger and father, father, father and mother. The infants in order 2 experienced the following: mother and father, mother, mother and stranger, stranger, stranger and father, father, mother and father, father, father and stranger, stranger, stranger and mother, mother, mother and father. The child's play, crying, proximity to a person, vocalization, smiles, and attentiveness were coded throughout each of the thirteen, 3-minute conditions. Interrater reliabilities ranged from 0.80 to 0.90 and the behaviors were coded from an audiovisual tape. Since there were no order differences, orders were pooled across episodes.

The subjects did not show a statistically significant decrease in play or increase in crying (compared with behavior during the previous episode) until they were about 12 months of age. These behaviors increased until 18 months, then declined very slightly. Moreover, as long as one parent remained with the child he did not show significant inhibition of play or crying. A child only showed these behaviors when he was alone with the stranger. There was very little difference in the child's reaction to mother or father departures, except that 12-month-olds played a little less following maternal than paternal departure.

In a second study (Spelke, Zelazo, Kagan, & Kotelchuck, 1973) the subjects were also white, middle-class, firstborns, but all were 12 months old. The procedure used was identical to that just described, and the same laboratory room was used. In addition, the fathers were interviewed in some detail to determine the degree of their participation in interaction with the infant at home. This information permitted a division of the fathers into three groups—high, moderate, and low interactive with the child at home. Incidence of crying and inhibition of play were in accord with those found in the first study. The infants displayed inhibition of play and crying only when they were alone with the stranger, not when one parent remained following the departure of the other.

Of great interest was the observation that the children whose fathers interacted with them frequently at home showed less crying and inhibition of play than the children with low-interactive fathers. This relation also occurred in the original Kotelchuck study. One interpretation is that the children who had high-interacting fathers had a greater variety of experiences, hence were cognitively precocious. As a result, they were better able to assimilate the discrepant events.

This study produced data suggesting the influence of a temperamental attribute on the incidence of crying and smiling. Two weeks before the separation experiment, all the infants were seen in a different laboratory, where they were exposed to visual habituation–dishabituation procedures. In the first, the infant was shown six repetitions of a large block and then dishabituated to a small block for three trials. The same infants were also exposed eight times to a hand moving an orange rod in a semicircle; at the end of its traverse, the rod touched a bank of light bulbs that lit. During the dishabituation phase the hand appeared but the rod did not move, and the lights lit after 3 seconds. There were five dishabituation trials. The subjects who smiled most to these nonsocial events were least likely to cry during the separation episode two weeks later ($x^2 = 5.03, p < .10$). The infants who were most fretful to the nonsocial episodes—even though they were on mother's lap—were most likely to cry to the separations ($x^2 = 7.66, p < .05$).

The final study attempted to assess the effect of context by repeating the original Kotelchuck (1972) study with father, mother, and stranger in the child's home, with infants 12, 15, and 18 months old. As in the laboratory study, the infants typically cried more and played less when left alone with the stranger than when they were with one parent, and reactions to father and mother departures were generally similar. That result has occurred on three separate occasions!

The main finding was that infants tested in the laboratory cried more, spent more time proximal to their mothers, and showed more inhibition of play than the children tested at home.

One important result bears directly on the discrepancy interpretation of "fear to separation." *There was more crying when a person entered the room* (even when a parent was already present) *when the laboratory was the context than when this event occurred in the home.*

Since the experience of people entering the home should be familiar (i.e., not discrepant), assimilation should be easier. But in the laboratory, where the total setting is unfamiliar and the child has no expectations of who will arrive and leave, the one-year-old who is in the stage of activation of hypotheses should have great difficulty understanding why people are coming in and going out at 3-minute intervals. He would be expected to cry as a reaction to his failure to assimilate those events.

It is important to note that in these and other studies with similar procedures (see Fleener & Cairns, 1970) the occurrence of crying and inhibition of play to separation is infrequent prior to 9 to 12 months and increases from 12 to 24 months. We recently found no differences in frequency of crying or response latency to crying between home-reared and day care infants seen seven times longitudinally from 3½ to 20 months of age, following a procedure in which the mother left the child alone in a small room (Kearsley, Zelazo, Kagan, & Hartmann, unpublished). This finding is supported by Ricciuti in this volume. The corpus of data suggests that a maturational factor related to the ability to recognize the discrepancy contained in the "separation procedure," but the temporary inability to assimilate that complex event may be a major cause of the behavioral signs of fear generated by this procedure. The fact that crying and inhibition are much less likely to occur prior to 8 months implicates a maturing cognitive mechanism.

One implication of these data is that the event "parent leaves child with other parent and stranger in an unfamiliar room" is discrepant but assimilable. We know that the event is alerting, for the children look at the departing parent and stop their play for a second or two. Hence failure to cry or display wariness and prolonged inhibition suggests rapid assimilation of the event. Since smiling or vocalization rarely occurred under these conditions, it may be that the event was easily understood and did not require much psychic effort to assimilate. An alternative explanation implies that the event of parental departure, as long as one parent remains, should not be viewed as a discrepancy. This is not an unreasonable suggestion. Some of the one-year-olds may have been exposed to similar events in their own or neighbors' houses in which one parent left and the other remained. This possibility is not attractive because of the initial alerting shown by the children following the parental departure and the occurrence of crying in the home setting.

A third interpretation, implied by Sroufe et al. (see Chapter 3), makes the infant even more complicated than we have made him. Sroufe suggests that the child evaluates a discrepant stimulus as threatening or nonthreatening. If the former, he will become fearful. As long as one parent remains, Sroufe implies that the child's set is one of nonthreat; therefore, he does not cry or show wariness. This explanation has some appeal. We know that if a baby is on its mother's lap or close to her, events that would ordinarily elicit crying or wariness if the mother were 10 feet away or absent do not elicit either reaction and, on occasion, elicit smiling. This phenomenon is in accord with Sroufe's notion of "evaluation of threat."

The Significance of Proximity to the Familiar

Let us probe this explanation further. Why does the presence or proximity of a parent seem to prevent the appearance of crying and behavioral wariness? One possibility derives from the notion that the infant's representation of the contemporary context is based on one salient stimulus element, and all other elements are referred and subordinate to it. When he is close to or in contact with a parent, that familiar element dominates his schema at that moment. If a single discrepant element is introduced—a mask or a stranger—it is usually, but not always, assimilated quickly, for the dominant representation is one of familiari-ty. It is as if the familiar representation "I am with my parent," absorbs, trans-forms, or neutralizes the single discrepant element. But if we continue to add discrepant elements, or if we introduce a discrepancy more difficult to assimi-late (a large animal that behaves strangely), many children will cry even though they are on mother's lap. We recently created intense fear in a group of 2-year-olds by introducing a person wearing the mask of an animal who behaved in an odd way. Even though the children were in physical contact with their mothers, they all cried intensely. We also have observed 24 one-year-olds in a situation in which initially they played in a room while their mother read in a chair nearby. Signs of wariness rarely occurred in this situation. But when a strange mother and her unfamiliar child entered the room a half-hour later, more than half the children showed alerting, their faces displayed wariness, they ran to mother, and some asked to be held. Thus the presence of a parent does not always prevent "fear" to a discrepancy; it seems to depend on the ease of assimilation of the discrepant event. The presence of a parent does not guaran-tee protection against inhibition and distress; it may only raise the threshold for those states. However, there is still sufficient ambiguity surrounding the data to permit debate and discussion. It is not clear whether the presence of the care-taker buffers "fear" because the child believes he is not threatened, because of a raised threshold for this state, or because of other factors. The implications of each view are different. If evaluation of threat is critical, the child might show little change in crying when less easily assimilated events are introduced in a home situation in which the child is close to his mother. If passing a thresh-old were critical, he should begin to cling to mother and cry as the difficulty of assimilation increases. As suggested earlier, even when the child is on his mother's lap, a discrepant event that is difficult to assimilate elicits crying when a more easily assimilated one does not.

OTHER SOURCES OF DISTRESS

Finally, we should note that unassimilated discrepancy is only one source of crying or distress states. Admittedly, it is ontogenetically one of the first occa-sions, and since this volume is concerned with origins, it is appropriate to focus on this process. As we have stated elsewhere (Kagan, 1971), four other events can elicit similar, although we feel not identical, distress states and behavior later in development. They are (1) anticipation of an undesirable event, (2) unpredictability, (3) recognition of inconsistency between belief and behavior, and (4) recognition of dissonance between or among beliefs. In the first, the child anticipates future encounter with an event that he believes will be painful or distressing—such as rejection or physical harm. This phenomenon seems to emerge during the second year. This anticipation can be established through simple contiguity conditioning, observation of contingencies that occur to others, or, later in life, generation of an expectancy of distress based on symbolic knowledge. The case of Hans' phobia of horses and wagons is a simple example; most are more complicated.

A second source of a distress state is unpredictability of a future event. The 6-year-old child who says he is afraid of going to school, but cannot state why or what he fears, is illustrative of this phenomenon. The likelihood of this fear being conditioned or acquired through observation is less persuasive. Many mothers have reported an increase in distress in their 2- and 3-year-olds prior to the delivery of their next child. The 3-year-old becomes irritable, wants to be close to the mother, has night awakenings, and seems tense and anxious. This class of "fear" does not appear to be fixed on any specific target but seems to be associated with the child's attempt to predict what his experience will be like when the new baby is born and his being unable to answer that question.

A third source of distress is occasioned when the child behaves in a way inconsistent with a previously acquired standard—he has lied or stolen money. The inconsistency between his action and his standard can produce an uneasy state of distress.

Finally, a distress state—typically called anxiety—is generated when the older child, adolescent, or adult recognizes a logical inconsistency within his belief systems; when he feels he is cowardly but has a standard for bravery; when he feels he has feminine interests but has a standard for masculine ones—a phenomenon called cognitive dissonance by Festinger (1970).

Independence of Distress States

It is useful to assume that these four distress states are not identical and to assign different names to each. These states have different origins, eliciting conditions, ages of emergence, phenomenologies, and sequelae, and each of the four differs from the state created by unassimilable discrepancy. Existing empirical data, although equivocal, suggest no strong correlation among these sources of "distress." This is reasonable, for the base of experience and knowledge that permits a child to be unable to predict what will happen after he has soiled his clothes has no necessary relation to the knowledge base involved when one is unable to assimilate the discrepancy of a hurricane. There is no reason to expect a strong relation, positive or negative, between the frequency of crying to a stranger during infancy and the frequency of irritability as a reaction to experienced dissonance over sex role standards in adolescence.

The data summarized in *Birth to Maturity* (Kagan & Moss, 1962) support the prediction of no strong relation between crying in infancy, which is usually due to unassimilable discrepancy, and signs of anxiety in adulthood, which are usually due to dissonance and unpredictability. The 6-year-old boys who were most afraid of physical harm were neither more nor less anxious as adults. Similarly, infants who cried a lot during the first 3 years of life were neither more nor less anxious as adults in major areas of functioning. Each person is capable of distress to all five classes of events. The frequency of each will depend on acquired information, temperament, the vicissitudes of exposure and opportunity to resolve the distress. It is a matter of opportunity for distress, not competence.

Summary

I shall try to knit a few long sentences of summary to prevent the ideas from unraveling too quickly. It seems wise to differentiate among the various occasions for the distress states that have been called "fear"—the state of unassimilable discrepancy is an early source, but only one basis for "fear." With respect to the reaction to discrepant events, it is useful to distinguish the 3- to 5-second reaction of alerting and temporary behavioral inhibition from the events that follow either assimilation or nonassimilation of the event. We should recognize that individual temperamental disposition, perhaps genetic in origin, exerts partial control over whether assimilation will be followed by smiling or nonassimilation will be followed by crying. The presence of smiling or crying can be used to infer those states, but absence of those reactions cannot serve as a basis for assuming their opposites.

Existing data from many sources and investigators suggest that a special cognitive competence emerges between 7 and 9 months among Western infants and that this competence permits the infant to compare, actively, external events with existing schemata. Whether this competence should be viewed as an activation of hypotheses or as the ability to perform simultaneous comparisons is not clear. But it seems likely that this competence is one basis for the appearance of a correlated set of performances toward the end of the first year, separation fear being one of them.

Finally, we need to improve our methodologies for assessing the sequence of microevents that occurs when a discrepant element is introduced into a situation. Perhaps physiological indices like electromyograms and heart rate will help. It is likely that a careful cinematic analysis of motor patterns will help us ascertain the validity of the view that the state of unassimilable discrepancy is different from the original state of alerting and that each can occur without the display of the more extreme reaction of crying.

References

Bohr, N. *Atomic theory and the description of nature.* Cambridge, England: Cambridge University Press; New York: Macmillan, 1934.

Bronson, G. W. Fear of the unfamiliar in human infants. In H. R. Schaffer (Ed.), *The origins of human social relations.* London: Academic Press, 1971. Pp. 59–64.

Festinger, L. *The theory of cognitive dissonance.* Stanford, Calif.: Stanford University Press, 1957.

Fleener, D. E., & Cairns, R. B. Attachment behaviors in human infants: Discriminative vocalization on maternal separation. *Developmental Psychology,* 1970, **2**, 215–223.

Freedman, D. G., & Keller, B. Inheritance of behavior in infants, *Science,* 1963, **140**, 196.

Gillespie, C. C. *The edge of objectivity.* Princeton, N.J.: Princeton University Press, 1960.

Hinde, R. A., & Spencer-Booth, Y. Effect of brief separation from mother on rhesus monkeys. *Science,* 1971, **173**, 111–118.

Holton, G. *Thematic origins of scientific thought: Kepler to Einstein.* Cambridge, Mass.: Harvard University Press, 1973.

Kagan, J. *Change and continuity in infancy.* New York: Wiley, 1971.

Kagan, J. Do infants think? *Scientific American,* 1972, **226**, 74–81.

Kagan, J. *Understanding children.* New York: Harcourt Brace Jovanovich, 1971.

Kagan, J., & Moss, H. A. *Birth to maturity.* New York: Wiley, 1962.

Kearsley, R., Zelazo, P. R., Kagan, J., & Hartmann, R. Differences in separation protests between day care and home-reared infants. *Journal of Pediatrics,* in press.

Kotelchuck, M. The nature of a child's tie to his father. Unpublished doctoral dissertation, Harvard University, 1972.

Littenberg, R., Tulkin, S., & Kagan, J. Cognitive components of separation anxiety. *Developmental Psychology,* 1971, **4**, 387–388.

McCall, R. B., & Kagan, J. Stimulus schema discrepancy and attention in the infant. *Journal of Experimental Child Psychology,* 1967, **5**, 381–390.

Reppucci, C. M. Hereditary influences upon distribution of attention in infancy. Unpublished doctoral dissertation, Harvard University, 1968.

Rheingold, H. L., & Eckerman, C. O. The infant separates himself from his mother. *Science,* 1970, **168**, 78–90.

Ricciuti, H. N. Fear and the development of social attachments in the first year of life. Chapter 4, this volume.

Schaffer, H. R. Cognitive components of the infant's response to strangeness. Chapter 1, this volume.

Spelke, E., Zelazo, P. R., Kagan, J., & Kotelchuck, M. Father interaction and separation protest. *Developmental Psychology,* 1973, **9**, 83–90.

Sroufe, L. A., Matas, L., & Waters, E. Contextual determinants of infant's affective response. Chapter 3, this volume.

Super, C., Kagan, J., Morrison, F., & Haith, M. An experimental test of the discrepancy hypothesis. *Genetic Psychology Monographs,* 1972, **85**, 305–331.

Thomas, A., Chess, S., & Birch, H. G. The origins of personality. *Scientific American,* 1970, **223**, 102–109.

CHAPTER 10

General Issues in the Study of Fear

Section I

HARRIET L. RHEINGOLD
University of North Carolina

Fear, the main theme of this conference, was more conspicuous by its absence than by its presence. That the response of the child to the unfamiliar person (I limit my comments to the human studies) was so seldom fearful, although remarked, was not accorded the attention I think it deserves. Given the powerful hold the fear-of-stranger concept has on our minds, the investigators have attempted to produce a fearful response to an unfamiliar person rather than a friendly response, and to propose mechanisms to account for one and not the other. Noteworthy are the expressions of surprise when even with experimental manipulations designed to evoke fear, fear did not occur; noteworthy, too, are the summary statements that ignore the absence of a fearful response. Even when it is acknowledged that fear is not the common response, in the next sentence investigators slip into talking about fear of the stranger. Thus even those who early on disclaim the use of the term "fear" to index the child's response, nevertheless only a few paragraphs later use the term without qualification.

STRANGE PERSONS OR STRANGE PROCEDURES?

By now several procedures gauging the child's response to an unfamiliar person have become customary and all but stamped with approval. One set of procedures specifies the manner in which the unfamiliar person presents himself—his behavior; the other involves the sequence of his presence in relation to the presence or absence of familiar persons. The reasonableness of these customary procedures may be questioned.

The manner in which the unfamiliar person presents himself and his behavior must be standardized. Thus for all subjects the timing of the unfamiliar person's advances and pausings, his facial expressions, whether sober or smiling, his vocalizations, and his touching of the child, must be specified. But before we can ascribe the child's response to the unfamiliarity of the person, we should entertain the possibility that his response may well be to the usually stereotyped, contrived, and altogether unnatural behavior of the person—that is, to the differences between how this unfamiliar person presents himself and how most other unfamiliar persons characteristically have presented themselves in the course of his life, to the differences between this special experience and his usual experiences. What is strange may be not so much the stranger but his strange behavior. All the more remarkable, then, is the finding that most infants do not cry or show signs of distress.

The second set of now customary procedures entails a series of appearances, disappearances, and reappearances of the unfamiliar person and of such familiar persons as the mother, the father, or the caregiver. Even a mature person might find these procedures bewildering. What of the infant and child? To attribute his response to the unfamiliarity of the person alone ignores the extent to which the rest of the routines may also depart from his normal experience. In particular, if we have to have the mother leave to produce a "negative" response, are we measuring the child's response to an unfamiliar person or his response to the mother's departure *and* to being left alone with an unfamiliar person?

From the foregoing it follows that a distinction should be made between the child's usual response to unfamiliar persons in everyday situations and his response in controlled investigations designed to produce fear, whether in the laboratory or the home. Especially since even the contrived situations do not produce fear, but some milder forms of avoidance, one must ask why we are trying to produce fear, rather than its absence or its opposite? Not too many years ago the child's response to an unfamiliar person was studied as a measure of attachment to his mother and was viewed as related to separation anxiety (his response to the mother's absence). Currently, however, the relationships between the response to an unfamiliar person on the one hand, and attachment and separation anxiety on the other, are questioned. To obtain the young organism's response to an unfamiliar person, we must therefore ask what important facts about the development of its social and emotional behavior can be learned from customary procedures. What information of consequence for understanding development will be gained? These questions have nowhere been explicitly formulated.

Although arguments can be presented for carrying out almost any set of procedures, at the very least the effect of a set of procedures, themselves strange by their departure from normal events, should not be confused with the response to the usual, ordinary set of events. The two avenues of study therefore should be separated: the first is the charting of the usual response of infants and children in everyday settings to unfamiliar persons who behave naturally; the second is the attempt to see what setting events and what behavior by the unfamiliar person can produce fear or an avoiding response—how it can be produced and what it will consist of. A careful separating of these questions is necessary before we can speak of fear of the stranger as a normative behavior.

CRITERIA OF FEAR AND WARINESS

As remarkable as the absence of fear is the absence of a *definition* of fear. Exactly what responses of an infant or young child would qualify as fear? Never mind! We proceed as though all know what we mean by the term. The term persists in the phrase "fear of stranger"; but the more popular term now seems to be "wariness," in itself an admission that the term "fear" was inaccurate. But what of wariness? Which behaviors are used to index it? Common in these reports are prolonged visual regard, looking away, inhibition of other activity (sometimes of play with toys), and the lack of approach and contact. If the theme of the conference were not fear, if fear of the stranger were not imbedded in our minds, would prolonged inspection by itself be characterized as wariness? Or, tensing of the muscles of the face and widening of the eyes? Or, occasional precryface and infrequent whimpering (behaviors often observed in infants at home with their mothers)? Furthermore, does not a cessation of activity accompany the visual regard of any new stimulus or change in the environment? And how long is prolonged? Although I run the risk of being labeled pedantic (I am!), I urge a more exact definition of terms in this area of investigation.

Furthermore, if fear were not the theme of the conference, some of the investigators might have made more of the extent to which their ratings of the child's response to the unfamiliar person fell higher on the "positive" side of the ordinate than on the "negative," and "affiliative" responses might have been emphasized more than "wary" responses. How different might the emphasis and interpretations have been if the theme of the conference had been *acceptance* of an unfamiliar person!

SOME METHODOLOGICAL CONSIDERATIONS

The confounding effects of many changes in the stimulating conditions have been mentioned earlier. It is natural for an investigator to wish to obtain as much behavior from a subject as possible, given the effort of bringing him into the laboratory or visiting the home. Still, one ought to resist the impulse, in the interest of obtaining an uncontaminated measure of the primary question. If the investigator cannot so constrain himself, he must try to compensate for the effect of one "episode" on another. At the least, he ought not to characterize the child's response to an unfamiliar person *following* the mother's departure as fear of the stranger. Especially does this stricture hold if the child showed no such response to an encounter with the unfamiliar person while in the presence of his mother.

A further word of caution, related to the confounding of effects produced by a series of different stimulating conditions, concerns the statistical treatment of the data. When all possible comparisons are drawn among experimental conditions within a sequence of events, and between conditions in two different sequences of events, the comparisons lack independence. Furthermore, the behavior in any experimental condition is undoubtedly influenced by the preceding condition; the presumption of carryover effects is strong. Although an investigator may make as many comparisons as he wishes, comparisons lacking independence do not provide the same quality of information as independent comparisons. He therefore must weigh the advantages of a limited set of independent comparisons with a less restrictive set of comparisons lacking independence. If he chooses the latter course, he should remind the reader of the nature of his comparisons.

The use of multivariate analyses of variance should be considered when such variables as visual regard, facial expressions, vocal behavior, locomotion, and manipulation of toys are measured on the same subject. The effect of the varying experimental conditions, if they must be used, might also be best evaluated by a multivariate analysis of variance.

The use of rating scales, even though here given an underpinning of specific behaviors, is still subject to the criticism that to a considerable extent they represent the behavior of raters rather than the behavior of children. Their use raises the old question of whether the mind does in fact see more than the eye.

A final note concerns observer agreement. In some papers an incomplete account is given of the effort to substantiate the measures by gauging how closely two independent observers agree. Especially when the behaviors of interest are as difficult to measure by an observer (usually outside the room) as are the direction of visual regard, duration of regard, such facial expressions as cryface or smile, and the tensing of facial muscles, the safeguard of agreement between observers seems to be required. Often these behaviors are not clear-cut; often they are open to subjective bias. We ought to use the most stringent methods, and we should view with caution data that do not meet some high level of agreement. We ought also to conduct these studies on all subjects, not just the first few, because of the possible altering of definitions during the course of the study, as well as the greater alertness and cautiousness of observers when they know that the agreement between their measures will be assessed. Percentages of agreement are preferred to correlations because they generally provide a stricter measure; in any case, correlations should be accompanied by statements of the amount of difference between observers. In this connection, a note of appreciation is extended to Ricciuti for using as data the average of the two observers' measures.

EXPLANATORY CONCEPTS

What progress do these chapters reveal toward explaining the psychological mechanisms that account for the child's response to an unfamiliar person? Since the response has been shown to be nonuniform among subjects, even within one sharply circumscribed age range and with identical stimulating events, an adequate theory must account for the entire range of responses from the most friendly to the most distressing. As most of the reports indicate, the response of the majority of children fell at neither extreme; this fact too must be accounted for.

The mechanism most often proposed in these papers is labeled by the investigators as perceptual-cognitive, a compound adjective describing the discrepancy hypothesis. The hypothesis posits that the child's response is produced by the amount of difference between the unfamiliar person (his appearance or behavior) and other familiar persons. The label *perceptual-cognitive* is used, I believe, in contrast to conditioning. The mechanism proposes that the child processes information from (perceives) the unfamiliar person and then matches the set of stimuli presented by the unfamiliar person with the set presented by familiar persons (the standard, the schema), the matching qualifying as cognitive. If the two sets match, the child responds in a friendly fashion; if they do not, he is distressed. Specifying that the amounts of difference take on an inverted U-function offers a further refinement.

Some objections may now be raised. First, the theory is untestable, since amounts of discrepancy are not manipulated (although they could be) but are postulated on the nature of the child's response. Second, no theory has yet been advanced to explain why differences in conspecifics uniquely arouse fear when differences in other objects often arouse interest and approach. That a difference in a conspecific only spells danger has not been demonstrated but has been advanced in default. Last, the adjective "perceptual-cognitive" could apply to explanations based on conditioning as well as to the discrepancy hypothesis, for here too the organism must perceive the unfamiliar person (organize his sense impressions into a whole) and compare them with past experiences (a cognitive process).

In the foregoing paragraph I used the conditioning mechanism as a contrast to the perceptual-cognitive mechanism so popular in these chapters, but not because it had been anywhere proposed or even suggested in the conference. Differences in temperament, to be sure, were suggested, but explanations based on conditioning, not at all. Why? One reason is the current penchant for things cognitive. And although in contrast to the discrepancy hypothesis, a conditioning hypothesis is testable, the investigator would face many difficulties in conducting such inquiries. As we know, both theories in principle can be stretched to encompass the full range of the child's response to an unfamiliar person. What is needed, however, is a theory that can predict what the response will be. Until then we cannot be satisfied.

CONCLUDING REMARKS

In 1972 Carol Eckerman and I (Rheingold & Eckerman, 1973) concluded a critical review of the literature on fear of the stranger with some directions for future study. It is satisfying indeed to see in these chapters fresh attempts that increase the scope and detail of previous work. We have in them finer and more precise descriptions of the child's behavior. The unfamiliar person is no longer just an adult female; the category now includes persons of both sexes, different ages, and varying degrees of familiarity. The unfamiliar person's behavior in different studies ranges from exact prescription to natural responsivity. In some, toys are present, in others not. The effect of settings—home, day care nursery, and laboratory—also comes under scrutiny, as do different rearing experiences. No one study, of course, investigates all these variables, but each extends our knowledge. The studies show that the term ''fear-of-stranger'' has obscured the richness and variety of the infant's and child's behavior. It allowed no room for the interest and pleasure he often accords new people. These papers take us a long way toward qualifying the absoluteness and universality heretofore adhering to the concept, hence toward understanding an important component of the child's social development.

References

Rheingold, H. L., & Eckerman, C. O. Fear of the stranger: A critical examination. In H. W. Reese (Ed.), *Advances in child development and behavior*. Vol. 8. New York: Academic Press, 1973, 185–222.

Section II

GORDON W. BRONSON
Mills College

It often is assumed that behaviors such as crying, arrest of motion, retreat, or gaze aversion might properly be conceived as diverse manifestations of a single phenomenon, fear. Our discussions have followed a rather uneven pattern with regard to this initial position: on some occasions we have spoken as though fear had indeed been firmly established as a core concept; on others we have taken a more critical position by raising thorny issues of definition, or by questioning the functional significance of particular behaviors. On the latter occasions the matter of definition seemed to be neither simple nor trivial. Latent in the definitional uncertainty is a fundamental question: should the various behaviors at issue be encompassed within the single construct, or might they be manifestations of more than one basic type of phenomenon? Let me begin by examining critically the various lines of inference that might lead us to subsume them all within the single unifying construct.

First, I suspect that the initial grouping originated in the feelings of empathy with our various subjects; we sensed that if adults were to show comparable behaviors, they would indeed be experiencing fear. This perhaps is a useful beginning, but it is clear that we need corroborating evidence—particularly when studying organisms different from ourselves, such as young infants or subjects of another species.

Second, we were led to posit fear as a unifying construct because we approached the issue from an evolutionary perspective. We recognized that man, like other species, must have evolved various behaviors whose function was the avoidance of danger, and then we identified such behaviors as manifestations of fear. However, it need not follow that all behaviors so identified actually are the diverse manifestations of a single mechanism—we may have evolved multiple systems for the avoidance of hazard. Moreover, when our discussions turned to the possible survival value of particular behaviors, we realized how little we know of the actual environmental and social conditions in which we evolved. Because of our ignorance, we could entertain grossly different views about just how a given behavior might have acted to enhance survival. It is possible, for example, that some of the behaviors at issue, such as turning away or the propitiatory smile, might be the initial manifestations of a conspecific signaling system; hence they could be viewed as quite distinct from other behaviors that served as protection from environmental hazard. It also might plausibly be argued that some infant reactions are quite devoid of functional significance, being simply the necessary precursors to subsequently emerging adaptive mechanisms. In sum, any classification of early behaviors based solely on their presumed adaptive functions must be regarded as tenuous. (Despite such ambiguities, I would defend the evolutionary view of man as a corrective to the empiricist bias that characterizes much of our developmental theory.)

In the course of our discussions we became aware of a third form of inferential hazard—the latent assumption that a given response always is in the service of the same adaptive function. We have found that the behaviors that followed a particular kind of reaction could differ markedly in different eliciting contexts, suggesting that the reaction at issue must serve different functions in different circumstances. It is not possible, therefore, simply to equate fear with some select set of behaviors whose sole function is to foster escape or avoidance.

Finally, we have tended to interpret our subjects' behaviors in light of our presuppositions: when we anticipate that a stimulus might elicit signs of fear or wariness, we so label the responses. The effect is a subtle one. Being aware of this pitfall, we note in our formal reports that we are merely using a provisional label for the observed reactions; however, subsequent generalizations that subsume a variety of studies tend to focus only on the descriptive labels, overlooking the possibility that the behavioral bases for positing fear differed in the various studies. Before we can properly be reassured by the similar patterns reported in studies conducted with different age groups, in different circumstances, or with different species, we must establish that the various reactions do imply the existence of homologous states within the various sets of subjects.

In sum, we must recognize that we cannot be sure whether the behaviors at issue are manifestations of one, or of several, phenomena. If the latter is true, there will be no single answer to questions regarding when fear first appears, what might be the scope and stability of individual differences, how fear typically might modify exploratory interest, and so on.

One approach to the problem of behavioral classification is through an analysis of the mediational processes. If we can accurately infer the mechanisms that underlie the various fear behaviors, we will have a more satisfactory basis for specifying similarities or identifying differences. Let me illustrate this by offering a reinterpretation of some longitudinal data on infants' changing reactions to strangers (Bronson, 1972). I focus on encounters in which a stranger was close by, and on one infant reaction—crying.

Rather to my surprise, a large portion of the babies in the sample occasionally cried in the stranger's presence when they were only 3 or 4 months old. Whether this can be properly classified as an early "fear of strangers," or should be considered to be a different phenomenon, can be clarified by examining the behavioral sequences in which the crying was imbedded at this and at subsequent ages. At 3 or 4 months it was not an immediate reaction: crying always was preceded by a long period of continuous and intense examination of the stranger's face. By 6.5 months the long periods of staring had vanished: the infants typically turned away from the stranger as soon as he came near; crying, if it appeared, came only after the stranger repeatedly insisted that the baby turn to look at him. At 9 months immediate turning away remained the most frequent response—however, instances of crying began within a few seconds of the stranger's appearance.

When infants 3 or 4 months old stared long and intently at the stranger, they appeared to be having difficulty in fitting the stranger's face into an existing facial schema. Some babies eventually smiled, appearing to have reached a resolution of their uncertainty. For others, it appears that continued difficulties in assimilation eventually led to crying. As evidence of a buildup of tension, the infants frequently began to breathe more heavily in the period before crying. In brief, prolonged unsuccessful attempts at assimilation seemed to underlie these earliest instances of crying at a stranger.

By 6½ months, however, it was evident that the babies no longer had difficulty in identifying the stranger as different (cf. the characteristic immediate turning away). Therefore, difficulties in assimilation no longer provide an adequate explanation for the now frequent instances of crying. By this age, how-ever, babies typically have developed well-defined patterns for promoting social commerce with familiar persons; accommodation to a stranger now would en-tail fitting the stranger's sequential activities with the baby's established expec-tancies for interpersonal exchange. When these expectancies are severely vio-lated tensions would be generated by the unusual and unpredictable behavior—i.e., when the stranger rather obtusely persisted in commanding attention, despite baby's turning away.

By 9 months infants could be expected to possess a more diversified set of interpersonal schemata, permitting an easier accommodation to the diverse man-ners of new persons. Recall, however, that the occasional instances of crying now began within a few seconds of the stranger's appearance, making it diffi-cult to explain the reaction in previous terms. Rather, it is as though the baby knew almost immediately that he was not going to like the encounter. In cogni-tive terms, the stranger's appearance was readily assimilated, but into a schema derived from previous unhappy encounters with similar persons.

Whether the foregoing interpretations are correct, they will serve as a brief illustration of the proposed approach to classification. We now could con-sider whether it is more useful to classify together "crying-at-stranger" reac-tions across the three ages or to treat them as distinct phenomena. Such deci-sions, however, should be made within the broader context of data on the entire array of fear reactions. For example, in reinterpreting the extensive literature on fear, Bowlby (1973) includes as fear phenomena not only the above-mentioned reactions to a stranger but responses elicited by a sudden intense stimulus, events previously associated with pain, the recognition of impending danger, feeling alone, and the misinterpretations of parental communications that can induce imaginary fears. Bowlby considers the various phenomena may be diverse manifestations of a single adaptive system; and he points out that the simultaneous presence of more than one kind of eliciting circumstance may produce a greatly intensified reaction, which does indeed lend support to the position. On the other hand, some of these phenomena are present from birth (e.g., crying at a sudden event), others begin to appear as the infant becomes able to identify discrepant pattern (e.g., the 3- to 4-month-olds' crying at a stranger), and at still older ages we find yet more sophisticated fear phenomena. Unfortunately our data in these domains generally are not sufficient to permit inferences regarding mediational processes. Pending the acquisition of such evi-dence, however, we should be cautious in attributing this ontological sequence to the progressive elaboration of a single fear-mediating system. The different phenomena may, at onset, reflect several discrete mechanisms, and only later as they come under the control of developing cognitive structures may they coalesce (or wane) to form a defensive pattern unique to the given individual.

References

Bowlby, J. *Attachment and loss*. Vol. 2. *Separation*. London: Hogarth; New York: Basic Books, 1973.

Bronson, G. W. Infants' reactions to unfamiliar persons and novel objects. *Monographs of the Society for Research in Child Development*, 1972, **37**(3, Serial No, 148).

Section III

DANIEL N. STERN
New York State Psychiatric Institute

This discussion focuses on children's behavioral acts rather than on the eliciting conditions or cognitive operations associated with those acts. Ultimately, the child's behavior is the main indicator of the perceptual, cognitive, and motivational processes that occur. In any given situation (e.g., exposure to a stranger), the child's behavior is most often an integrated performance consisting of combinations and sequences of many separate behaviors, some of them belonging to or being the expression of different motivational systems. A closer look at how different behaviors from various motivational systems are integrated and how those integrations may change developmentally may prove valuable.

There have been relatively minor disagreements within the chapters about what the motivational or behavioral systems are that appear to operate when a child is placed in a strange situation. Bretherton and Ainsworth have proposed a set of four systems: exploratory, attachment, affiliative, and peer-wariness. Others have conceptualized either explicitly or implicitly two systems: fear-wariness and affiliation, or a positive and negative affect system, which may or may not be considered to be in direct opposition. In discussing the behaviors that reflect the activation of such systems, we need not debate which systems are the most fruitful to conceptualize or what their labels should be. The central point, which was highlighted in almost every paper, is that we cannot speak of only one motivational system (e.g., fear) being in a state of activation, at least in a situation featuring a child exposed to a stranger, and perhaps in any human situation. Several systems are simultaneously activated to different extents. Accordingly, Sroufe argues that we must now formulate an integrated view of infant emotional development which encompasses the simultaneous emergence and activation of both positive and negative affect systems. Bretherton and Ainsworth document this point well in finding that the vast majority (85%) of children, in the presence of a stranger, display separate behaviors that belong both to an affiliative system and to a fear-wariness system.

The first problem, then, is how we assess and understand a child's acts that consist of some "mix" of separate behaviors from different systems (i.e., an integrated "performance" of many separate behaviors in various combinations and sequences). What combinations of behaviors may occur, and what "rules" apply to the integration of these behavioral combinations or sequences? Also, what developmental changes may the nature of these integrations undergo? In reviewing the ethological literature, Eibl-Eibesfeld has described many different combinations of simultaneously elicited separate behaviors from different systems (1970). Bretherton and Ainsworth described an example of superposition in which behavior A, smiling, combines with behavior B, gaze aversion, to form an act, gaze aversion with smiling, which is a composite of both (A + B) and in fact has an additional signal value interpreted as coyness. This can be written as: $A + B \rightarrow (A + B)$.

There have also been several examples of an infant who shows some fearful behaviors and affiliative behavior who then "resolves" the "conflict" by directing some third behavior to a toy: $A + B \rightarrow C$ (toy behavior). Other combinations of separate behaviors from different systems would present major interpretive problems in the experiments described in this volume. For instance, if the simultaneous activation of two behaviors from different systems resulted in each canceling or suppressing the other $(A + B \rightarrow 0)$, we might assume that neither system (e.g., fear and affiliation) had been activated, when in fact both may have been highly activated. Or again, if the performance of one behavior, A, prevented the appearance of B $(A + B \rightarrow A)$ or simply attenuated its appearance $[A + B \rightarrow (A + B/2)]$, we might assume that the motivational system associated with B was not activated at all, or only weakly so. The many other possibilities need not be elaborated. Until we know the various ways in which separate behaviors from different motivational systems combine or are integrated, our interpretations will be limited.

So far we have only considered behaviors that, relatively speaking, belong to or are the expressive movements of a single motivational system (e.g., smiling and crying). There are also behaviors that may be recruited by many different motivational systems. Gazing is an example, as several authors have pointed out. Gaze by itself does not reflect the activation of any one particular system. The problem of the signal value and interpretation of any set or sequence of behaviors is thus compounded by the way in which a behavior such as gaze, which does not specifically belong to either of the major motivational systems involved, is integrated into the performance of the combination of other behaviors.

To complicate the issue further, developmental changes in the nature and types of combinations of separate behaviors must be considered. Most of these studies concern infants from 6 to 12 months of age. It is likely that during this period developmental changes occur not only through the acquisition of new behaviors and the extension of the fullness of display of already present behaviors, but also in the possible combinations of separate behaviors from different systems. Many of our conclusions about developmental changes in cognitive processes rest on the assumption that the same behaviors seen at 6 and 12 months reflect the same internal events. Schaffer points out that the ability to inhibit a behavioral response tends to occur later in maturation than the ability to perform the response. The maturational timetable for the appearance and the inhibition of each behavior from the separate motivational systems is likely to be somewhat different; thus, given the same level of activation of several motivational systems, different resulting combinations of behavior would be predicted on maturational grounds alone. For instance, if the mutual inhibition or suppression of behaviors ($A + B \rightarrow 0$) was more likely for developmental reasons in the year-old child compared to the 6-month-old, we would expect more expressionless staring at strangers from the one-year-old when in fact the level of activation of his fear and affiliative system need be no different from that of the 6-month-old. Several authors have reported a trend toward more neutral affect expression in the one-year-old.

Another interpretive problem occurs because there may be significant individual variability in the types of integration of separate behaviors that a given child tends to form. Kagan and others have mentioned individual temperamental differences. These may be due not only to differences in thresholds but also to differences in styles of the integration of separate behaviors. This line of argument is not without the pitfall of creating a different type of black box—one in which differences in behaviors are attributed to differences in the integration of separate action patterns rather than differences in level of activation of the separate motivational or behavioral systems. This discussion is exploring the former black box not because of its relative importance, which is unclear, but because of its relative neglect.

One way of further investigating this area is to gain a greater developmental perspective to aid in identifying behaviors and combinations of behaviors relevant for the age group of study. With the exception of Smith's work, all the chapters on human infants concern mainly the latter half of the first year of life. The reasons for this intense focus on a relatively short but important developmental epoch are clear. However, with regard to our understanding of the differentiation and integration of expressive movements into signals, this narrow time focus may be limiting. An understanding of the behaviors seen and chosen to score at 6 to 12 months would be aided by a fuller knowledge of the developmental history of the fixed action patterns from which they develop and the later, more complicated behavioral signals that will emerge. For instance, in a recent study of 3- to 5-year-olds asked to approach a nonfriendly stranger, Stern and Bender (1974) found that most of the children's smiles had more the character of appeasement behavior than affiliative behavior. Bretherton and Ainsworth suggest that propitiatory smiles can be seen as early as 12 months. When trying to assess the relative activation of an affiliative versus a fear-wariness system, such smiles cannot be lumped with the more purely affiliative smiles; and to distinguish appeasement smiles from affiliative smiles requires a finer evaluation of the cluster of other behaviors accompanying each. We must have better behavioral definitions of these two smiles, and we must discover at what point in development they can be distinguished.

Similarly, results of the Stern and Bender (1974) study indicate that by the age of 3 the exact approach distance to a stranger, the orientation of the head, and the orientation of the body (i.e., angular distance from the stranger), as well as many hand gestures, represent separate behaviors that 3-year-olds can vary separately or together in a predictable fashion, depending on the posture and position of the stranger. Furthermore, established patterns of use of these separate behaviors are not only present by the age of 3 but change little over the next 2 years. The observation of these behaviors or their precursors in the one-year-old may be valuable additions, not only in their own right but as the behavioral context within which currently scored behaviors such as smiling or sobering acquire some of their signal value.

A longer developmental view also allows for the identification of combinations or integrations of separate behaviors that may not be obvious at the developmental epoch of their first appearance. For instance, Stern and Bender (1974) also found that many children perform "ambivalent" smiles combining elements of both affiliative and fearful mouth behaviors performed simultaneously. The "lip-in smile" (Brannigan & Humphries, 1972) is such an example. It consists of an "upper smile" (upper teeth showing) from the affiliative system, plus a "bite-lower-lip" from the fear-wariness system; it looks like a smile in which the lower lip is drawn into the mouth and held between the teeth. Would a closer analysis of the facial behavior of one-year-olds reveal similar or developmentally related compound expressions? If so, the identification of such behaviors may allow for a finer precision in assessing cognitive events.

Clearly then, the pursuit of these issues of the integration of separate behaviors into signals will necessitate greater reliance on television and film methods of data collection and analysis, use of analytic methods that focus on integrations of separate behaviors rather than treating each behavior as a separate index, and coordination of physiological measures, along with finer behavioral assessment.

The thrust of these remarks is less to present caveats than to suggest further lines of inquiry, thus permitting analyses of behaviors to become an even better indicator of the cognitive operations of developmental interest.

References

Brannigan, C. R., & Humphries, D. A. Human non-verbal behavior, a means of communication. In N. B. Jones (Ed.), *Ethological studies of child behavior*. Cambridge, England: Cambridge University Press, 1972. P. 37.

Eibl-Eibesfeld, I. *Ethology, the biology of behavior*. New York: Holt, Rinehart & Winston, 1970.

Stern, D. N., & Bender, E. P. An ethological study of preschool children approaching a strange adult: Sex differences. In R. Friedman (Ed.), *Sex differences in behavior*. New York: Wiley, 1974.

Section IV

WILLIAM R. CHARLESWORTH

University of Minnesota

What we just witnessed here is an instance of a concept being empirically differentiated and conceptually expanded very rapidly. As all this scientific progress was being made, however, I kept expecting someone to suggest that the everyday concept of fear has finally proved itself too unwieldy, hence should be replaced by more precise, relatively uncomplicated, situationally specific, and operationally more rigorous concepts. Maybe this will have to be done someday. For now, however, I feel that everyday fear is still a worthwhile concept (as global as it is) for scientists to retain.

All would agree that much work is required before we can say that the full range of behavioral and situational phenomena subsumed under the term 'fear' has been empirically explored. Many also would agree that we are still far from putting together what we know about fear into a comprehensible picture. Yet how many of us would agree that before very long we will have to make some hard practical decisions about what is reasonable to include in this picture and what is not? Will our picture, for example, include fear as it is known only in the laboratory or well-structured psychometric situations, or will it also include fear as known and dealt with in everyday natural environments? As I see it, this question is going to have to be answered very soon, mainly because society is beginning to ask that very vexatious question with increasing frequency, What knowledge is worth having? I want to expand on this a bit later. For the moment it is worth noting briefly what we already know about fear, so that the point about a comprehensible picture will make some substantive sense.

We know now that there is a large, but not infinitely large, cluster of behavioral, situational, and internal events that collectively make up what most of us at one time or other mean by fear. The whole cluster need not be present for us to identify a fear situation or to distinguish it from another situation. We also know that some items in the cluster appear in other clusters. The vigilance that frequently attends the orienting reaction is a case in point—it could be a fearful vigilance or a fearless vigilance.

Research, as well as common-sense observation, tells us that fear is seldom, if ever, confused with joy, affection, play, or other forms of relaxed approach behavior. Momentary arresting or slowing of ongoing behaviors or prolonged freezing, heightened vigilance or wariness, stimulus–distance maintaining or expanding behavior, serious or fearful facial expressions—these are some of the distinctive features of fear that as a group at least set fear apart from many other psychological phenomena. We know that fear can be accompanied or immediately followed by (but not necessarily identified with) withdrawal, flight, wary exploration, and various overt signals in the form of such behaviors as smiling, laughing, or crying, all of which could have important social value.

The conditions precipitating fear include social novelty, unfamiliarity, and strangeness, which all involve some form of incongruity or discrepancy from expectations, the sudden onset of an intense stimulus that produces startle, the presence or absence of certain persons, or being in a totally unfamiliar surrounding.

We know too that many long-termed or short-termed dispositional factors are implicated in a fear response, such as level of cognitive maturity, being able to discriminate stimuli in general, being sensitive to discrepancies, incongruity, and novelty; and all these presuppose at least some form of recognitory memory. Contextual and prior situational factors are also involved. Many of these consist of expectations or anticipations that can subtly interact one way or the other to predispose the individual to laugh or cry, approach warmly, remain coolly neutral, or avoid in great panic. We are also slowly beginning to learn that in addition to strangeness, familiar situations in which there is aggression or potential for aggression can elicit fear. Repeated elicitations of fear responses may lead to a prolonged, characteristic response referred to as timidity, which interferes with normal approach behaviors such as play and exploration.

From this information alone we now have good justification to insist that any fear study done in the future should pay attention to at least four factors or dimensions: (1) *the nature of the fear responses* themselves—the overt behaviors, whether they be expressive (such as facial or postural expressions), instrumental (such as locomotion away or limb withdrawal from, receptor aversion as in the case of averting the eyes), or autonomic in the form of heart rate changes, and so on; (2) *the nature of the stimulus conditions* preceding and accompanying the fear stimulus, as well as the nature of the stimulus itself—variables that would include both physical environmental variables such as size and familiarity of the locus and social environmental variables such as who is present, and how many; (3) *the dispositional nature of the subject,* his age, sex, species, his known personality, as well as cognitive-perceptual characteristics; (4) *the conse-quences of the fear situation* for the subject and for those around him including the fear-arousing object. If we are to retain fear as a worthwhile phenomenon to study, the need to consider at least these dimensions seems to be unavoid-able.

Although our knowledge of fear has grown rapidly in the last decade or so, there are still areas that have not been investigated with the care and vigor that have characterized the studies reported here. These areas, in my estimation, must still be explored to create a comprehensible, hence potentially useful, pic-ture of fear. I would like to mention a few of these areas.

1. In many respects researchers have concerned themselves primarily with the determinants of fear—its causal aspects—and have tended to neglect the conse-quences of fear, thereby its possible functional role in general and in ontogene-sis in particular. We have not done enough empirical studies to determine how those around the infant, for example, respond to his fear—whether they assist him, distract him, comfort him, remove him from the scene of the fear-eliciting stimulus, and so on. Nor have we examined the function of fear at later ages— the possibility that fear has an appeasement function, facilitates aggression, eli-cits avoidance, lowers esteem for the fearful person, or elicits nurturance. Fear must certainly have some of these functions—at least that is what everyday experience seems to strongly indicate.

2. Most studies of humans have focused on fear of a particular object or per-son. With the exception of the work of such ethologically oriented researchers as Bowlby (1969, 1973) the fear of being left completely alone or abandoned has not been given much emphasis in human research. In animal research the opposite is true; the number of open field studies on defecating rats far exceeds anything even closely comparable among humans. Total abandonment is a ser-ious problem for human infants. Common sense tells us that it would be better for infants to cry when abandoned, thus attracting a stranger, than not to cry at all. That infants do not consistently and vigorously respond negatively to a stranger may be relevant here. Also the physical locus of the abandonment or isolation has not been systematically investigated. Sroufe and his colleagues have only begun to explore this area empirically. Fear of losing contact with others because of decreases in specific or ambient stimulation is another area that has not been studied in detail. Fear of being in the dark is an example,

and this fear may fit roughly in the same class as abandonment in the sense that no particular object is involved. Bowlby's (1973) recent thoughts on this represent the first serious attempt to conceptualize what is involved in such a response and its significance for the infant.

3. There is a relative dearth of research on fear of certain objects or people because they possess properties that release innately determined fear tendencies. "Innate" here refers to a genetic predisposition to respond to certain classes of stimuli, a predisposition that is not necessarily impervious to modification by experience. I am thinking here of some of the early pioneer work on children's fear by Jones and Jones (1928), for example, Hebb's work (1946), as well as the interests of ethologists in various agonistic encounters between animals in which various expressive behaviors have fear-releasing properties in animals sensitive to such signals (see Hinde, 1970; Jolly, 1972). Knowing the animal literature and the role of innate dispositions involved in sending and responding to fear signals, it is inconceivable that similar phenomena are not present in humans.

4. So far nearly all the studies (there are a few exceptions), have focused on fear of the novel, the unfamiliar, the incongruous. There are very few studies on fear of the familiar. If one did a frequency count of every fearful situation an individual ever experienced, surely a large number would be situations with which the individual is very familiar. When and why, for example, does an infant become afraid of the parent, of his sibs, and of peers? Is it because of classically conditioned pain or discomfort, or because threatening acts by the parent are incongruous? Satisfactory answers to these questions are, in my estimation, still lacking.

These are some of the areas still to be explored and especially explored developmentally. It is obvious that three of the areas—function, abandonment, and innate factors—are of great interest to ethologists and those interested in evolution in general. And this brings me to my final point.

What has been most evident in all that has gone on in fear research with humans is the almost total lack of a unifying theory for giving organization and meaning to our data and ideas about fear. Not only are our studies of fear often totally unlike one another in substance, methodology, and interpretation, but the basic questions that such studies attempt to answer are also frequently very different from one another as well as unrelated. There are at least two major paths we can follow in our study of fear. We can systematically explore those parameters and variables we have already identified—for example, we can vary speeds with which strangers approach babies, vary length of intertrial intervals, specify more exactly the nature of expectancies, and determine whether looming pictures of faces produce more or less fear than live looming faces. In effect, we can continue what we have been doing, but in a much more sophisticated, molecular, and simultaneously somewhat broader way than we have been doing.

Or we can stop our empirical work momentarily and ask what kind of research is still worthwhile doing in this area. In addition to expanding fear research to include some of the areas mentioned previously, we can ask whether there is anything we can do to organize and guide research in a better way. I believe that there is a way, and it involves taking seriously the synthetic theory of evolution and its implications for behavioral research. Like all theories, this one puts constraints on our behavior and forces us to think hard about exclusion and inclusion criteria to govern what we do, how we do it, and what area we work in. Most of us work with constraints, consciously or unconsciously, well thought out and not so well thought out; hence I do not feel it is unnecessarily directive to push for one that has proved itself very powerful in the biological sciences.

Since most evolutionists of behavior are ethologists today, they can be singled out as a worthwhile group for psychologists to pay attention to, especially as they try to grapple with human behavior from an evolutionary point of view. It is not possible in the space allotted to do justice to their approach, and only a few points are made here.

1. The ethologist is a behavioral biologist. The adjective means that his first emphasis is on overt behavior (rather than, e.g., verbal reporting or cognitive operations)—see Blurton Jones (1973) and Smith (1974)—and the need to observe it in terms of fundamentally reliable and theoretically meaningful units. The ethologist is very analytic in this respect, hence very concerned with the precision and objectivity of his measurement.

2. The ethologist's selection of the behavior area and the units he breaks it into is conditioned by two major concerns (this accounts for him being a "biologist")—the distribution of the behavior units in the life of the animal as well as the distribution of the units in other species (the part of his concern that is comparative) and, second, the function of behavior both currently in the life of the individual and historically in the evolution of the species of which the individual is a member (the part of his concern that is phylogenetic). Function in the ethologist's mind is a relational concept which necessitates viewing the behavior in terms of physical environmental as well as social factors. Consequently, the ethologist's ties to and dependency on ecological considerations are very great. The comparative approach forces the ethologist to consider the behavior under interest in terms of other individuals, other species, and situations outside his own immediate realm of interest. This dimension of his obligation has the salutary effect of forcing him to extend the perspective of what he is doing. Such an extension takes him into research areas that deal with phenomena antedating the existence of the subject he is studying. Hence he cannot avoid questions concerning the innateness and learnedness of the behavior he is focused on. None of this means, however, that he need achieve a defini-

tive solution to the nature–nurture problem (his operations have to be limited at some point) or that he argue a strict nativist position. The notion that an ethologist is de facto a nativist is an anachronism. For most ethologists the innate–learned dichotomy is a useful conceptual tool for posing questions and organizing hypotheses, not an emotional commitment.

3. The ethologist emphasizes the organization of his investigatory procedure. Most ethologists are interested in behavior that occurs when the animal is in his natural habitat or a close approximation to it. This is usually the starting point for the ethologist's work and for answering questions concerning the nature of the behavior, how frequently it occurs, and what its apparent function is under natural conditions. When these questions are answered to one degree or another in the form of descriptions, frequency analyses, or correlations, his interest can legitimately shift toward attempts to explain the behavior. Such attempts necessitate artificializing or idealizing conditions under which the behavior occurs. The investigator's choice of variables to manipulate in such conditions is determined by the first phase of his efforts, not by his intuitions or by such considerations as convenience. In short, the direction is from field to lab and ideally back again to field to check the lab findings. In all this the field research is taken seriously because it contributes the fundament on which all the other forms of his research rest. Psychologists frequently claim to operate in a similar way, but the history of psychology does not bear this out. How many fear studies have been begun with field observations of fear behavior in the home or playground? Peter Smith and a few other ethologists have done most of this research. Who knows with any degree of scientific certainty what the distribution of fearful moments are in the life of humans, what their primary and secondary determinants are, and what consequences they have? We have many data obtained from our psychometric-laboratory studies, but almost nothing about how representative they are of real-life fear. There are an infinite number of variables and parameters that can be studied and manipulated in the laboratory in an infinite number of ways. Hence choosing which to study is extremely crucial. It seems justifiable to suppose that such choices can be made reasonably on the basis of what we know about fear in nature rather than on what we think we know about fear or what is convenient to find out about fear. Knowing scientifically what fear is in nature is knowledge not easily obtained, but it has to be obtained if we wish to proceed rationally as well as economically. Once we have a good approximation to such knowledge, we can proceed to more designed, artificial ways of clarifying it. Egon Brunswik (1947) recognized this years ago and provided concrete examples of how it can be done.

My comments are almost over. The chapters have made me aware of great progress in the study of fear. They have also sensitized me to the great need to guide future progress. In the old days factory builders could erect factories almost anywhere and almost in any way. They could get by simply by asking a few standard questions that required relatively little knowledge about the environment or people outside the factory. Once these few questions were answered, the rest of the factory building went according to standard, unquestioned plans. Today the scene has changed radically. Building a factory is no longer an isolated enterprise for a specialized gain. The same has become true for epistemic enterprises. They cannot be carried out in isolation and for the gain of a specialized few. They must face up to questions of interdisciplinary cooperation (questions concerning their ecology), and questions of the potential gains they offer other epistemic enterprises, as well as pragmatic enterprises involved with social needs (questions concerning their function). Answering these questions for an epistemic enterprise—and fear research in such an enterprise—will take a systematic interdisciplinary approach combined with a greater respect for phenomena as they occur outside the laboratory.

References

Blurton Jones, N. Characteristics of ethological studies of human behavior. In N. Blurton Jones (Ed.), *Ethological studies of child behavior*. Cambridge, England: Cambridge University Press, 1972. Pp. 3–33.

Bowlby, J. *Attachment and loss*. Vol. 1. *Attachment*. London: Hogarth; New York: Basic Books, 1969.

Bowlby, J. *Attachment and loss*. Vol. 2. *Separation*. London: Hogarth; New York: Basic Books, 1973.

Brunswik, E. *Systematic and representative design of psychological experiments*. University of California Syllabus Series #304. Berkeley: University of California Press, 1947.

Hebb, D. O. On the nature of fear. *Psychological Review*, 1946, **53**, 259–276.

Hinde, R. A. *Animal behavior*. (2nd ed.) New York: McGraw-Hill, 1970.

Jolly, A. *The evolution of primate behavior*. New York: Macmillan, 1972.

Jones, H. C., & Jones, M. C. A study of fear. *Childhood Education*, 1928, **5**, 136–143.

Smith, P. Ethological studies. In B. M. Foss (Ed.), *New perspectives in child development*. London: Penguin Books, 1974, in press.

Author Index

Numbers in *italics* indicate the pages on which the full references appear.

Subject Index